# THE HARLEM RENAISSANCE

**Recent Titles in Historical Explorations of Literature**

American Slavery: A Historical Exploration of Literature
*Robert Felgar*

# THE HARLEM RENAISSANCE

*A Historical Exploration of Literature*

**Lynn Domina**

HISTORICAL EXPLORATIONS OF LITERATURE

 GREENWOOD

AN IMPRINT OF ABC-CLIO, LLC
Santa Barbara, California • Denver, Colorado • Oxford, England

**Library of Congress Cataloging-in-Publication Data**

Domina, Lynn.
  The Harlem Renaissance : a historical exploration of literature / Lynn Domina.
      pages cm. — (Historical Explorations of Literature)
    Includes index.
    ISBN 978-1-61069-649-4 (hardback : acid-free paper) — ISBN 978-1-61069-650-0 (ebook)  1. American literature—African American authors—History and criticism.  2. Harlem Renaissance. 3. Literature and society—United States—History—20th century. 4. African Americans in literature.  5. Harlem (New York, N.Y.)— Intellectual life—20th century.  I. Title.
    PS153.N5D596  2015
    810.9'896073—dc23        2014026323

ISBN: 978-1-61069-649-4
EISBN: 978-1-61069-650-0

19  18  17  16  15    1  2  3  4  5

This book is also available on the World Wide Web as an eBook. Visit www.abc-clio.com for details.

Greenwood
An Imprint of ABC-CLIO, LLC

ABC-CLIO, LLC
130 Cremona Drive, P.O. Box 1911
Santa Barbara, California 93116-1911

This book is printed on acid-free paper ∞

Manufactured in the United States of America

# Contents

# I

# Introduction and Background to the Harlem Renaissance

The Harlem Renaissance refers to a period, primarily during the 1920s and 1930s, when African American literature, music, and other arts flourished. Many poets, dramatists, and novelists who would profoundly affect later writers published their most memorable work during this time. Although the energy of this movement was centered in Harlem, a neighborhood on the northern end of Manhattan in New York City, its influence spread throughout the country and then internationally. Most of the writers who became prominent during the Harlem Renaissance lived in New York City for at least a time, although many of them had been born elsewhere, and some produced much of their work while living in other locations. They were generally young, however, having come of age when the 20th century was new, and their expectations mirrored this expectantly new time.

Of course, no movement, literary or otherwise, springs fully formed out of nothing. The conditions that made the Harlem Renaissance possible had begun to form soon after (or even before) the American Civil War. The abolition of slavery was not at all synonymous with racial equality. During the last decades of the 19th century and the first few of the 20th, progressive Americans debated the best strategies to incorporate former slaves and their descendants as full citizens. Two major figures in the generation immediately preceding the Harlem Renaissance were Booker T. Washington (1856–1915) and W.E.B. Du Bois (1868–1963). Literary critic Houston Baker argues that a profound change occurred in American thinking generally and African American thinking particularly as a result of Washington's Atlanta Exposition Address in 1895. The founder of Tuskegee Institute in Alabama, Washington urged African Americans to focus their energies on vocational education, acquiring skills that would permit them to support themselves, demonstrating their responsibility to white southerners who resisted integration and political enfranchisement for African Americans. In contrast, W.E.B. Du Bois argued for more immediate political and civil rights; he used the term "talented tenth" to refer to African American leaders who would help others achieve this goal. Because Du Bois was not a southerner, his experience of discrimination was different from Washington's, and he could propose actions that would be more feasible in metropolitan regions of the northeast United States than they would be in the more rural South. Du Bois was one of the founders of the National Association for the Advancement of Colored People (NAACP), and he also participated in Pan-African Congresses that sought to address European colonialism in Africa as well as the situations of people of African descent who lived in Europe and the United States.

As the Harlem Renaissance began, World War I had just ended. Initially, most Americans did not support U.S. entry into the war, and the war raged in Europe for three years before the United States became directly involved. During these years, approximately half a million African Americans migrated from southern states to the North, creating new homes in major cities like New York, Detroit, and Chicago. Economic as well as social conditions affected desires to move north. Most African American farmers in the South did not own their land and had very little opportunity to improve their status. Then the boll weevil decimated cotton crops throughout the South during 1915 and 1916, further impoverishing African American sharecroppers. The comparative freedom these migrants experienced in the North, combined with southern traditions of music and storytelling, influenced much of the literature that writers would create during the 1920s and 1930s and later. When the United States entered the war in 1917 in order to, as President Wilson declared, make the world "safe for democracy," many African Americans perceived this goal as hypocritical, given the level of discrimination and segregation that was often enforced by law within the United States. Nevertheless, African Americans responded to the national call for military service by the thousands, even though the military itself remained segregated. After the war, returning soldiers understandably hoped that their patriotic service would result in a warmer reception by their fellow citizens in their own country.

Such was not to be, at least not immediately. World War I ended in November, 1918. The summer of 1919 was plagued with race riots in several cities, especially in Washington, D.C., and Chicago, and the number of lynchings increased through the South. The Ku Klux Klan, originally established immediately after the Civil War, saw a resurgence in membership during the first few decades of the 20th century. In 1925, over 50,000 Klan members participated in a march in the nation's capital. It looked as if African Americans would not be able to define their patriotism during the war as a cultural victory, but their military experience and sacrifice did galvanize many people to assert their rights with much more energy.

The fear of social disruption in the United States following the war was significantly influenced by the Communist Revolution in Russia that had occurred in 1917. Although the most dramatic panic over Communism in the United States would not occur until the McCarthy era during the 1950s, these fears were planted decades earlier. Simultaneously, many Americans, including some of the writers affiliated with the Harlem Renaissance, were genuinely interested in communism and explored its application to American problems of poverty and racism. Langston Hughes and Claude McKay, for example, visited the Soviet Union.

Many American writers during this period lived for at least brief periods overseas. Known as expatriates, these writers were most attracted to Paris, considered the cultural capital of the western world at that time. They included such notable figures as Ernest Hemingway, F. Scott Fitzgerald, Sherwood Anderson, Ezra Pound, and Gertrude Stein, who coined the phrase "The Lost Generation" to refer to the group which reached young adulthood at this time. Langston Hughes also visited France, though he lived there more briefly than did many of the other writers. Because so many English speaking writers (and other artists) resided in Paris at this point, several English language presses and periodicals, and even bookstores specializing in literature written in English, flourished there for a few years. Most of these presses suspended publication as the Great Depression lengthened, and many of the writers also found living abroad much more economically difficult during the Depression.

During this period, racial identity was still strictly enforced, and though terms existed for mixed-race people, one's identity was determined from the outside, culturally and legally. Social segregation was often as powerful as legal segregation. Interracial marriage, for example, was illegal in all southern states until 1967, when the Supreme Court declared these anti-miscegenation laws unconstitutional. Some people of African descent chose to "pass" as white if their complexion and other features permitted it. These people would have also had white ancestry, however, and the fact that they are perceived as "passing" for white demonstrates how intently racial categories were (and to some extent still are) monitored.

Not all of the influences on the Harlem Renaissance were directly political, however. When the Eighteenth Amendment to the U.S. Constitution went into effect in 1920, prohibiting the manufacture and sale of alcohol (although individuals were still permitted to make wine for personal use), many people hoped that social problems affiliated with alcohol use, such as domestic violence and child neglect, would decrease as Americans adopted sobriety. Positive behavioral changes likely did occur in some instances, but the decade of the 1920s saw the development of speakeasies which served bootlegged liquor, often of poor quality, but because of prohibition, these establishments were often quite profitable. They were frequently raided by local police or federal agents, but they were too numerous to ever be fully eradicated.

Other more liberalizing social changes also occurred during the 1920s. The decade isn't known as the Quiet Twenties, after all, but the "Roaring Twenties." It's also called the Jazz Age. People not only listened to new styles of music, but they also went to dance halls where they engaged in new dances like the foxtrot or the tango or the Charleston. The tone of this decade was exceptionally modernist, when innovation was valued above tradition. It was an age of celebrity, as technological advances permitted new forms of entertainment, including the movies. Because the economy was booming, many middle class Americans could afford luxuries they wouldn't have dreamed of during the war, from comparatively modest items like radios to more expensive products like automobiles.

Fashions also changed, especially for women. The Nineteenth Amendment, which granted women the right to vote in 1920, initiated profound political changes, and these were mirrored in greater social freedoms for women. They abandoned their corsets, shortened their skirts, and bobbed their hair. They wore cosmetics without fear of being perceived as prostitutes. Although women certainly did not achieve social equality with men during this era, they did begin to acquire more public roles. They attended college in greater numbers and pursued careers, at least for the short term if not for the entirety of their adult lives.

Much of the exuberance of the 1920s ended abruptly on October 29, 1929, when the stock market crashed. Wealth evaporated overnight, and with it much American optimism. The Great Depression began, and it would last until the United States entered World War II over a decade later. Writers of the Harlem Renaissance continued to work and publish throughout this next more trying decade, however, and some of them produced their most memorable work during the 1930s.

We can't conclude a discussion of influences on writers of the Harlem Renaissance without a brief reference to literary modernism, a movement that emerged most forcefully during the aftermath of World War I. Reflecting writers' perceptions of the human consciousness, literature became more fragmented; modernist writing can seem anarchic, and it demands more of the reader than earlier styles of writing such as realism. Poetry became more focused on the image and less driven by narrative; free verse emerged as a more popular structural choice than received forms. Visual art became more abstract. The most significant piece of American modernist literature is probably T. S. Eliot's long poem, "The Wasteland." Although the poets and novelists most closely associated with the Harlem Renaissance are not always identified as modernist writers, the influence of modernism on their work is undeniable.

The following chapters discuss the work of some of the most important writers during the Harlem Renaissance. After the chronology that immediately follows this introduction, a chapter focuses on the poetry of Langston Hughes and Claude McKay, two poets whose styles differed dramatically but whose thematic concerns overlapped significantly. Much of their poetry describes racial violence; and they both address historical events that affected the lives of hundreds of thousands, even millions, of people. Following that is a chapter about the lyrical novel *Cane,* composed by Jean Toomer. Stylistically, *Cane* is the most on unusual text explored in this book. It links the North with the South in prose and poetry that is sometimes highly romanticized and sometimes implicitly sinister. The next chapter considers two novels by Nella Larsen, *Quicksand* and *Passing.* In each of these novels, the protagonists must negotiate their mixed-race identity, identifying primarily as white or as black. Finally, the last chapter focuses on Zora Neale Hurston's *Their Eyes Were Watching God.* This novel is partly a bildungsroman, or coming of age story, partly an exploration of gender roles, and partly an examination of African American rural life. Each chapter highlights several cultural and political events that informed the literature, placing the poetry and fiction in a broader cultural context.

# II

# Chronology

**1909**   The National Association for the Advancement of Colored People (NAACP) is founded on February 12.

**1912**   Claude McKay immigrates to the United States.

**1917**   The United States enters World War I.

Russian Revolution climaxes on October 25 (November 7 for countries using the Gregorian calendar, such as the United States), eventually resulting in Communist government of Russia and eventually the Soviet Union.

**1918**   World War I ends with armistice on November 11.

**1919**   Claude McKay moves to London.

W.E.B. Du Bois organizes Pan-African Congress in Paris, February.

Race riots occur throughout the summer in major cities, including Washington, D.C., and Chicago.

**1920**   Eighteenth Amendment to the U.S. Constitution begins prohibition of the manufacture and sale of alcohol.

Nineteenth Amendment to the U.S. Constitution is passed guaranteeing women the right to vote.

*Spring in New Hampshire* by Claude McKay is published.

**1921**    Langston Hughes moves to New York.

Second Pan-African Congress is held.

**1922**    *The Book of American Negro Poetry,* edited by James Weldon Johnson, is published.

*Harlem Shadows* by Claude McKay is published.

**1923**    The magazine *Opportunity: A Journal of Negro Life* is founded.

Claude McKay speaks at the Third International, a Communist organization, in Moscow during June.

The Cotton Club opens in Harlem.

Third Pan-African Congress is held.

*Cane* by Jean Toomer is published.

Louis Armstrong and Duke Ellington begin careers.

**1924**    Jean Toomer begins study at the Gurdjieff Institute for Harmonious Development in France.

**1925**    The New Negro movement begins.

The Ku Klux Klan holds massive march with 40,000 participants in Washington, D.C., on August 8.

*Opportunity* magazine honors Langston Hughes, Countee Cullen, and Zora Neale Hurston.

*The Book of American Negro Spirituals,* edited by James Weldon Johnson and J. Rosamond Johnson, is published.

*The New Negro* by Alain Locke is published.

*There Is Confusion* by Jessie Redmon Fauset is published.

**1926**    *The Weary Blues* by Langston Hughes is published.

*Nigger Heaven* by Carl Van Vechten is published.

**1927**    *Caroling Dusk* by Countee Cullen is published.

*Fine Clothes to the Jew* by Langston Hughes is published.

*God's Trombones: Seven Negro Sermons in Verse* by James Weldon Johnson is published.

**1928**    *Quicksand* by Nella Larsen is published.

*Plum Bun* by Jessie Redmon Fauset is published.

*Home to Harlem* by Claude McKay is published.

1929    Black Thursday, stock market crash, occurs on October 29.

*The Black Christ and Other Poems* by Countee Cullen is published.

*Banjo* by Claude McKay is published.

*Passing* by Nella Larsen is published.

1930    *Black Manhattan* by James Weldon Johnson is published.

*Not Without Laughter* by Langston Hughes is published.

1931    Trial of Scottsboro Boys occurs in April–July.

*The Chinaberry Tree* by Jessie Redmon Fauset is published.

*Dear Lovely Death* by Langston Hughes is published.

*The Negro Mother* by Langston Hughes is published.

*Scottsboro Limited* by Langston Hughes is published.

*Essentials* by Jean Toomer is published.

1932    Langston Hughes travels to Soviet Union.

*One Way to Heaven* by Countee Cullen is published.

*The Dream Keeper* by Langston Hughes is published.

*Ginger Town* by Claude McKay is published.

1933    Twenty-first Amendment to the U.S. Constitution repeals Eighteenth Amendment, ending prohibition of alcohol.

*Comedy, American Style* by Jessie Redmon Fauset is published.

*Along This Way* by James Weldon Johnson is published.

*Banana Bottom* by Claude McKay is published.

1934    Apollo Theatre opens.

*The Ways of White Folks* by Langston Hughes is published.

*Jonah's Gourd Vine* by Zora Neale Hurston is published.

*Negro Americans: What Now?* by James Weldon Johnson is published.

1935    Race riot occurs in Harlem on March 19.

*Porgy and Bess* by white composers George Gershwin, DuBose Heyward, and Ira Gershwin, with entirely African American cast opens on Broadway.

*Mulatto* by Langston Hughes opens on Broadway.

*The Medea and Other Poems* by Countee Cullen is published.

*Mules and Men* by Zora Neale Hurston is published.

**1937**    *Long Way from Home* by Claude McKay is published.

*Their Eyes Were Watching God* by Zora Neale Hurston is published.

**1939**    *Moses: Man of the Mountain* by Zora Neale Hurston is published.

**1940**    *The Big Sea* by Langston Hughes is published.

*Harlem: Negro Metropolis* by Claude McKay is published.

# The Poetry of Claude McKay and Langston Hughes

## HISTORICAL BACKGROUND

Discussing the background of poetry is slightly different from discussing the background of a novel or book-length piece of nonfiction because separate poems are obviously less united than most novels, even if the individual poems were written in close proximity to each other. Even when published in the same collection, poems do not usually depend on the surrounding work in order to make sense, although individual poems may enhance the meaning of other poems in a collection. Both poets whose work is considered in this chapter, Claude McKay and Langston Hughes, wrote and published their work within and beyond the temporal boundaries of the Harlem Renaissance. Claude McKay published his first collection of poetry in 1912, when Langston Hughes was only 10 years old. Although McKay published very little after the Harlem Renaissance had peaked, Hughes published many collections of poetry as well as fiction and nonfiction for several more decades, up until the year of his death. Because this book focuses on the Harlem Renaissance, however, this chapter will focus primarily on the poems written during the 1920s and 1930s and the

Claude McKay was a Jamaican American writer and significant influence on the Harlem Renaissance. (Library of Congress)

historical issues that influenced them. Although many of the political and social concerns of the two writers were similar, their styles differed dramatically.

Claude McKay is most well-known for his sonnets. The sonnet, consisting of 14 lines of rhymed iambic pentameter, is easily the most canonical poetic form in English, in part because the English language falls fairly naturally into an iambic pattern—stressed syllables alternating with unstressed syllables. Traditionally, this form has been used for love poems—think of Shakespeare's sonnet 18, "Shall I Compare Thee to a Summer's Day," or his sonnet 116, beginning "Let me not to the marriage of true minds / admit impediment," or Edna St. Vincent Millay's sonnet beginning "What lips these lips have kissed." McKay adapted this canonical form as a vessel for protest poetry. Readers who recognized the form would have their expectations disrupted; social protest within the sonnet is in some ways more disorientating than social protest poetry written in free verse.

One reason for McKay's adept use of received forms in his poetry is his early education in Jamaica, a former English colony which did not become fully independent of England until 1962. Through McKay's entire life, in other words, Jamaica remained an English colony, and his literary education would have placed greater emphasis on the English poets who wrote in similar received forms than an American student's might have. While many of McKay's literary influences might have been English, many of the poems he wrote during the Harlem Renaissance responded to cultural and political events in the United States. For example, his poem "If We Must Die," perhaps his most famous, is a protest against lynchings of black men that occurred throughout the South and in some other places during the early 20th century. This poem was written in 1919, when race riots erupted in several American cities, a series of events that will be discussed in more detail later in this chapter. Another of McKay's well-known sonnets,

"America," written soon after "If We Must Die," critiques America for its rejection of its black citizens, yet it also reveals the speaker's attraction to the sweeping energy of this country. It is not, in other words, simply a bitter poem about racism, but a poem in which the speaker acknowledges the complicated relationship between bitterness and desire, for always lying behind the racial reality of America is its idealism. Both of these poems, however, can apply to other situations, for although their language is concrete and precise, their genesis in McKay's experience of racism is implicit rather than explicit.

Others of McKay's poems are more explicitly racial. His poem "Enslaved," for example, speaks directly of resentment at the losses of black people and cries out for vengeance as a component of complete liberation. In this sense, the tone of the poem is psalm-like. His sonnet "Africa" is a complicated response to African and specifically Egyptian history as a region that has its own experience of enslaving people, a country that achieved great things scientifically and architecturally and yet also lost its grasp on power. McKay's influence on the Harlem Renaissance is also revealed in poems set in the neighborhood of Harlem itself, poems such as "Harlem Shadows" and "The Harlem Dancer." Both of these poems initially appear to be erotically driven, but they both turn on themselves to reveal the brittleness inherent in sexuality expressed as a commodity. In all of these poems, McKay reveals the complexity of human relationships, whether or not those relationships are overtly political.

Langston Hughes, in contrast to McKay, wrote frequently in free verse; when his poems exhibit a formal influence from tradition, it is often the tradition of blues music more than Shakespeare's sonnets. Several of his poems repeat phrases or rely on parallel phrasing to develop their themes, after the manner of blues lyrics. And several even identify themselves as heirs of blues music through their titles: "Minnie Sings Her Blues," "Listen Here Blues,"

Langston Hughes, African American writer best known for his work during the Harlem Renaissance (1902–1967). (Library of Congress)

"Fortune Teller Blues," "Homesick Blues." When Hughes uses rhyme, it is often simple rhyme, such as "die / fly" and "go / snow" from his early poem "Dreams." Like McKay, Hughes sets some of his poems explicitly in Harlem, and he also frequently alludes to Africa and African American experiences. Hughes's poems are often spoken in the voices of ordinary people.

Because of the two writers' similar concerns, some of their poems can be paired to comment on each other. For example, Hughes's poem "I, Too" can be paired with McKay's "America" to explore not only America's treatment of African Americans but also African American response to America. Hughes's poem, though its content centers on discrimination, can also be read optimistically, for it concludes with a promise of inclusion, when America will repent of its racism. In this poem, the speaker displays a prophetic if also painful confidence in his right to belong. The speaker speaks not only for himself, however, but for all of the poem's readers who may experience discouragement at justice so long delayed. Another of Hughes's well-known poems, "Mother to Son," provides similar encouragement. In this poem, a mother is speaking to her son who has apparently grown weary of his difficult life. The mother reminds her son that her life, too, has been challenging, but she has met her challenges time and again. The son's task—and the reader's—is to rise now to meet similar challenges.

Hughes's first published poem, "The Negro Speaks of Rivers," is also frequently anthologized in current literature textbooks and collections of American and African American poetry. In this poem, Hughes suggests that his spiritual identity is bound up in his racial history, not simply in his direct experience as a young man in the United States during the early 20th century, but as a man descended from Africans. The rivers in this poem function as symbols for ancestral influence, as the speaker identifies himself not only with the Mississippi, but with African rivers, the Nile and the Congo, and also with the Euphrates, a river frequently identified as flowing through the cradle of civilization. The speaker is therefore not simply an individual but a representative of human continuity.

Yet Hughes also writes of fun-loving people who occasionally find themselves in trouble. He writes about rent parties and crap games and dancers and drinkers. His collected poems illustrate a full human experience, of which discrimination and oppression comprise a significant part but are nevertheless less than the whole of human experience. The breadth of Hughes's poems illustrates one problem with reading only one or two poems by an individual poet. The half-dozen or so poems by Langston Hughes that are frequently anthologized are undoubtedly important and accomplished poems, but they are a narrow representation of his work. Readers will acquire a much fuller understanding of the poetry—Hughes's poetry as well as McKay's and any other poet's—if they immerse themselves in fuller collections of the author's work.

# ABOUT CLAUDE MCKAY

Claude McKay was born in Jamaica on September 15, 1889. His full name was Festus Claudius McKay. McKay's parents were farmers but apparently financially secure. He was educated initially by his brother, who was a teacher and introduced him to many literary classics. Then his education was turned over to an English instructor, Walter Jekyll, who influenced McKay's eventual development as a writer and also assisted in the publication of his early work. McKay's first two collections of poetry, *Constab Ballads* and *Songs of Jamaica,* were published in 1912 when he was only 23 years old.

In 1912, McKay also left Jamaica and moved to the United States in order to attend Tuskegee Institute, which had been founded by Booker T. Washington. He was shocked by the racism in the American South, and his experiences and observations of discrimination informed much of his subsequent poetry. McKay grew disenchanted with Tuskegee and transferred to Kansas State University, where he still intended to major in agronomy, but he left without taking a degree. While at Kansas State, he read W.E.B. Du Bois's *The Souls of Black Folk,* a collection of essays that had been published in 1903. He found Du Bois's more radical attitudes toward African American experience more appealing than Washington's emphasis on practical education, and he moved to New York in 1914.

He began to publish poetry and also worked as an editor of a periodical, *The Liberator.* His politics grew increasingly radical, and he grew increasingly restless. In 1919, he moved to London, where he continued to write and became involved in socialist and communist activities. He published another volume of poetry, *Spring in New Hampshire and Other Poems,* while living in England; it was later published in the United States, as was his next and final volume of poetry, *Harlem Shadows.* McKay was also a novelist and nonfiction writer. He published three novels during the Harlem Renaissance, although his novels were not as appreciated as his poetry had been. He published an autobiography, *A Long Way from Home,* in 1937, the same year that Zora Neale Hurston published *Their Eyes Were Watching God.* His final book was a collection of essays, *Harlem: A Negro Metropolis,* published in 1940.

During 1922 and 1923, he visited the Soviet Union, and he subsequently remained in Europe for several years. Although McKay denied ever formally joining the Communist Party, some scholars suspect that he was at least briefly a member. By the 1930s, however, he had become disillusioned with Communism and became more publicly critical of it. By then, he had returned to the United States and lived in Harlem. He was profoundly influential on the development of the Harlem Renaissance, particularly with younger poets such as Langston Hughes.

Like many others, McKay participated in the Federal Writers Project during the Great Depression. He experienced financial difficulties for the rest of his life, even as much of the country became more prosperous during World War II. McKay moved to Chicago in 1944, and he died there of heart failure in 1948.


## ABOUT LANGSTON HUGHES

A true man of the 20th century, Langston Hughes was born in 1902 in Joplin, Missouri; his full given name was James Mercer Langston Hughes, after his father, James Nathaniel Hughes. He was raised primarily by his mother, Carrie Mercer Langston Hughes, and grandmother, Mary Langston, because his father had abandoned the family when Langston Hughes was very young. Both of Hughes's parents were mixed race. James Hughes eventually moved to Mexico, where Langston would visit him as a young man. Demonstrating the surprising connections that sometimes exist among people, an interesting detail of Langston Hughes's ancestry is that his grandmother had been married to Lewis Sheridan Leary, one of the men who had accompanied radical abolitionist John Brown during his raid on Harpers Ferry and had been killed there. Hughes's grandmother then married another abolitionist, Charles Langston.

During his childhood, Langston Hughes lived in Kansas, Illinois, and Ohio. When he was 19, he moved to New York to begin studies at Columbia University. The summer before, he had published "The Negro Speaks of Rivers" in *The Crisis,* his first national publication. While living in New York, Hughes met several other African American writers, some who had been prominent for years, such as W.E.B. Du Bois, and others who would become prominent during the Harlem Renaissance, such as Jessie Redmon Fauset and Countee Cullen. Hughes left Columbia University a year after he had enrolled and spent several years traveling in Africa and Europe. During this period, he wrote another of his well-known poems, "The Weary Blues," which eventually won him first prize in a poetry contest sponsored by *Opportunity* magazine. This prize led to a book contract, and Hughes published his first collection of poetry, *The Weary Blues,* when he was just shy of 24 years old. In 1926, Hughes enrolled at Lincoln University, a historically black college in Pennsylvania; he graduated from Lincoln in 1929.

Hughes continued to write and travel for several years, though after that he lived much of the time in Harlem. One of his trips was to the Soviet Union, where he participated in a film about race relations in the United States. By this point, Hughes had published additional poetry and fiction, as well as the play he coauthored with Zora Neale Hurston, *Mule Bone.* Hughes was emerging as a preeminent writer, and he was viewed as one of the most prominent African American writers for several more years. His critiques of racism and other social problems in the United States, together with his sympathetic views of the Soviet Union, led to him being called before the House Committee on Un-American Activities during the

Poet and author Langston Hughes speaks before the House Un-American Activities Committee (HUAC) in Washington, D.C., March 26, 1953. Hughes testified before the Senate investigations subcommittee that he formerly had been sympathetic to the Soviet form of government, but never had he joined the Communist party. Hughes did not name names. (AP Photo)

McCarthy era in the 1950s. Hughes began to lose his influence during the late 1950s, not because he'd been accused of being a Communist but because other more radical African American writers were beginning to garner attention. Hughes never married, and most scholars believe he was gay.

During his lifetime, Hughes published over a dozen collections of poetry, over a dozen books of fiction and nonfiction, nearly a dozen plays, and several books for children. He won numerous awards. Even after his death, he is honored with schools and streets named after him and with his home declared a landmark. Hughes died in 1967 following surgery. His ashes were deposited in the Arthur Schomburg Center for Research in Black Culture, a significant Harlem institution.

# HISTORICAL EXPLORATION: RACE RIOTS OF 1919

The summer of 1919 was one of discontent for many African Americans. During World War I, many African Americans had migrated to industrialized cities in the North, and the African American population of Chicago nearly tripled between 1910 and 1920. As soldiers returned from the war, they expected recognition as full citizens, with all of the rights and privileges granted citizens (similar feelings would arise after World War II, when frustration at continued discrimination would contribute to the civil rights movement that emerged in the 1950s and 1960s). Yet discrimination continued, and housing shortages contributed to racial tension in Chicago, as African Americans moved into neighborhoods that had traditionally been reserved for white people. Other cities, particularly Washington, D.C., and Omaha, Nebraska, also experienced racial violence during the summer of 1919. Chicago's situation, however, was particularly tense.

Then on July 27, a 17-year-old African American boy named Eugene Williams drowned in Lake Michigan, which forms the eastern border of much of Chicago. The beach was as segregated as the rest of the city, and when a few African American men entered the white area of the beach, violence erupted, with members of both races throwing rocks at each other. Meanwhile, Eugene Williams, who was already in the water, had drifted into the white section. When a white boy approached him, Williams tried to swim away but went under water and died, apparently too afraid to try to swim to shore. No one was arrested as a result of his death. When a police officer arrested an African American man without arresting any white people soon after Williams's death, the riot broke out.

Rumors circulated around the city, and that night many white and black people were attacked—some beaten, some stabbed, some shot. Rioting continued over the next several days. By the time it was over, 38 people were killed. Hundreds of others were wounded, and thousands of people lost their homes through fires set during the rioting.

Among Claude McKay's most well-known poems is "If We Must Die," which he wrote as a direct response to the rioting in 1919. In this poem, he urges people who are being attacked to fight back, to refuse to cower even in the face of death. Because this poem does not specifically mention race, it has been read in and applied to many other circumstances. Langston Hughes did not write such a direct response to these riots; yet several of his poems mention Chicago and object to segregated housing and employment in Chicago and elsewhere. These poems include "Migration," "Visitors to the Black Belt," "Restrictive Covenants," "Migrant," "Little Song on Housing," "Chicago Blues," and "Chicago."

### Newspaper Reports of Riots

The first three sources below are articles from three different newspapers, *The Chicago Daily Tribune,* among Chicago's most well-read papers, though it was sometimes accused of biased reporting; *The New York Times,* the nation's newspaper of record, whose reporting of these riots demonstrates the national attention these events received; and *The Chicago Defender,* the city's African American newspaper, published in part as an attempt to compensate for the biases and neglect of the white press. Much of the reporting of these riots was later discovered to be inaccurate, an inherent danger of the quick deadlines under which reporters work, but one that nevertheless must be guarded against as much as possible.

## From "A Crowd of Howling Negroes," 1919

Report Two Killed, Fifty Hurt, in Race Riots
Bathing Beach Fight Spreads to Black Belt
All Police Reserves Called to Guard South Side

Two colored men are reported to have been killed and approximately fifty whites and negroes injured, a number probably fatally, in race riots that broke out at southside beaches yesterday. The rioting spread through the black belt and by midnight had thrown the entire south side into a state of turmoil.

Among the known wounded are four policemen of the Cottage Grove avenue station, two from west side stations, one fireman of engine company No. 9, and three women.

One Negro was knocked off a raft at the Twenty-ninth street beach after he had been stoned by whites. He drowned because whites are said to have frustrated attempts of colored bathers to rescue him. The body was recovered, but could not be identified.

A colored rioter is said to have died from wounds inflicted by Policeman John O'Brien, who fired into a mob at Twenty-ninth street and Cottage Grove avenue. The body, it is said, was spirited away by a colored man.

## Drag Negroes from Cars

So serious was the trouble throughout the district that Acting Chief of Police Alcock was unable to place an estimate on the injured. Scores received cuts and bruises from flying stones and rocks, but went to their homes for medical attention.

Minor rioting continued through the night all over the south side. Negroes who were found in street cars were dragged to the street and beaten.

They were first ordered to the street by white men and if they refused the trolley was jerked off the wires.

Scores of conflicts between the whites and blacks were reported at south side stations and reserves were ordered to stand guard on all important street corners. Some of the fighting took place four miles from the scene of the afternoon riots.

When the Cottage Grove avenue station received a report that several had drowned in the lake during the beach outbreak, Capt. Joseph Mullen assigned policemen to drag the lake with grappling hooks. The body of a colored man was recovered, but was not identified.

## Boats Scour Lake

Rumors that a white boy was a lake victim could not be verified. The patrol boats scoured the lake in the vicinity of Twenty-ninth street for several hours in a vain search.

John O'Brien, a policeman attached to the Cottage Grove avenue station, was attacked by a mob at Twenty-ninth and State streets after he had tried to rescue a fellow cop from a crowd of bawling Negroes. Several shots were fired in his direction and he was wounded in the left arm. He pulled his revolver and fired four times into the gathering. Three colored men dropped.

## Man Cop Shot Dies

When the police attempted to haul the wounded into the wagon the Negroes made valiant attempts to prevent them. Two were taken to the Michael Reese hospital but the third was spirited away by the mob. It was later learned that he died in a drug store a short distance from the shooting.

Fire apparatus from a south side house answered an alarm of fire which was turned in from a drug store at Thirty-fifth and State streets. It was said that more than fifty whites had sought refuge here and that a number of Negroes had attempted to "smoke them out." There was no semblance of a fire when the autos succeeded in rushing through the populated streets. . . .

## Shot at His Window

Charles Cromier was sitting in his window at 2839 Cottage Grove avenue watching the clashing mobs. A stray bullet lodged in his head and he fell back into the room. Spectators saw him being helped to a chair by a woman.

Racial feeling, which had been on a par with the weather during the day took fire shortly after 5 o'clock when white bathers at the Twenty-ninth street improvised beach saw a colored boy on a raft paddling into what they termed "white" territory.

A snarl of protest went up from the whites and soon a volley of rocks and stones were sent in his direction. One rock, said to have been thrown by George Stauber of 2904 Cottage Grove avenue struck the lad and he toppled into the water.

## Cop Refuses to Interfere

Colored men who were present attempted to go to his rescue, but they were kept back by the whites, it is said. Colored men and women, it is alleged, asked Policeman Dan Callahan of the Cottage Grove station to arrest Stauber, but he is said to have refused.

Then, indignant at the conduct of the policeman, the Negroes set upon Stauber and commenced to pummel him. The whites came to his rescue and then the battle royal was on. Fists flew and rocks were hurled. Bathers from the colored Twenty-fifth street beach were attracted to the scene of the battling and aided their comrades in driving the whites into the water.

### Negroes Chase Policeman

Then they turned on Policeman Callahan and drove him down Twenty-ninth street. He ran into a drug store at Twenty-ninth street and Cottage Grove avenue and phoned the Cottage Grove avenue police station.

Two wagon loads of cops rolled to the scene, and in a scuffle that ensued here Policeman John O'Brien and three blacks were shot.

Riot calls were sent to the Cottage Grove avenue station and more reserves were sent into the black belt. By this time the battling had spread along Cottage Grove avenue and outbreaks were conspicuous at nearly every corner.

Meanwhile the fighting continued along the lake. Miss Mame McDonald and her sister, Frances, had been bathing with a friend, Lieut. Runkie, a convalescing soldier. A colored woman walked up to the trio and made insulting remarks, it is said.

Runkie attempted to interfere, but the colored woman voiced a series of oaths and promptly struck the soldier in the face. Negroes in the vicinity hurled stones and rocks at the women and both were slightly injured.

### Reserves Called Out

In less than a half hour after the beach outbreak, Cottage Grove avenue and State street from Twenty-ninth south to Thirty-fifth were bubbling caldrons of action.

When the situation had gotten beyond the control of the Cottage Grove police, Acting Chief of Police Alcock was notified. He immediately sent out a call to every station in the city to rush all available men to the black belt.

Before they arrived colored and white men were mobbed in turn. The blacks added to the racial feeling by carrying guns and brandishing knives. It was not until the reserves arrived that the rioting was quelled.

### Whites Arm Selves

News of the afternoon doings had spread through all parts of the south side by nightfall, and whites stood at all prominent corners ready to avenge the beatings their brethren had received. Along Halsted and State streets they were armed with clubs, and every Negro who appeared was pummeled.

Lewis Phillips, colored, was riding in a Thirty-ninth street car, when a white man took a pot shot from the corner as the car neared Halsted street. Phillips was wounded in the groin and was taken to the provident hospital.

Melvin Davies, colored of 2816 Cottage Grove avenue, was waiting for a Thirty-fifth street car in Parnell avenue when he was slugged from behind. His assailant disappeared.

*Source:* "A Crowd of Howling Negroes." *The Chicago Daily Tribune,*
July 28, 1919.

# From "Street Battles at Night," 1919

Five Negroes Are Killed in One Fight—Rioting Subsides at
  Midnight
Nine Whites Among Dead
Negroes Storm Armory in Effort to Obtain Arms and Ammunition
South Side Terrorized
Gangs Stone Vehicles and Beat Up and Stab Lone Whites and
  Blacks
Special to the New York Times

Chicago, July 28—Rioting that ended in looting, arson, and murder broke loose in Chicago's "black belt" tonight. It was the most serious race rioting that has ever stained the history of Illinois. Before midnight fourteen had been killed and seventy-six injured. Of the dead nine were white. Twenty-nine white persons were hurt and forty-seven negroes.

The disorder, which had been going on all day, grew serious at night with the hurling of bricks and the firing of revolvers at Thirty-fifth Street and Wabash Avenue at 7:30 o'clock. Before many hours passed the outbreaks had spread to the Stock Yards district, to Thirty-fifth and Halstead Streets, all through the "black belt" and into the Hyde Park district.

Every available policeman in the city was rushed to the scene; former soldiers and sailors were sworn in; the National Guard and the reserve militia regiments had been called out and were being mobilized; the hospitals were crowded with victims; the street cars and the elevated trains had ceased to run on the south side; telephone wires were cut; scores of white men and black were under arrest. . . .

The fighting at Thirty-fifth Street was fiercest in the early evening. Here five Negroes were killed and scores wounded, two policemen were wounded, one of them after he had made a barricade of his horse and fought, Indian fashion, from the cover of his mount.

The battle started when Negroes, in groups of 50 and 100, began firing on isolated policemen. . . .

Brooks, when hit, forced his horse to lie down and fired from behind him. Traffic policeman Otto Newman was reported to have been killed in this battle. . . .

At the same time a report came in that Negroes were breaking into the old Eighth Infantry Armory at Thirty-fifth Street and Forest Avenue to obtain rifles and ammunition, and part of the reserve policemen were diverted there, checking the attack. . . .

## Lone Negro Is Stabbed

Early in the afternoon white men gathered in groups and stoned, stabbed, or shot at lone colored men wherever they appeared. The negroes in retaliation formed gangs and began to stab, shoot, and throw missiles at automobiles, street cars, or wagons containing white men, and to attack those on the street who were not under actual protection of the police. . . .

Those killed in the early fighting were:
Eugene Cappel, laundryman, white, 3,642 South State Street.
Kaspar Kazzouran, white, peddler, address unknown.
Unidentified negro.

Cappel had operated a laundry at the South State Street address for fifteen years. At 5 o'clock this afternoon, he, with his wife and daughter, closed the laundry and started for their automobile. He had a revolver in his hip pocket, four negroes saw him, rushed for him, and took his weapon from him. He was stabbed in the scuffle, once in the back and three times in the chest. His wife and daughter were severely beaten. All three were taken to the Providence Hospital. Cappel died there fifteen minutes later.

The killing of Kazzouran was witnessed by a large group. He sat on his wagon in front of 3,618 South State Street. A car stopped at the corner of Thirty-sixth and State, colored man stepped off, ran to where Kazzouran sat, stabbed him in the back, ran half a block further north and boarded a northbound car. No one attempted to stop him.

The unidentified man who was killed was in the riot at Thirty-ninth and Wallace Streets. Thirty whites and nearly as many colored men began by throwing bricks and ended by shooting and stabbing. The negro ran toward Policeman John Condon in front of the Walker Vehicle Company, stumbled into his arms and died. Condon said he had to draw his revolver and threaten to shoot to protect the body from mutilation. . . .

To save their employees from danger, the Chicago Telephone Company announced tonight that it would allow none of the girls living on the south side to go home and would make accommodations for them. . . .

Today's riot caused the most complete concentration of the police force in a given district which the city has seen in years. . . .

At a meeting of the City Council Alderman John Passmore of the Police Committee declared that both whites and colored men in the affected area must be disarmed if a catastrophe is to be averted.

Politics is to blame for the race rioting in the opinion of State's Attorney MacLayhoyne.

"The present race riots," said the Prosecutor, "are no surprise to me, and I do not believe they are a surprise to the officers of the

Police Department. The Police Department is so demoralized by politicians, both black and white, on the south side that the police are afraid to arrest men who are supposed to have political backing.

"I am investigating a case in which it is charged a certain white politician has gone about distributing revolvers and cartridges among vicious colored persons who would be likely to engage in race rioting.". . .

*Source:* "Street Battles at Night." *The New York Times,* July 29, 1919.

# From "Ghastly Deeds of Race Rioters Told," 1919

For fully four days this old city has been rocked in a quake of racial antagonism, seared in a blaze of red hate flaming as fiercely as the heat of day—each hour ushering in new stories of slaying, looting, arson, rapine, sending the awful roll of casualties to a grand total of 40 dead and more than 500 wounded, many of them perhaps fatally. A certain madness distinctly indicated in reports of shootings, stabbings and burning of buildings which literally pour in every minute. Women and children have not been spared. Traffic has been stopped. Phone wires have been cut.

### Stores and Offices Shut

Victims lay in every street and vacant lot. Hospitals are filled: 4,000 troops rest in arms, among which are companies of the old Eighth regiment, while the inadequate force of police battles vainly to save the city's honor.

### Few to Care for Bodies

Undertakers on the South Side refused to accept bodies of white victims. White undertakers refuse to accept black victims. Both for the same reason. They feared the vengeance of the mobs without.

Every little while bodies were found in some street, alley or vacant lot—and no one sought to care for them. Patrols were unable to accommodate them because they were being used in rushing live victims to hospitals. Some victims were dragged to a mob's "No Man's Land" and dropped.

The telephone wires in the raging districts were cut in many places by the rioters as it became difficult to estimate the number of dead victims.

### Hospitals Filled with Maimed

Provident hospital, 36th and Dearborn streets, situated in the heart of the "black belt," as well as other hospitals in the surrounding districts, are filled with the maimed and dying. Every hour, every minute, every second finds patrols backed up and unloading the human freight branded with the red symbol of this orgy of hate. Many victims have reached the hospitals, only to die before kind hands could attend to them. So pressing has the situation become that schools, drug stores and private houses are being used. Trucks, drays and hearses are being used for ambulances.

### Monday Sees "Reign of Terror"

Following the Sunday affray, the red tongues had blabbed their fill, and Monday morning found the thoroughfares in the white neighborhoods thronged with a sea of humans—everywhere—some armed with guns, bricks, clubs and an oath. The presence of a black face in their vicinity was a signal for a carnival of death, and before any aid could reach the poor, unfortunate one his body reposed in some kindly gutter, his brains spilled over a dirty pavement. Some of the victims were chased, caught and dragged into alleys and lots, where they were left for dead. In all parts of the city, white mobs dragged from surface cars, black passengers wholly ignorant of any trouble, and set upon them. An unidentified man, young woman and a 3 month old baby were found dead on the street at the intersection of 47th street and Wentworth avenue. She had attempted to board a car there when the mob seized her, beat her, slashed her body into ribbons and beat the Baby's brains out against a telegraph pole. Not satisfied with this, one rioter severed her breasts and a white youngster bore it aloft on a pole, triumphantly, while the crowd hooted gleefully. All the time this was happening, several policemen were in the crowd, but did not make any attempt to make rescue until too late.

## Kill Scores Coming from Yards

Rioters operating in the vicinity of the stock yards, which lies in the heart of white residences west of Halsted street, attacked scores of workers—women and men alike returning from work. Stories of these outrages began to fluster into the black vicinities and hysterical men harangued their fellows to avenge the killings—and soon they, infected with the insanity of the mob, rushed through the streets, drove high powered motor cars or waited for street cars which they attacked with gunfire and stones. Shortly after noon all traffic south of 22nd street and north of 55th street, west of Cottage Grove avenue and east of Wentworth avenue, was stopped with the exception of trolley cars. Whites who entered this zone were set upon with immeasurable fury.

Policemen employed in the disturbed sections were wholly unable to handle the situation. When one did attempt to carry out his duty he was beaten and his gun taken from him. The fury of the mob could not be abated. Mounted police were employed, but to no avail.

## 35th Vortex of Night's Rioting

With the approach of darkness the rioting gave prospects of being continued throughout the night. Whites boarded the platforms and shot through the windows of the trains at passengers. Some of the passengers alighting themselves from cars were thrown from the elevated structure, suffering broken legs, fractured skulls, and death. . . .

The trouble climaxed when white occupants of the Angelus apartments began firing shots and throwing missiles from their windows. One man was shot through the head, but before his name could be secured he was spirited away. The attack developed a hysterical battling fervor and the mob charged the building and the battle was on.

Police were shot. Whites were seen to tumble out of automobiles, from doorways, and other places, wounded or suffering from bruises inflicted by gunshots, stones or bricks. A reign of terror literally ensued. Automobiles were stopped, occupants beaten and machines wrecked. Street cars operating in 35th street were wrecked as well as north and south bound State street cars. Windows were shattered and white occupants beaten. . . .

## Stores Looted: Homes Burned

Tiring of street fights rioters turned to burning and looting. This was truly a sleepless night and a resume on the day's happenings nourished an inclination for renewed hostilities from another angle. The homes of blacks isolated in white neighborhoods were burned to the ground and the owners and occupants beaten and thrown unconscious in the smoldering embers. Meanwhile rioters in the "black belt" smashed windows and looted shops of white merchants on State street. . . .

## Rioting Extends Into Loop

Tuesday dawned sorrowing with a death toll of 20 dead and 300 injured. In early morning a 13-year-old lad standing on his porch at 51st and Wabash avenue was shot to death by a white man who, in an attempt to get away, encountered a mob and his existence became history. A mounted policeman, unknown, fatally wounded a small boy in the 48th block on Dearborn street and was shot to death by some unknown rioter.

Workers thronging the loop district to their work were set upon by mobs of sailors and marines roving the streets and several fatal casualties have been reported. Infuriated white rioters attempted to storm the Palmer house and the postoffices, where there are a large number of employees, but an adequate police force dispersed them and later the men were spirited away to their homes in closed government mail trucks and other conveyances. White clerks have replaced our clerks in the main postoffice temporarily and our men have been shifted to outlying postoffices. The loop violence came as a surprise to the police. Police and reserves had been scattered over the South Side rioting districts, as no outbreaks had been expected in this quarter. Toward noon stations therein were overwhelmed with calls.

Frederick Smith, 33 years old, who spent three years in the Canadian army overseas and bears three wounded chevrons, was attacked by a mob of hoodlums as he was passing Harrison street on S. State street. Smith had just stepped from the train, here to visit relatives, and was wholly ignorant of the disturbance. Monroe Gaddy, 3712 S. State street, and Halbert L. Bright, 3005 S. State street both employees of the custodians office in the Federal building, were attacked and severely beaten by a crowd of whites at Jackson boulevard and S. State street.

Excitement ran high all through the day July 28. Groups of men whose minds were inflamed by rumors of brutal attacks on men, women and children crowded the public thoroughfares in the South Side district from 27th to 39th streets. Some voicing sinister sentiments, others gesticulating and the remainder making their way home to grease up the old family revolver.

Added to the already irritable feeling was the fact that some whites had planned to make a "fore day" visit to the South Side homes with guns and torches. This message was conveyed to a group of men who were congregated near 36th street, on State. I elbowed my way to the center of the maddened throng as a man with his face covered with court plaster recited the story of his experience at the hands of a mob which had pounced upon him unannounced at 31st street and Archer ave. His story proved convincing enough to hasten the death of Casper Kazzourman (Greek), a peddler who was struck down from his wagon in front of 3618 South State street. It was men from this crowd who stole silently away and knifed the peddler to death.

*Source:* "Ghastly Deeds of Race Rioters Told." *The Chicago Defender,* August 2, 1919.

## Responses to the Riots

The next two excerpts attempt to analyze the contributing factors to the riots. Walter White, who was assistant executive secretary of the NAACP (National Association for the Advancement of Colored People) identified eight issues that affected the rioting, but he argued that the primary cause was simply the long history and ingrained practices of racial prejudice. This analysis was published in the *Crisis* magazine, affiliated with the NAACP. The next excerpt is taken from a report issued by the Chicago Commission on Race Relations. This group gathered thousands of pages of evidence from multiple sources before releasing their report, which itself was several hundred pages long. The commission identified many factors and also made several recommendations for response by the city.

# From Walter White, "N.A.A.C.P.—Chicago and Its Eight Reasons," 1919

Many causes have been assigned for the three days of race rioting, from July 27 to 30 in Chicago, each touching some particular phase of the general condition that led up to the outbreak. Labor union officials attribute it to the action of the packers, while the packers are equally sure that the unions themselves are directly responsible. The city administration feels that the riots were brought on to discredit the Thompson forces, while leaders of the anti-Thompson forces, prominent among them being State's Attorney Maclay Hoyne, are sure that the administration is directly responsible. In this manner charges and counter-charges are made, but, as is usually the case, the Negro is made to bear the brunt of it all—to be the "scapegoat." A background of strained race relations brought to a head more rapidly through political corruption, economic competition and clashes due to the over-flow of the greatly increased colored population into sections outside of the so-called "Black Belt," embracing the Second and Third Wards, all of these contributed, aided by magnifying of Negro crime by newspapers, to the formation of a situation where only a spark was needed to ignite the flames of racial antagonism. That spark was contributed by a white youth when he knocked a colored lad off a raft at the 29th Street bathing beach and the colored boy drowned. Four weeks spent in studying the situation in Chicago, immediately following the outbreaks, seem to show at least eight general causes for the riots, and the

Portrait of Walter Francis White, executive secretary of the National Association for the Advancement of Colored People (NAACP), in 1942. A magazine published by the NAACP, *The Crisis,* was a prominent venue for writers of the Harlem Renaissance. (Library of Congress)

same conditions, to a greater or less degree, can be found in almost every large city with an appreciable Negro population. These causes, taken after a careful study in order of their prominence, are:

1. Race Prejudice.
2. Economic Competition.
3. Political Corruption and Exploitation of Negro Voters.
4. Police Inefficiency.
5. Newspaper Lies About Negro Crime.
6. Unpunished Crimes Against Negroes.
7. Housing.
8. Reaction of Whites and Negroes from War. . . .

Prior to 1915, Chicago had been famous for its remarkably fair attitude toward colored citizens. Since that time, when the migratory movement from the South assumed large proportions, the situation has steadily grown more and more tense. This was due in part to the introduction of many Negroes who were unfamiliar with city ways and could not, naturally, adapt themselves immediately to their new environment. Outside of a few sporadic attempts, little was done to teach them the rudimentary principles of sanitation, of conduct or of their new status as citizens under a system different from that in the South. During their period of absorption into the new life, their care-free, at times irresponsible and sometimes even boisterous, conduct caused complications difficult to adjust. But equally important, though seldom considered, is the fact that many Southern whites have also come into the North, many of them to Chicago, drawn by the same economic advantages that attracted the colored workman. The exact figure is unknown, but it is estimated by men who should know that fully 20,000 of them are in Chicago. These have spread the virus of race hatred and evidences of it can be seen in Chicago on every hand. This same cause underlies each of the other seven causes. . . .

During the riots the conduct of the police force as a whole was equally open to criticism. State's Attorney Hoyne openly charged the police with arresting colored rioters and with an unwillingness to arrest white rioters. Those who were arrested were at once released. In one case a colored man who was fair enough to appear to be white was arrested for carrying concealed weapons, together with five white men and a number of colored men. All were taken to a police station; the light colored man and the five whites being put into one cell and the other colored men in another. In a few minutes the light colored man and the five whites were released and their ammunition given back to them with the remark, "You'll probably need this before the night is over."

Fifth on the list is the effect of newspaper publicity concerning Negro crime. With the exception of the *Daily News,* all of the papers of Chicago have played up in prominent style with glaring, prejudice-breeding headlines every crime or suspected crime committed by Negroes. Headlines such as "Negro Brutally Murders Prominent Citizen," "Negro Robs House" and the like have appeared with alarming frequency and the news articles beneath such headlines have been of the same sort. During the rioting such headlines as "Negro Bandits Terrorize Town," "Rioters Burn 100 Homes—Negroes Suspected of Having Plotted Blaze" appeared. In the latter case a story was told of witnesses seeing Negroes in automobiles applying torches and fleeing. This was the story given to the press by Fire Attorney John R. McCabe after a casual and hasty survey. Later the office of State Fire Marshall Gamber proved conclusively that the fires were *not* caused by Negroes, but by whites. As can easily be seen such newspaper accounts did not tend to lessen the bitterness of feeling between the conflicting groups. Further, many wild and unfounded rumors were published in the press—incendiary and inflammatory to the highest degree. . . .

*Source:* White, Walter. "N.A.A.C.P.—Chicago and Its Eight Reasons." *Crisis* 18 (October 1919): 293–97.

# From The Chicago Commission on Race Relations, 1922

Wild rumors were in circulation by word of mouth and in the press throughout the riot and provoked many clashes. These included stories of atrocities committed by one race against the other. Reports of the numbers of white and Negro dead tended to produce a feeling that the score must be kept even. Newspaper reports, for example, showed 6 per cent more whites injured than Negroes. As a matter of fact there were 28 per cent more Negroes injured than whites. The

*Chicago Tribune* on July 29 reported twenty persons killed, of whom thirteen were white and seven colored. The true figures were exactly the opposite.

Among the rumors provoking fear were numerous references to the arming of Negroes. In the *Daily News* of July 30, for example, appeared the subheadline: "Alderman Jos. McDonough tells how he was shot at on South Side visit. Says enough ammunition in section to last for years of guerrilla warfare." In the article following, the reference to ammunition was repeated but not elaborated or explained.

The alderman was quoted as saying that the mayor contemplated opening up Thirty-fifth and Forty-seventh streets in order that colored people might get to their work. He thought this would be most unwise for, he stated, "They are armed and white people are not. We must defend ourselves if the city authorities won't protect us." Continuing his story, he described bombs going off: "I saw white men and women running through the streets dragging children by the hands and carrying babies in their arms. Frightened white men told me the police captains had just rushed through the district crying, "For God's sake, arm; they are coming; we cannot hold them."

Whether or not the alderman was correctly quoted, the effect of such statements on the public was the same. There is no record in any of the riot testimony in the coroner's office or state's attorney's office of any bombs going off during the riot, nor of police captains warning the white people to arm, nor of any fear by whites of a Negro invasion. In the Berger Odman case before a coroner's jury there was a statement to the effect that a sergeant of police warned the Negroes of Ogden Park to arm and to shoot at the feet of rioters if they attempted to invade the few blocks marked off for Negroes by the police. Negroes were warned, not whites (598–599).

### To the Press
#### *Handling of News Involving Negroes*
In view of the recognized responsibility of the press in its general influence upon public opinion concerning Negroes—especially important as related to the suppression of race rioting—we recommend: (a) that the newspapers generally, including the foreign-

language press, apply the same standards of accuracy, fairness, and sense of proportion, with avoidance of exaggeration, in publishing news about Negroes as about whites; in this connection special attention is called to the fact that emphasis, greatly out of proportion to that given their creditable acts, is frequently placed on the crimes and misdeeds of Negroes, who, unlike other groups, are identified with each incident and thus constantly associated with discreditable conduct; (b) that the manner of news treatment be no different in the case of Negroes than in that of whites, to the end that there shall always be the unwritten assumption that the same responsibility for equal consideration of the rights of the one by the other rests on whites and Negroes alike, in respect of the matter involved in the publication; (c) that, in consideration of the great ease with which the public is influenced against the whole Negro group by sensational articles and headlines, the press should exercise great caution in dealing with unverified reports of crimes of Negroes against white women, and should avoid the designation of trivial fights as race riots; (d) that in recognition of the dangers of racial antagonism on the part of the ignorant, the unthinking, and the prejudiced of both races, publication be made, as opportunities offer, of such matters as shall in their character tend to dispel prejudice and promote mutual respect and good will.

We specially recommend more frequent publications concerning: (1) creditable achievements of consequence by Negroes; (2) their efforts toward a higher cultural and social life, and (3) their improvement of the physical conditions of their own communities; (4) the common obligation of all citizens of all races to recognize in their interrelations the supreme duty of strict obedience to the law, in spirit as well as in deed; (5) verification, so far as practicable, of all news concerning Negroes and their activities by reference to recognized Negro agencies or responsible representative Negroes. . . .

### Handling of News Involving Negroes and Whites

To the Negro press we recommend greater care and accuracy in reporting incidents involving whites and Negroes, the abandonment of sensational headlines and articles on racial questions, and more attention to educating Negro readers as to the available means and opportunities of adjusting themselves and their fellows into more harmonious relations with their white neighbors and fellow-citizens, and as to the lines of individual conduct and collective effort which will tend to minimize interracial friction, promote their own social and economic development, and hasten interracial adjustment.

*Source:* The Chicago Commission on Race Relations. *The Negro in Chicago: A Study of Race Relations and a Race Riot in 1919.* Chicago: The University of Chicago Press, 1922: 650–51.

## Discussion Questions

1. Read several poems by Langston Hughes and/or Claude McKay. What do the poems have to say about racial violence?

2. Compare the poems of Langston Hughes or Claude McKay to the work of other poets who wrote during the Harlem Renaissance. Examples include James Weldon Johnson, Anne Spencer, Georgia Douglas Johnson, Sterling A. Brown, Gwendolyn Bennett, and Countee Cullen.

3. Compare the poems of Langston Hughes or Claude McKay to the work of more contemporary African American poets. Discuss whether Hughes or McKay seems to retain greater influence. Some poets you might consider include Rita Dove, Yusef Komunyakaa, and Elizabeth Alexander.

4. Write a poem in which you imitate the style of Claude McKay and one in which you imitate the style of Langston Hughes. Consider differences between received forms like the sonnet and free verse, but also consider how the two poets arrange their lines, how they use figures of speech and imagery, and how they incorporate alliteration, rhyme, and other devices that appeal to the reader's ear.

5. Lorraine Hansberry chose one of Langston Hughes's lines as the title for her play, *A Raisin in the Sun,* and John Howard Griffin chose another of Hughes's lines as the title of his memoir, *Black Like Me.* Read several poems by McKay or Hughes and choose one line to use as a title for a story, essay, or play. Then write that story, essay, or play.

6. Read the newspaper accounts above and identify any discrepancies among them. Consider whether they report contradictory facts or simply different facts and whether they interpret those facts similarly or differently.

7. Read African American newspapers published in other cities and compare the content of their coverage or editorial stance to another newspaper from the same city.

8. Choose a current event and read reporting on that event from multiple sources. You might choose newspapers published in different cities, news magazines, online reporting, or television news programs. Do the different sources complement or contradict each other? Which sources do you find most reliable? Why?

9. Research racial violence from another time period and write a paper comparing and contrasting that violence with the riots of 1919.

10. Read other poems, plays, or novels set in Chicago. How do different authors present this city? Examples include *Sister Carrie* by Theodore Dreiser, *The Jungle* by Upton Sinclair, "Chicago" by Carl Sandburg, *Native Son* by Richard Wright, *A Raisin in the Sun* by Lorraine Hansberry, *The Adventures of Augie March* by Saul Bellow, *Clybourne Park* by Bruce Norris, and the poetry of Gwendolyn Brooks.

11. Research whether your city or town has a commission on civil rights, race relations, or human rights. If so, interview someone who sits on that commission in order to discover the type of work that group does.

12. On a map of Chicago, identify the locations of the events discussed in the sources included in this chapter.

## Suggested Readings

Abu-Lughod, Janet L. *Race, Space, and Riots in Chicago, New York, and Los Angeles.* New York: Oxford University Press, 2012.

Baldwin, Davarian L. *Chicago's New Negroes: Modernity, the Great Migration, and Black Urban Life.* Chapel Hill: University of North Carolina Press, 2007.

Bellow, Saul. *The Adventures of Augie March.* New York: Penguin, 2006.

Chicago Commission on Race Relations. *The Negro in Chicago: A Study of Race Relations and a Race Riot in 1919.* New York: Arno Press and The New York Times, 1968.

Collins, Ann V. *All Hell Broke Loose: American Race Riots from the Progressive Era Through World War II.* Santa Barbara, CA: Praeger, 2012.

Doreski, C. K. "From News to History: Robert Abbott and Carl Sandburg Read the 1919 Chicago Riot." *African American Review* 26, no. 4 (Winter 1992): 637–51.

Drayton, Arthur D. "Claude McKay's Human Pity: A Note on His Protest Poetry." In *Introduction to African Literature: An Anthology of Critical Writings from "Black Orpheus,"* edited by Ulli Beier, 76–88. London: Longmans, 1967.

Dreiser, Theodore. *Sister Carrie.* New York: Simon & Schuster, 2008.

Ellsworth, Scott and John Hope Franklin. *Death in a Promised Land: The Tulsa Race Riot of 1921.* Baton Rouge: Louisiana State University Press, 1992.

Hansberry, Lorraine. *A Raisin in the Sun.* New York: Vintage, 2004.

Harper, Michael S. and Anthony Walton. *The Vintage Book of African American Poetry.* New York: Vintage, 2000.

Hoagwood, Terence. "Claude McKay's 'Harlem Shadows.'" *Explicator* 68, no. 1 (2010): 51–54.

Hudson, Cheryl. "'The Negro in Chicago': Harmony in Conflict, 1919–1922." *European Journal of American Culture* 29, no. 1 (2010): 53–67.

Jenkins, Lee M. "'If We Must Die': Winston Churchill and Claude McKay." *Notes and Queries* 50, no. 3 (Sept. 2003): 333–37.

Keating, Ann Durkin. *Chicago Neighborhoods and Suburbs: A Historical Guide.* Chicago: University of Chicago Press, 2008.

Lewis, Thabiti. "'Home to Harlem' Again: Claude McKay and the Masculine Imaginary of Black Community." In *Escape from New York: The New Negro Renaissance Beyond Harlem,* edited by Davarian L. Baldwin and Minkah Makalani. Minneapolis: University of Minnesota Press, 2013.

McWhirter, Cameron. "Carl Sandburg's Reporting Foretold the Chicago Race Riots of 1919." *Nieman Reports* 65, no. 3 (Fall 2011): 31–34.

Mellis, Delia. "'Literally Devoured': Washington, D.C. 1919." *Studies in the Literary Imagination* 40, no. 2 (Fall 2007): 1–24.

Norris, Bruce. *Clybourne Park.* New York: Faber and Faber, 2011.

Pacyga, Dominic A. *Chicago: A Biography.* Chicago: University of Chicago Press, 2011.

Rice, Miyiti Sengstacke. *Chicago Defender.* Mt. Pleasant, SC: Arcadia Publishing, 2012.

Sandburg, Carl, Paul Buhle, and Walter Lippmann. *The Chicago Race Riots: July 1919.* New York: Harcourt, Brace and Howe, 1919.

Sinclair, Upton. *The Jungle.* New York: W. W. Norton, 2002.

Tuttle, William M. *Race Riot: Chicago in the Red Summer of 1919.* New York: Atheneum, 1970.

Voogd, Jan. *Race Riots and Resistance: The Red Summer of 1919.* New York: Peter Lang, 2008.

Williams, Lee E., and Lee E. Williams II. *Anatomy of Four Race Riots: Racial Conflict in Knoxville, Elaine (Arkansas), Tulsa, and Chicago, 1919–1921.* Jackson: University Press of Mississippi, 1972.

Wright, Richard. *Native Son.* New York: HarperPerennial, 2005.

# HISTORICAL EXPLORATION: RE-INVIGORIZATION OF THE KU KLUX KLAN

The Ku Klux Klan is a white supremacist organization that has undergone multiple transformations since its genesis soon after the Civil War. In addition to its racist philosophy, it has also often expressed ideas that are anti-Catholic, anti-Semitic, anti-immigrant, and anti-Communist. A short-lived version of the Ku Klux Klan was created in the South during the late 1860s, but it lasted only until the 1870s. Then a new version materialized during World War I, as the aesthetic energy that would inform the Harlem Renaissance was also emerging. Finally, the latest version appeared after World War II in reaction against the budding Civil Rights movement of the mid-20th century.

The stereotypic disguise of Klan members—white robes, masks, pointed white hats—was part of the Klan identity virtually since its beginning. This costume served not only to conceal the identity of the members but also to further terrify Klan victims, especially because many Klan attacks and threats occurred at night. The Klan originated in Pulaski, Kentucky, through the activities of a small group of men who resented the changes that had come to the South following its defeat in the Civil War. Reconstruction policies empowered freed slaves and disempowered their former white masters. The federal government responded quickly with legislation intended to restrict Klan activity. During this period, the Klan did not become a highly organized network, and it died out as a formal organization within a decade; similar white supremacist groups arose to replace it however.

During the second phase of Klan development, it created a much more formal structure and gained significant membership in metropolitan areas of the country rather than operating primarily in the rural South. A significant factor contributing to this revised identity was the intensity of immigration to the United States from Eastern Europe and Russia, as well as migration of southerners (often black southerners) to the North. During this period, the Klan adopted its stereotypic activity of burning crosses. At one point it claimed membership of several million, though by the end of the 1920s, membership had dropped to approximately 30,000.

Two decades later, the Klan reenergized itself, entering its third phase, again in response to other social and political changes within the United States. Courts have found that many Klan members were involved in violence, including murder, against civil rights workers during the 1950s and 1960s. Some of these crimes were difficult to prosecute at the time because Klan membership included police officers and sheriffs. Even when powerful political figures weren't formal members, they often agreed with the Klan's agenda and cooperated in its tactics. During this third phase, the Klan did not achieve the widespread national membership that it had during the 1920s, although it was still a pronounced force in the South. Currently Klan membership has diminished dramatically, but other white supremacist organizations with similar goals, though often more loosely organized, have emerged to replace or at least supplement it. Currently, the Klan makes the news as often for lawsuits focused on freedom of speech as for actual activity.

More than Claude McKay, several of Langston Hughes's poems directly mention the Klan, and others describe lynchings of black citizens, a crime consistent with Klan philosophy and objectives. In "Ballad of Ozie Powell," for example, Hughes describes a shooting by a sheriff and directly states that the "Law" is property of the Klan. Almost by chance, Ozie Powell had been arrested and tried as a defendant in the infamous "Scottsboro Boys" case. Powell was shot by a sheriff, though he survived and spent much of his life in prison. The poem "Ku Klux" is told in the voice of a black man who is beaten by members of the Klan, and "Note to All Nazis Fascists and Klansmen" suggests by its title that fascist organizations and political parties bear much in common, whether or not their primary agenda is identical. This poem concludes by suggesting that victims of fascism will prevail over fascists. "The Ballad of Sam Solomon" tells the story of an African American man determined to vote despite threats by the Klan. Sam Solomon insists on his rights and dignity as a citizen and human being. Additional poems by Langston Hughes exploring similar topics include "The White Ones," "A New Song," "Lynching Song," "Southern Mammy Sings," "The Bitter River," "Ballad of Walter White," and "Song After Lynching."

The documents below focus primarily on the activities of the Klan and on responses to it during the period immediately preceding the Harlem Renaissance, although the first two provide earlier context. Because of its extremism, and despite its frequent insistence on disguise and avoidance of open activity, the Klan often garners significant publicity. Newspapers and magazines have, since its beginning, printed articles and commentary on Klan behavior. As other forms of mass communication have developed in the 20th and 21st centuries, the Klan is also featured on radio and television programs. Today, the Klan itself operates several websites, and other organizations host sites criticizing the Klan.


## Legal Responses to the Ku Klux Klan

The first document below contains the text of the Fourteenth Amendment to the U.S. Constitution. This amendment was adopted July 9, 1868, during the Reconstruction era. It addresses several issues regarding the position of African Americans, particularly former slaves, and of individuals who had supported or fought for the Confederacy, within the United States. In the notorious three-fifths clause, the Constitution itself states that slaves will be counted as three-fifths of a person for the purpose of representation in Congress. And in the equally notorious Dred Scott case, the Supreme Court had decided in 1857 that African Americans were not citizens and could never be granted the rights of citizens. This amendment specifically states in Section 1 that everyone born in the United States, regardless of race, is a citizen, and in Section 2 that each person now counts fully for the purposes of representation in Congress. While protecting the rights of African Americans, however, this amendment would now give southern states more power in Congress, since their populations would now appear to be so much higher. Section 3, however, denies the right to hold any political office to anyone who has "engaged in insurrection or rebellion" against the United States. In other words, no man who had been a Confederate soldier or political representative of a Confederate state, could hold office in the newly reunified United States. This meant that virtually no white person from the South could be elected to Congress unless two-thirds of the members of both houses of Congress voted to permit it.

Following this amendment is an excerpt from a law passed soon afterward, providing for means of enforcing it and responding specifically to attempts by the Ku Klux Klan to thwart it. For example, members of the Klan would threaten African Americans if they attempted to vote or exercise other political rights held by citizens. Because this law was passed specifically in response to the Klan, it acquired the nickname of "The Ku Klux Klan Act," although it would be enforceable against any similar organization. The excerpt included here states that individuals who interfere with people attempting to vote, serving on juries, exercising their responsibilities as judges or other legal authorities, can be punished with both jail time and fines. This excerpt also prohibits individuals from going about "in disguise upon the public highway," probably the most obvious reference to the Klan.

# Fourteenth Amendment to the Constitution of the United States, 1868

**Section 1.** All persons born or naturalized in the United States, and subject to the jurisdiction thereof, are citizens of the United States and of the State wherein they reside. No State shall make or enforce any law which shall abridge the privileges or immunities of citizens of the United States; nor shall any State deprive any person of life, liberty, or property, without due process of law; nor deny to any person within its jurisdiction the equal protection of the laws.

**Section 2.** Representatives shall be apportioned among the several States according to their respective numbers, counting the whole number of persons in each State, excluding Indians not taxed. But when the right to vote at any election for the choice of electors for President and Vice President of the United States, Representatives in Congress, the Executive and Judicial officers of a State, or the members of the Legislature thereof, is denied to any of the male inhabitants of such State, being twenty-one years of age, and citizens of the United States, or in any way abridged, except for participation in rebellion, or other crime, the basis of representation therein shall be reduced in the proportion which the number of such male citizens shall bear to the whole number of male citizens twenty-one years of age in such State.

**Section 3.** No person shall be a Senator or Representative in Congress, or elector of President and Vice President, or hold any office, civil or military, under the United States, or under any State, who, having previously taken an oath, as a member of Congress, or as an officer of the United States, or as a member of any State legislature, or as an executive or judicial officer of any State, to support the Constitution of the United States, shall have engaged in insurrection or rebellion against the same, or given aid or comfort to the enemies thereof. But Congress may, by a vote of two-thirds of each House, remove such disability.

**Section 4.** The validity of the public debt of the United States, authorized by law, including debts incurred for payment of pensions and bounties for services in suppressing insurrection or rebellion, shall not be questioned. But neither the United States nor any State shall assume or pay any debt or obligation incurred in aid of insurrection or rebellion against the United States, or any claim for the loss or emancipation of any slave; but all such debts, obligations and claims shall be held illegal and void.

**Section 5.** The Congress shall have power to enforce, by appropriate legislation, the provisions of this article.

*Source:* The Fourteenth Amendment (Amendment XIV) to the United States Constitution, adopted on July 9, 1868.

# From the Ku Klux Klan Act, 1871

An Act to enforce the Provisions of the Fourteenth Amendment to the Constitution of the United States, and for other Purposes. . . .

Section 2: That if two or more persons within any State or Territory of the United States shall conspire together to overthrow, or to put down, or to destroy by force the government of the United States, or to levy war against the United States, or to oppose by force the authority of the government of the United States, or by force, intimidation, or threat to prevent, hinder, or delay the execution of any law of the United States, or by force to seize, take, or possess any property of the United States contrary to the authority thereof, or by force, intimidation, or threat to prevent any person from accepting or holding any office or trust or place of confidence under the United States, or from discharging the duties thereof, or by force, intimidation, or threat to induce any officer of the United States to leave any State, district, or place where his duties as such office might lawfully be performed, or to injure him in his person or property on account of his lawful discharge of the duties of his office, or to injure his person while engaged in the lawful discharge of the duties of his office, or to injure his property so as to molest, interrupt, hinder, or impede him in the discharge of his official duty, or by force, intimidation, or threat to deter any party or witness in any court of the United States from attending such court, or from testifying in any matter pending in such court fully, freely, and truthfully, or to injure any such party or witness in his person or property on account of his having so attended or testified, or by force, intimidation, or threat to influence the verdict, presentment, or indictment, of any juror or grand juror in any court of the United States, or to injure such juror in his person or property on account of any verdict, presentment, or indictment lawfully assented to by him, or on account of his being or having been such juror, or shall conspire together, or go in disguise upon the public highway or upon the premises of another for the purpose, either directly or indirectly, of depriving any person or any class of persons of the equal protection of the laws, or of equal privileges or immunities under the laws, or for the purpose of preventing or hindering the constituted authorities of any State from giving or securing to all persons within such State the equal protection of the laws, or shall conspire together for the purpose in any manner impeding, hindering, obstructing or defeating the due course of justice in any State or Territory, with intent to deny to any citizen of the United States the due and equal protection of the laws, or to injure any person in his person or his property for lawfully enforcing the right of any person or class of persons to the equal protection of the laws, or by force, intimidation, or threat to prevent any citizen of the United States lawfully entitled to vote from giving his support or advocacy in a lawful manner towards or in favor of the election of any lawfully qualified person as an elector of President or Vice-President of the United States, or as a member of the Congress of the United States, or to injure any such citizen in his person or property on account of such support or advocacy, each and every person so offending shall be deemed guilty of a high crime, and upon conviction thereof in any district or circuit court of the United States or district or supreme court of any Territory of the United States having jurisdiction of similar offences, shall be punished by a fine not less than five hundred nor more than five thousand dollars, or by imprisonment, with or without hard labor, as the court may determine, for a period of not less than six months nor more than six years, as the court may determine. . . .

*Source:* The Ku Klux Klan Act. 42nd Congress, 1st Session. 17 U.S. Statutes at Large 13 (1871).

## William Garrott Brown's Interpretation of the History of the Ku Klux Klan

This next document is an excerpt from a lengthy article that originally appeared in *The Atlantic Monthly,* a national general interest magazine whose audience was and is comparatively educated. This article provides a history of the original foundation of the Klan, and because it was written at the turn of the 20th century, after the first phase of the Klan had been completed but over a decade before it would reemerge, the author assumes that the Klan existed as a response to one historic moment that was now over. Reading this article a century afterward provides an interesting perspective—and perhaps also a lesson in the necessity of intellectual humility—for contemporary students and scholars who know what followed. William Garrott Brown, the author, treats original Klan members sympathetically. He implies that white southerners were so traumatized and confused by the changes in their culture that their repressive treatment of freed persons is understandable, even excusable. He describes black people stereotypically as noisy and idle. He also suggests that young men accustomed to the excitement of war could not reasonably be expected to settle into the peacetime calm of a rural town. Brown also discusses what he perceives as unfair carpet-bag rule, that is, by northerners who moved South to take advantage of postwar political opportunity, people who had not suffered the types of effects the war brought to the South. In his conclusion, Brown asserts that the actions of the Ku Klux Klan were necessary to turn an upside-down culture right-side up. Yet, he also states that the repressive tactics of southern government deprive not only African Americans of true freedom but also the white rulers themselves.

## From William Garrott Brown, "The Ku Klux Movement," 1901

Without attempting any elaborate argument, we may, I think, take it for granted that the Ku Klux movement was an outcome of the conditions that prevailed in the Southern states after the war. It was too widespread, too spontaneous, too clearly a popular movement, to be attributed to any one man or to any conspiracy of a few men. Had it existed only in one corner of the South, or drawn its membership from a small and sharply defined class, some such explanation might serve. But we know enough of its extent, its composition, and the various forms it took, to feel sure that it was neither an accident nor a scheme. It was no man's contrivance, but an historical development. As such, it must be studied against its proper background of a disordered society and a bewildered people. . . .

It is doubtful, however, if even the injury to his [the Southern taxpayer's] fortunes had so much to do with his state of mind as the countless humiliations and irritations which the rule of the freedman and the stranger brought upon the most imperious, proud, and sensitive branch of the English race.

If the white man of the lately dominant class in the South were permitted to vote at all, he might have literally to pass under bayonets to reach the polls. He saw freedmen organized in militia companies, expensively armed and gayly caparisoned. If he offered his own military services, they were sure to be rejected. He saw his former slaves repeating at elections, but he learned that he had no right of challenge, and that there was no penalty fixed by law for the crime. In the local courts of justice, he saw his friends brought, by an odious system of informers, before judges who were not merely incompetent or unfair, like many of those who sat in the higher courts, but often grotesquely ignorant as well, and who intrusted the execution of their instruments to officials who in many cases could not write an intelligible return. In the schools which he was so heavily taxed to support, he saw the children of his slaves getting the book-learning which he himself thought it unwise to give them from strangers who would be sure to train them into discontent with the only lot he thought them fit for, and the only sort of work which, in the world he knew, they ever had a chance to do. He saw the Freedmen's Bureau deliberately trying to substitute its alien machinery for that patriarchal relation between white employers and black workmen which had seemed to him right and inevitable. He saw the Loyal League urging freedmen to take up those citizenly powers and duties which he had never understood emancipation to imply, when he gave up his sword. In every boisterous should of a drunken negro before his gate, in every insolent glance from a group of idle negroes on the streets of the county seat, in the reports of fisticuffs with little darkies which his children brought home after school, in the noises of the night and the glare of occasional conflagrations, he saw the hand or heard the harshly accented voice of the stranger in the land. . . .

When the Civil War ended, the little town of Pulaski, Tennessee, welcomed home a band of young men who, though they were veterans of hard-fought fields, were for the most part no older than the mass of college students. In the general poverty, the exhaustion, the lack of heart, naturally prevalent throughout the beaten South, young men had more leisure than was good for them. A Southern country town, even in the halcyon days before the war, was not a particularly lively place; and Pulaski in 1866 was doubtless rather tame to fellows who had seen Pickett charge at Gettysburg or galloped over the country with Morgan and Wheeler. A group of them, assembled in a law office one evening in May, 1866, were discussing ways and means of having a livelier time. Some one suggested a club or society. An organization with no very definite aims was effected; and at a second meeting, a week later, names were proposed and discussed. Some one pronounced the Greek word "Kuklos," meaning a circle. From "Kuklos" to "Ku Klux" was an easy transition . . . and "Klan" followed "Ku Klux" as naturally as "dumpty" follows "humpty" . . . one can fancy what sort of badinage would have greeted a suggestion that in six years a committee of Congress would devote thirteen volumes to the history of the movement that began in a Pulaski law office. . . .

In the beginning it was, in fact, no "movement" at all. It was a scheme for having fun, more like a college secret society than anything else. Its members were not "lewd fellows of the baser sort," but young men of standing in the community, who a few years earlier would also have been men of wealth. . . . The only important clause in the oath of membership was a promise of absolute secrecy. The disguise was a white mask, a tall cardboard hat, a gown or robe that covered the whole person, and, when the Klan went mounted, a cover for the horses' bodies and some sort of muffling for their feet. . . . While the club adhered to its original aim and character, only men of known good morals were admitted. Born of the same instinct and conditions that gave birth to the "snipe hunt" and other hazing devices of Southern country towns, it was probably as harmless and as unimportant a piece of fooling as any to be found inside or outside of colleges. . . .

From this time [1867] the Klan put itself more clearly in evidence, generally adhering to its original devices of mystery and silence, but not always successfully resisting the temptation to add to these violence. On the night of July 4, by well-heralded parades, it exhibited itself throughout Tennessee, and perhaps in other states, more impressively than ever before. In Pulaski, some four hundred disguised horsemen marched and countermarched silently through the streets before thousands of spectators, and not a single disguise was penetrated. The effect of mystery even on intelligent minds was well illustrated in the estimate, made by "reputable citizens," that the number was not less than three thousand. . . .

The remaining facts in the history of the Ku Klux Klan proper need no lengthy recital. The effectiveness of the order was shown wherever, by its original methods, it exerted itself to quiet disturbed communities. Wherever freedmen grew unruly, disguised horsemen appeared by night; and thereafter the darkies of the neighborhood inclined to stay under cover after daylight failed. But the order had grown too large, it was too widespread, the central authority was too remote from the local "dens," and the general scheme was too easily grasped and copied, to permit of the rigid exclusion from membership of such men as would incline to use violence, or to cover with the mantle of secrecy enterprises of a doubtful or even criminal cast. . . . So, a few weeks later, by an order of the Grand Wizard, the Klan was formally disbanded, not only in Tennessee, but everywhere. It is generally understood that the Grand Wizard who issued that order was no less a person than Nathan Bedford Forrest. How many dens received the order at all, and how many of those that received it also obeyed it, will never be known, any more than it will be known how many dens there were, or how many members. However, the early spring of 1869 may be taken as the date when the Ku Klux Klan, which gave its name and its idea to the secret movement which began the undoing of reconstruction, ceased to exist as an organized body. . . .

If one asks of the movement, "Was it necessary?" this much, at least, may be answered: that no other plan of resistance would have served so well. If one asks, "Was it successful?" the answer is plain. No open revolt ever succeeded more completely. If one asks, "Was it justifiable?" the "yes" or "no" is harder to say. There must be much defining of terms, much patient separating of the accidental from the essential, much inquiry into motives. Describe the movement broadly as a secret movement, operating by terror and violence to nullify laws, and one readily condemns it. Paint all the conditions, enter into the minds and hearts of the men who lived under them, look at them through their eyes, suffer with their angry pain, and one revolts as their pride revolted. Weigh the broad rule, which is less a "light to guide" than a "rod to check," against the human impulse, and the balance trembles. One is ready to declare, not, perhaps, that the end justified the means, but that never before was an end so clearly worth fighting for made so clearly unattainable by any good means.

Nor does our hindsight much avail us. The end attained was mainly good. Southern society was righted. But the method of it survives in too many habits of the Southern mind, in too many shortcomings of Southern civilization, in too many characteristics of Southern life. The Southern whites, solidified in resistance to carpet-bag rule, have kept their solidarity unimpaired by any healthful division on public questions. Having learned a lesson, they cannot forget it. Seeing forms of law used to cloak oppression, and liberty invoked to countenance a tyranny, they learned to set men above political principles, and good government above freedom of thought. For thirty years they have continued to set one question above all others, and thus debarred themselves from full participation in the political life of the country. As they rule by fear, so by fear are they ruled. It is they themselves who are now befooled, and robbed of the nobler part of their own political birthright. They outdid their conquerors, yet they are not free.

*Source:* Brown, William Garrott. "The Ku Klux Movement." *The Atlantic Monthly* 87, no. 523 (May 1901).

## Newspaper Reports on the Ku Klux Klan

These last four documents are articles that appeared in the *New York Times*. While all of them are straightforward news articles, two contain so much quotation of participant views that they border on commentary or editorial. Notice that the date of the first article appears to contradict the statement in the second that rejuvenated Klan had been established only six years previously, which would have been 1915. The first article suggests that this local branch of the Klan was organized as a response to alleged attacks by African American men against white women. The article states that although six attacks had occurred, only one man had been "lynched" while the others had escaped. Despite earlier laws intended to guarantee equality under the law to all citizens, these men are able to state openly that lynching—capital punishment, often through torture, without a trial—is not only acceptable but desirable. The articles also reveal fear and anger that African American men might be sexually attracted to white women; although these fears often bordered on paranoia, they are nevertheless ironic given the number of white male slave owners who raped or otherwise coerced their female slaves into having sex with them. The third article, "Klan Denounced from Many

Pulpits," quotes several members of the clergy who all, with only one exception, vigorously oppose Klan activities, despite the Klan's statements, as exemplified in the final document, that they represent Protestant Christianity and uphold the teachings of the Bible. Some of the Protestant clergy who object to being represented by the Klan, however, do acknowledge that suspicion of Catholicism can be valid, especially if the American government were to be unduly influenced by the Pope and Catholic bishops through the election of Catholic politicians. This fear would not be fully alleviated until the election of John F. Kennedy as president of the United States in 1960. As a group, these four newspaper articles present a good representative range of perceptions of the Ku Klux Klan during the early part of the 20th century, and they also provide details of the racialized context in which the writers of the Harlem Renaissance were working.

## "Atlanta's Ku-Klux Klan," 1906

Whites Are Alarmed by Recent Attacks by Negroes.

Atlanta, Aug. 25.—Spurred by the advice of The Atlanta News, which is owned by Col. James W. English, Jr., Gov. Terrell's Chief of Staff, the white men of Atlanta and the suburban towns began to-day to organize a Ku-Klux Klan for the purpose of avenging attacks on white women by negroes.

In the last two weeks six white girls have been attacked by negroes in Atlanta and its suburbs, and only one negro has been lynched, the others having escaped. The assault which led the citizens to organize Ku-Klux Klan was committed last night in the western part of the city. Miss Kate Waites, 18 years old, a school teacher, being the victim.

All last night and to-day white men armed with rifles have been patrolling the negro settlements in search of Miss Waites's assailant. This afternoon it was announced that formation of a Ku-Klux Klan had been determined upon to protect white women, and that the Klan would begin operations to-night.

The business men of Atlanta have offered a large sum to aid in the protection of white women, and this money will be placed at the Klan's disposal. The feeling between the races is bitterer than it has been in years, and conservative citizens fear there may be serious trouble.

*Source:* "Atlanta's Ku-Klux Klan." *The New York Times,*
August 26, 1906.

# "Ku Klux Klan Celebrates," 1921

Five Thousand Knights to Meet in Atlanta Today

Atlanta, Ga., May 4— Knights of the Ku Klux Klan from all parts of the United States will gather in Atlanta tomorrow and Friday for a great ceremonial and two-day celebration commemorating the founding of the order six years ago. Incoming trains brought several hundred members today. Other hundreds will arrive tomorrow, and by Friday 5,000 members of the white robe and fiery cross are expected to be in the city.

The principal event of the gathering will be a big initiation ceremonial tomorrow night. More than 1,000 candidates are to be initiated into the mysteries of the Klan, it is said—the largest single class of candidates in the history of the organization. The meeting will be

Ku Klux Klan members attend an initiation ceremony in Baltimore, Maryland, in 1923. The Klan was founded in the South after the Civil War for the purpose of intimidating the newly freed slaves and preventing them from taking advantage of their new rights. Klan members dressed in white robes and hoods to conceal their true identities. The Klan experienced a resurgence of interest during the period leading up to the Harlem Renaissance. (The Illustrated London News Picture Library)

the first general celebration held since the order began to organize in the North, East, and West. Colonel W. J. Simmons is Imperial Wizard of the Klan.

The Klan of reconstruction days was formed on May 6. Reorganization of the Klan under Colonel Simmons took place on Thanksgiving Day six years ago on the Summit of Stone Mountain.

*Source:* "Ku Klux Klan Celebrates." *The New York Times,*
May 5, 1921.

# "Ku Klux Denounced from Many Pulpits," 1922

Dr. Fosdick Says Klan Methods Are a Menace to American Institutions.

Jews Advised Not to Fight.

Gerard Declares Invisible Empire Breeds Racial Dissension—Straton Is Silent.

The Ku Klux Klan was denounced, not only as un-American and sinister but as misrepresentative of the Protestantism it professed to uphold, by clergymen and other speakers yesterday, at Thanksgiving Day services here. The Rev. Dr. Harry Emerson Fosdick, one of the ministers of the First Presbyterian Church, declared that to commit American institutions to the care of a secret order of "oath-bound Protestants, making the night its covering and tar and feathers its instrument," would be to lose those institutions, and that the Protestant churches of the country should say so.

A warning to Jewish organizations that attacks by them on the Klan would only intensify the conflict between them was issued by James W. Gerard, former Ambassador to Germany, in an address to the congregation B'nai Jeshurun, 257 West Eighty-eighth Street. After condemning the Klan as a menace to American democracy, Mr. Gerard referred to newspaper reports of a resolution adopted by the Independent Order of B'rith Abraham last Wednesday, and said:

> I think it would be a mistake for Jews to wage war against the Ku Klux Klan. It would simply increase the very racial and religious antipathies which the Klan seeks to stir up. It is for us to attend to the Klansmen, and we shall do it. Leave them to us.
>
> For masked men pretend to fight in the name of religion and morality is out of place in a democracy like ours. If they are really fighting for these things, they have no need for masks. The practices of the Ku Klux Klan in the present day are contrary to the American principles of democracy and fair-mindedness. The Klan is breeding racial and religious dissension. If changes in our institutions of government are needed, they can be brought about by lawful means.

## Denounces Klan Methods

"One of the most considerable of our present dangers is an astonishing organization, ostensibly pledged to the support of the Protestant cultural tradition—an oath-bound, secret order of masked men who work in the dark," said Dr. Fosdick at the First Presbyterian Church.

One never would have supposed it likely that in a New York pulpit it would be necessary to refer to the Ku Klux Klan. Yet here is an organization pretending to represent Protestantism, which, having swept across the country, is now proposing to organize in this city its oath-bound secret order of sheeted men.

But whatever may be its professions, its methods and principles are perilously un-American. It says that it wishes to keep the Roman Church out of politics. For Catholic Christians I have only respect. They are my spiritual brethren, and for their service to this country in the interests of personal purity, decency and piety we may well be grateful. But I, too, fear the Roman hierarchy with its temptation to use spiritual power for political purposes. Nevertheless, if we wish to keep the Roman hierarchy from baneful political activity, we must not try to do it by substituting the baneful political activity of a Protestant secret order. We must appeal rather on the basis of a broad Americanism to the whole body of our citizens, Jews, Protestants and Catholics alike.

The Roman Church in America is full of free spirits who, with sincere loyalty to the spiritual authority of their church, are for all that determined not to be political serfs of a foreign potentate in Rome, or an ecclesiastical hierarchy here. The one thing that will never do any good is this utterly un-American thing—this secret order of Protestants oath-bound, making the night its covering, and tar and feathers its instruments.

## Violation of Constitution

The Rev. William Carter, pastor of Throop Avenue Presbyterian Church, Brooklyn, attacked the Klan in a sermon at a union Thanksgiving service at the Marcy Avenue Baptist Church. He said:

Based, as they say, upon the Constitution and so upholding the majesty of the law, they daily violate the Constitution and break the holiest laws of the land. The Constitution guarantees to every man the right of trial by a jury of his peers. The Ku Klux Klan constitutes itself judge and jury and without any trial, condemns not only criminals, but oftentimes innocent men to punishment and death.

Are they any better than criminals? Are not they all law-breakers, and is it not time that we should consider that judgment and righteousness begin at home and that we cannot save others until we save ourselves?

A brief reference to the Klan was made by the Rev. Dr. Cornelius Woelfkin, pastor of the Fifth Avenue Baptist Church. He said he did not know the tenets of the Klan from the inside and could not condemn it from the outside. "Neither do I know the objects of the Knights of Columbus," he added. "It is the American spirit to tolerate no organizations that do not stand for American principles. All for each and each for all."

Rabbi Stephen S. Wise also referred to the Klan in a sermon at a union service of the Community Church and several synagogues at Temple Israel, Ninety-first Street and Broadway. "Such un-Americanism of intolerance and inhospitality as lifts up its head and yet masks itself behind the veil of the Ku Klux Klan must be driven out of America," he said.

The Rev. Dr. John Roach Straton, pastor of Calvary Baptist Church, the general evangelist of which, the Rev. Dr. Oscar Haywood, is the accredited lecturer of the Klan in New York City, made no reference to the Klan in his sermon. Dr. Straton urged that the United States should participate more actively in European affairs and that the time had come for America to be the servant of the world.

In his address at Temple Anche Chesed, Rabbi Jacob Kohn said:

"Strange, sinister phenomena are making themselves felt in American life. A huge organization, secret in its method and arrogant in its claim, is spreading like wild-fire throughout the land. The Protestant white race which it presumes to champion, is a myth, but the bigoted hate it is stirring up against all who are not white, or who, being white, are not Protestant, is a reality that is fast dividing the citizenship of our beloved land. Even the Universities, which should be centres of liberalism, are not free from the taint of racial and religious bigotry. God calls to America to preserve in America that freedom and toleration for which the soil of America has been kept inviolate."

*Source:* "Ku Klux Denounced from Many Pulpits." *The New York Times,*
December 1, 1922.

# "Ku Klux Klansmen March into Church," 1922

Hooded Band of Ten Give Kearny (N.J.) Pastor Letter, Which He Reads from Pulpit

The visit of ten members of the Ku Klux Klan, in full regalia of hoods and gowns, to the Grace Methodist Episcopal Church at Kearny, N.J. Sunday evening was the chief local topic of interest there yesterday, and disclosed the presence of an organized Klan in that town. The ten klansmen, the largest number who have participated in such a visitation in the neighborhood of New York City, entered the church by the main door while the congregation was singing "Onward Christian Soldiers." They walked to the pulpit and presented a letter to the pastor, the Rev. Frederick L. Rounds.

At the end of the hymn the klansmen left the church and rode away in an automobile. The envelope containing the letter bore the inscription, "Read this to your congregation," but the pastor preached his sermon first on the topic, "Why I believe the Protestant Bible is the Word of God." After his sermon Mr. Rounds read the letter, which was as follows:

"Rev. Frederick L. Rounds, Pastor:
Grace M.E. Church, Kearny, N.J.:

"Dear Sir, with a sincere desire to assist in all things, we, the members of the Kearny Provisional Klan, Realm of New Jersey, Invisible Empire, Ku Klux Klan, offer this slight donation for your building fund, and ask that it be received as a gift from the klansmen, who in their humble way try to follow the teachings of Jesus Christ.

"The K.K.K. is ever ready to assist in a worthy cause, without regard to race, creed, or color. You will find us at all times ready and willing to answer any call of charity that may be brought to our attention.

"We have been attacked by the enemies of pure Americanism, and our only reply has been, 'God forgive them, for they know not what they do.'

"To you sir, and your congregation we extend our greetings and pledge anew our faith in Him who gave his life that we might be saved. As Klansmen, we are pledged to the Bible, our country and the flag, and to protect the chastity of pure womanhood. Can men be banded together in a more noble cause? While our enemies and near-enemies are attacking our organization from all angles, we are standing on four-square, picking our men by the thousands, men of dependability and character, who accept Christ as their saviour. In due time, when the storm of vile abuse has passed over as a dark cloud, the sunshine will appear and the whole world will know the truth."

(Signed)
"THE KNIGHTS OF THE K.K.K."

The letterhead bore the name of the "Kearny Provisional Klan," but did not contain the names of any of its officers.

*Source:* "Ku Klux Klansmen March into Church." *The New York Times,*
December 19, 1922.

## Discussion Questions

1. Several of Langston Hughes's poems refer to actual people. Research the biographies of these people and analyze how Hughes uses the details of their lives in his poems. Examples include Ozie Powell, Booker T. Washington, Franklin D. Roosevelt, Tom Mooney, Helen Keller, Anne Spencer, and Captain Hugh Mulzac.
2. Write a poem in the form of a ballad about the life of a historical person you admire.
3. Read the work of other poets who wrote during the Harlem Renaissance and compare their social protest poems to those by Hughes or

McKay. Some other poets are Countee Cullen, Anne Spencer, Georgia Douglas Johnson, and Gwendolyn Bennett.

4. Research the literary period known as Modernism. Write an essay analyzing whether the poetry of Langston Hughes or Claude McKay exhibits the characteristics of modernist literature.

5. Both Langston Hughes and Claude McKay wrote fiction and non-fiction as well as poetry. Read a novel or book of nonfiction by one of these writers and write an essay comparing and contrasting the themes of that book with the themes developed in the poetry.

6. Watch movies that feature Ku Klux Klan activity and compare how the Klan is presented from film to film and time period to time period. Examples include *Birth of a Nation* directed by D. W. Griffith, *Mississippi Burning* directed by Alan Parker, or *Places in the Heart* directed by Robert Benton.

7. Read the full U.S. Constitution, including all of the amendments, keeping track of its statements on race. Which statements in the original version of the Constitution are revised through amendments? To what extent have amendments to the Constitution affected the legality of Klan activities over the three phases of its existence?

8. Hold a debate in your class focusing on whether the activities of the Ku Klux Klan are protected under the Constitution.

9. Read further about the beginnings of the Ku Klux Klan and then write an essay agreeing or disagreeing with William Garrott Brown's interpretation of those events.

10. Research other white supremacist organizations and discuss how they are similar to the Ku Klux Klan and how they differ.

11. Visit your local historical society to research events affected by racial tensions in your own city, town, or region.

12. After reading the article "Ku Klux Denounced from Many Pulpits," write an essay in which you choose one of the quoted members of the clergy as most representative of your own views and state why. If you disagree with all of the people quoted in this article, discuss the weaknesses of their views.

13. Interview a minister, priest, rabbi, imam, or other religious leader about his or her denomination's teachings on racial or ecumenical interactions.

14. Read articles focused on the Ku Klux Klan in other early 20th-century newspapers and compare their coverage with that of the *New York Times*.

## Suggested Readings

Bailey, Amy Kate and Karen A. Schnedker. "Practicing What They Preach: Lynching and Religion in the American South, 1890–1929." *Journal of Sociology* 117, no. 3 (2011): 844–87.

Baker, Kelly J. *The Gospel According to the Klan: The KKK's Appeal to Protestant America, 1915–1930.* Lawrence: University Press of Kansas, 2011.

Banks, Kimberly. "'Like a Violin for the Wind to Play': Lyrical Approaches to Lynching by Hughes, Du Bois, and Toomer." *African American Review* 38, no. 3 (2004): 451–65.

Blee, Kathleen and Amy McDowell. "The Duality of Spectacle and Secrecy: A Case Study of Fraternalism in the 1920s U.S. Ku Klux Klan." *Ethnic and Racial Studies* 36, no. 2 (2013): 249–65.

"A Brief History of the Ku Klux Klan." *The Journal of Blacks in Higher Education* 14 (Winter 1996–1997): 32.

Carcasson, Martin and James Arnt Aune. "Clansman on the Court: Justice Hugo Black's 1937 Radio Address to the Nation." *Quarterly Journal of Speech* 89, no. 2 (2003): 154–70.

Chalmers, David M. *Hooded Americanism: The History of the Ku Klux Klan.* New York: New Viewpoints, 1976.

Cunningham, David. *Klansville U.S.A.: The Rise and Fall of the Civil-Rights Era Ku Klux Klan.* New York: Oxford University Press, 2012.

Davis, David A. "Not Only War Is Hell: World War I and African American Lynching Narratives." *African American Review* 42, no. 3–4 (2008): 477–91.

Dixon, Thomas, Jr. *The Leopard's Spots: A Romance of the White Man's Burden.* New York: A. Wessels, 1906.

Dixon, Thomas, Jr. *The Clansman: An Historical Romance of the Ku Klux Klan.* Lexington: University Press of Kentucky, 1970.

Goldberg, David J. "Unmasking the Ku Klux Klan: The Northern Movement against the KKK, 1920–1925." *Journal of American Ethnic History* 15, no. 4 (1996): 32–49.

Horn, Stanley F. *Invisible Empire: The Story of the Ku Klux Klan 1866–1871.* New York: Haskell House, 1973.

Jackson, Keneth. *The Ku Klux Klan in the City, 1915–1930.* Chicago: Ivan R. Dee, 1992.

Laats, Adam. "Red Schoolhouse, Burning Cross: The Ku Klux Klan of the 1920s and Educational Reform." *History of Education Quarterly* 52, no. 3 (2012): 323–50.

Leeper, Ray. "The Ku Klux Klan, Public Highways, and the Public Forum." *Communications and the Law* 22, no. 4 (2000): 39–60.

McGee, Bryan R. "Speaking About the Other: W.E.B. Du Bois Responds to the Klan." *Southern Communication Journal* 63, no. 3 (1998): 208–20.

MacLean, Nancy. *Behind the Mask of Chivalry: The Making of the Second Ku Klux Klan.* New York: Oxford University Press, 1994.

McVeigh, Rory. *The Rise of the Ku Klux Klan: Right Wing Movements and National Politics.* Minneapolis: University of Minnesota Press, 2009.

Miller, W. Jason. *Langston Hughes and American Lynching Culture.* Gainesville: University Press of Florida, 2012.

Mitchell, Koritha. *Living with Lynching: African American Lynching Plays, Performance, and Citizenship, 1890–1930.* Urbana: University of Illinois Press, 2012.

Moore, Leonard J. "Historical Interpretations of the 1920's Klan: The Traditional View and the Populist Revision." *The Journal of Social History* 24, no. 2 (1990): 341–58.

Pegram, Thomas R. *One Hundred Percent American: The Rebirth and Decline of the Ku Klux Klan in the 1920s.* Chicago: Ivan R. Dee, 2011.

Ray, Stephen G., Jr. "Contending for the Cross: Black Theology and the Ghosts of Modernity." *Black Theology: An International Journal* 8, no. 1 (2010): 53–68.

Wade, Wyn Craig. *The Fiery Cross: The Ku Klux Klan in America.* New York: Simon and Schuster, 1987.

Wood, Amy Louise. *Lynching and Spectacle: Witnessing Racial Violence in America, 1890–1940.* Chapel Hill: University of North Carolina Press, 2011.

# HISTORICAL EXPLORATION: THE RUSSIAN REVOLUTION AND ATTRACTION OF THE COMMUNIST PARTY AMONG AMERICAN WRITERS

Many Americans today associate Communism with the Soviet Union and the cold war that pitted the United States and its allies against the Soviet Union and its allies in an ideological battle. Fear of communism in the United States reached its height during the McCarthy Hearings in the 1950s. Both the cold war and the McCarthy Hearings occurred after the Harlem Renaissance had concluded, and writers who were attracted to the Communist Party during the 1920s had a different understanding of communism than many people would have following World War II.

At its root, communism is an economic system that rejects class distinctions. While people would still need to work for a living, of course, communism would dismantle the privileges of those who owned the means of production—things like factories—because those privileges permit the owners, or capitalists, to exploit the workers. Instead, the means of production would be owned by the workers collectively. While communism is sometimes spoken of as if it is the opposite of democracy, this is a misunderstanding. Communism is better understood in opposition to capitalism. It is hypothetically possible for a country to be both communist and democratic, just as there are in fact countries that legitimately define themselves as democratic and socialist. (Communist countries have also often defined themselves as democratic, but few outsiders would agree that they are in fact democratic.)

One of the most famous founding documents of communism is *The Communist Manifesto,* written by Karl Marx and Friedrich Engels in 1848. It begins with a famous line, "A spectre is haunting Europe," and concludes with an even more famous line, "Working men of all countries, unite!" The goal of this manifesto was to encourage workers to put aside other differences in order to unite against those who were, according to Marx and Engels, oppressing them. This desire is prominent in several of Langston Hughes's poems.

Half a century later, communism seemed to be achieving significant political victories, especially as the Russian Revolution in 1917 resulted in the formation of the Soviet Union as a communist country. During this period, communists supported racial equality, which was one of the reasons why African Americans were particularly drawn to it. For many people, this was a time of great hope, for it seemed as if vast economic inequalities among people might be eliminated. Both Langston Hughes and Claude McKay were attracted to communism at this point, and they both visited the Soviet Union. Both also eventually became disillusioned.

Despite the paranoia that later characterized the McCarthy era, and despite the continued existence of the Communist Party USA, communism never made many inroads into American politics. One significant factor in this failure is that Americans often feel more loyalty to other demographic markers, such as ethnicity, race, or religion, than they do to people who share their economic class. Part of the reason for that is the tendency of many Americans to identify themselves as middle class, whether they live near the poverty line or have excessive wealth. In addition, Americans often subscribe to an ideology of individual success and celebrate people who seem to have pulled themselves up by their own bootstraps, without assistance from anyone else. (Of course, when those lives are examined more closely, they often did benefit from the assistance of others.)

Claude McKay's references to communism occur more often in his nonfiction than in his poetry, including a speech he gave in the Soviet Union, referred to in the last article below. Langston Hughes, however, addressed communism more directly and more frequently in his poetry.

In "Open Letter to the South," for example, he urges white workers to join with black workers, becoming unified through their identities as workers. In "Good Morning Revolution," he refers directly to the Soviet Union and criticizes the bosses who have access to wealth and privilege while the workers remain destitute. Similarly, in "One More 'S' in the U.S.A.," he celebrates the Soviet Union and urges the United States to imitate it. Other poems that are significantly influenced by Hughes's interest in communism are "Chant for Tom Mooney," "Always the Same," "Letter to the Academy," "Song of the Revolution," "Ballads of Lenin," "Chant for May Day," "Salute to Soviet Armies," and "Lenin."

### Communist Party Writing

The first two documents below contain excerpts from early materials published by the Communist Party in the United States. These documents attempt to explain the goals of communism to Americans. They were very cheaply produced, costing a nickel or a dime, so that many people could afford them, even if most people did not buy them. Like many communists, the authors of these pamphlets interpreted the massive social and technological disruption that occurred internationally during the first decades of the 20th century as a sign that communism was about to achieve many of its goals. They stress, however, that their goal is to disrupt an entire system, not simply to attack individuals, and that attacks on individuals were often counterproductive. Communism would be successful only if masses of people joined the movement, for it defined itself as a movement of and for the masses. The pamphlets attempt two different though complementary tasks: first, they must explain what communism is, and second, they must also refute accusations that have been made against communism, accusations that their readers will likely have heard.

## From Communist Party of America, Pamphlet No. 1, 1919

The world is on the verge of a new era. Europe is in revolt. The masses of Asia are stirring uneasily. Capitalism is in collapse. The workers of the world are seeing a new life and securing new courage. Out of the night of war is coming a new day.

The spectre of Communism haunts the world of capitalism. Communism, the hope of the workers to end misery and oppression.

The workers of Russia smashed the front of international Capitalism and Imperialism. They broke the chains of the terrible war; and in the midst of agony, starvation and the attacks of the capitalists of the world, they are creating a new social order.

The class war rages fiercely in all nations. Everywhere the workers are in a desperate struggle against their capitalist masters. The call to action has come. The workers must answer the call!

The Communist Party of America is the party of the working class. The Communist Party proposes to end Capitalism and organize a workers' industrial republic. The workers must control industry and dispose of the products of industry. The Communist Party is a party realizing the limitations of all existing workers' organizations and proposes to develop the revolutionary movement necessary to free the workers from the oppression of Capitalism. The Communist Party insists that the problems of the American worker are identical with the problems of the workers of the world.

*Source:* Communist Party of America. Manifesto and Program, Constitution, Report to the Communist International. Pamphlet No. 1, 1919: 1.

# From *Manifesto of the Communist Party of America,* 1922

To the Workers of the United States:

Barbarous persecution is today being directed against Communists and all those whom it suits the Department of Justice to call Communists. In the eyes of the Attorney General, every one who is "red," every one who is a "radical," every one who is class-conscious and takes his part in the class struggle in a conscientious manner, every trade unionist who refuses to betray the interests of the workers, is a Communist.

This is the "legal" basis for the arrest of Ruthenberg, Dunne and their fifteen brother workers at Bridgeman, Mich. This is the "legal" basis for the arrest of William Z. Foster.

## Turn to Workers of America

It is only on such a "legal" basis that agents of the Department of Justice have arrested fifteen other workers at the convention of the Trade Union Educational League in Chicago.

This always is the only "legal" basis, and is now again the only "legal" basis for the issuance of forty more warrants for the arrest of the workers who are charged with having attended an alleged "secret," "underground," "conspiratorial" convention in Michigan.

Workers of America! We are now turning to you. We want to make it clear to you why we are being persecuted.

The Government, the hordes of spies and stoolpigeons, and the kept press, are howling day and night: "Persecute and crush the Communists; they are a dangerous secret band of conspirators!" The Gompers clique rushes to the rescue of this unholy Trinity. And even the Socialist New York Call and the Forward print documents and evidence to prove that the Communists are an underground party with secret objects and mysterious methods.

## Want Workers to Know Everything

Workers of America! We want to make it clear to you why all the Powers that be of American capitalism have solidly lined up against us.

They are persecuting us, not because we are a secret band of conspirators.

The Communist Party of America is not a secret band of plotters. We do not desire to conceal a single one of our objects from the great working class of America. It is an infamous lie that we Communists organize campaigns of bomb throwing, dynamiting and sabotage. On the contrary, we Communists, as all of our manifestoes, books and press show, are in principle opposed to all such individual actions—instead of action of the masses—not because we want to save the capitalists, but because we know that all such terroristic acts are ineffective and would serve to confuse the working masses and poison public opinion against the workers' cause, and would afford the capitalist government an excuse to proceed against the workers.

We can perfectly well understand how honest, striking workers, embittered by the brutal oppression suffered by them under capitalism, resort to acts of sabotage, and we look upon the persecution of such workers with utmost disdain. But we do not look upon such methods as methods of the Revolution.

### Revolutionists Not Bomb Throwers

We are revolutionists and not bomb throwers. We want to destroy the whole building of capitalist society and not the building of some railway station.

We are after the life of the political and economic rule of the bourgeoisie and not after the life of this banker or that governmental official.

The road to the Workers' Revolution does not lie in train wrecks and petty dynamiting feats, but in broad, huge mass actions, that is thru the organized mass movements of the organized workers.

It is base and senseless slander to brand the Communists a small, sinister band in ambush. Face to face with all the workers of America, we openly declare that we have neither arms nor an armed organization. We know very well, however, that capitalism cannot be abolished without the use of force.

The capitalist magnates will hand over power to the workers only as willingly and as peacefully as the British Crown and Feudal Forces handed it over to the American bourgeoisie in 1776, and as peacefully and as willingly as the Southern slave owners freed their Negro slaves in the Civil War.

*Source: Manifesto of the Communist Party of America.* Milwaukee:
Labor Press Syndicate, 1922: 5–7.

### Newspaper Report on Communism and Race

The final document is an article from *The New York Times* that directly links communism to racial struggles in the United States and elsewhere. The article specifically mentions Claude McKay, who had attended the meeting though he did not have the authority there of an actual delegate. In his address to the delegates, McKay argued that one reason communism struggled to gain African American members was that racial tensions in the United States exceeded class tensions. McKay suggested that the amplification of racial tensions was at least partially intentional on the part of capitalists as a means of preventing the unification of the working class.

# "Negro's Rights Here Derided in Moscow," 1922

Internationale Hears a Proposal That the Communists Support Race Movement Everywhere

Moscow, Nov. 29. (Associated Press) The negro question came before an open session of the Third Internationale today. President Kolaroff proposed that detailed reports on the negro be submitted for the purpose of clarifying the subject for European members who are unfamiliar with the problem in other countries.

One negro delegate suggested that the Communist parties support the negro movement everywhere in connection with a proposal to call a congress at Moscow of all the revolutionary negro organizations of the world "to realize a united front of all workers against capitalism and imperialism."

The speaker said that the political rights of the negro in the United States were mere scraps of paper and that for a long time capitalists had been spreading propaganda among the negroes in favor of white capitalists and against white workers. Until now, he said, the workers had done nothing to counteract this.

Claude McKay, who, it was announced, is not a delegate, also addressed the Internationale, asserting that the negroes of America were denied the right of free assembly and were often lynched, one purpose of the capitalists being to turn the mind of the worker from class war by inciting him to race war.

*Source:* "Negro's Rights Here Derided in Moscow." *The New York Times,* November 30, 1922.

## Discussion Questions

1. Read several of Langston Hughes's poems that urge workers to unite or that celebrate communist leaders such as Vladimir Lenin. Analyze how these poems represent communism.
2. Read biographies of Langston Hughes and/or Claude McKay. How do the biographers explain the poets' attraction to communism?
3. Examine several poetry anthologies that feature the work of Langston Hughes or Claude McKay. Which of their poems are included

most often? Do these anthologies include any poems that directly refer to communism, the Soviet Union, the Russian Revolution, or related topics? If not, what are the topics of the poems included in anthologies? Why do you think other poems have retained greater interest for editors?

4. Write an essay describing an occasion when you felt exploited by others. What contributed to this exploitation? Could you have done (or did you do) anything to counteract this exploitation?

5. Write an essay describing a time when you felt united with others. What factors contributed to that unity?

6. Write a speech you would like to deliver to an international political organization.

7. Research the differences between these economic and political terms: capitalism, socialism, communism, democracy, fascism.

8. Look up the meaning of the word "manifesto" and write a manifesto of your own that addresses one of your strongly held beliefs.

9. Research various utopian communities, such as the 19th-century Brook Farm, New Harmony, or Fruitlands, and compare their ideals and practice with communist philosophy.

10. With a group of your classmates, create a contract for a utopian community you would like to join. Consider what kinds of things the members will hold in common and what they might own individually. Consider how work will be distributed and how labor will be measured. Consider how the group will determine who has authority over others and how much authority they have. Be as specific as possible.

11. Research membership of Americans in the Communist Party during the 1920s. Compare that to membership in the Ku Klux Klan. What can you conclude from your discoveries?

## Suggested Readings

Aaron, Daniel. *Writers on the Left: Episodes in American Literary Communism.* New York: Harcourt, Brace and World, 1961.

Cooper, Wayne F. *Claude McKay: Rebel Soldier in the Harlem Renaissance: A Biography.* Baton Rouge: Louisiana State University Press, 1996.

Dawahare, Anthony. "Langston Hughes's Radical Poetry and 'The End of Race.'" *MELUS* 23, no. 3 (1998): 21–41.

Draper, Theodore. *The Roots of American Communism.* Chicago: Ivan R. Dee, 1989.

Foner, Phillip S. and James S. Allen. *American Communism and Black Americans: A Documentary History, 1919–1929.* Philadelphia: Temple University Press, 1987.

Glazer, Nathan. *The Social Basis of American Communism.* New York: Harcourt, Brace & World, 1961.

Goldman, Emma. *Living My Life.* 2 vols. New York: Dover, 1970.

Gould, Rebecca. "Jim Crow in the Soviet Union." *Callaloo* 36, no. 1 (2013): 125–41.

Haywood, Harry. *Black Bolshevik: Autobiography of an Afro-American Communist.* Chicago: Liberator Press, 1978.

Howe, Irving and Lewis Coser. *The American Communist Party: A Critical History (1919–1957).* Boston: Beacon, 1957.

Hudson, Hosea and Nell Irvin Painter. *The Narrative of Hosea Hudson His Life as a Negro Communist in the South.* Cambridge: Harvard University Press, 1979.

Kelley, Robin D. G. *Hammer and Hoe: Alabama Communists during the Great Depression.* Chapel Hill: University of North Carolina Press, 1990.

Kornweibel, Theodore Jr. *Seeing Red: Federal Campaigns against Black Militancy, 1919–1925.* Bloomington: Indiana University Press, 1999.

Leffler, Melvin P. *The Specter of Communism: The United States and the Origins of the Cold War, 1917–1953.* New York: Hill and Wang, 1994.

Marx, Karl and Friedrich Engels. *The Communist Manifesto.* New York: Signet, 1998.

Maxwell, William. *New Negro, Old Left: African American Writing and Communism between the Wars.* New York: Columbia University Press, 1999.

McDuffie, Erik S. *Sojourning for Freedom: Black Women, American Communism, and the Making of Black Left Feminism.* Durham, NC: Duke University Press, 2011.

Naison, Mark. *Communists in Harlem during the Depression.* Urbana: University of Illinois Press, 2005.

Rampersad, Arnold. *The Life of Langston Hughes: Volume I, 1902–1941, I Too Sing America.* New York: Oxford University Press, 2002.

Rampersad, Arnold. *The Life of Langston Hughes: Volume II, 1941–1967, I Dream a World.* New York: Oxford University Press, 2002.

Scott, Jonathan. *Socialist Joy in the Writing of Langston Hughes.* Columbia: University of Missouri Press, 2006.

Smethurst, James. "The Red Is East: Claude McKay and the New Black Radicalism of the Twentieth Century." *American Literary History* 21, no. 2 (2009): 355–67.

Smith, S.A. *The Oxford Handbook of the History of Communism.* New York: Oxford University Press, 2014.

Solomon, Mark. *The Cry Was Unity: Communists and African-Americans, 1917–36.* Jackson: University Press of Mississippi, 1998.

Wright, Richard. *Native Son.* New York: HarperPerennial, 2005.

Young, Robert. "Langston Hughes's 'Red' Poetics." *Langston Hughes Review* 18 (2004): 16–21.

Zumoff, J.A. "Mulattoes, Reds, and the Fight for Black Liberation in Claude McKay's Trial by Lynching and Negroes in America." *Journal of West Indian Literature* 19, no. 1 (2010): 22–53.

# WHY WE READ THE POETRY OF CLAUDE MCKAY AND LANGSTON HUGHES TODAY

In this chapter, we have examined many of the political concerns of the poetry of Langston Hughes and Claude McKay. Some of these concerns remain pertinent to contemporary readers, as issues of racial justice, violence, and political affiliation continue to affect the personal and public lives of all Americans, indeed of virtually all people in the world. Both Hughes and McKay exercised significant influence over the development of the Harlem Renaissance, influencing other writers aesthetically and personally. One could not become very familiar with the Harlem Renaissance or with American literature generally during the early 20th century without becoming familiar with the work of these poets. Although the topics of many of the poems of Langston Hughes and Claude McKay are similar, their styles are dramatically different, and those stylistic differences affect how the work is received today.

McKay writes in received forms, often sonnets. Free verse poetry became dominant over the second half of the 20th century and remains preferred by many working poets today. As a result, poets who write in received forms sometimes garner less attention from contemporary readers than they otherwise might. Yet McKay's work benefits from his attraction to form—his language is tight and compressed while also being straightforward. His use of a regular rhyme scheme permits his poems, especially the sonnets, to close with a definite click, reinforcing the tone.

McKay's most well-known sonnets, "If We Must Die" and "America," have been read, adopted, and proclaimed by later groups who have felt themselves also oppressed, and some of his poems do invite inclusive readings. However, readers need to be careful not to dilute the poems' force as protests against racism, and their historical context should not be ignored, particularly since some of the actions and attitudes that McKay objected to remain, even if they are no longer as widespread.

Langston Hughes's poetry remains very popular. As a driving force behind the Harlem Renaissance, he befriended and influenced many of the other writers associated with this period (although occasionally his relationships disintegrated, as the chapter on Zora Neale Hurston will illustrate). Another factor in Hughes's continued popularity is his prolific output—he wrote several hundred poems, as well as material in other genres. And he continued to write poetry until his death in 1967, so some of his work has a more contemporary frame of reference than does the work of many other writers of the Harlem Renaissance. Although some of his poems were very topical when they were written and so allude to events or people that may seem obscure to 21st-century readers, the style of many of his poems makes them very accessible; they can be enjoyed by people of all ages and levels of education. He may be as well known, though, for one particular line as for any of his poems, the line quoted by Lorraine Hansberry for the title of her play, *A Raisin in the Sun.* His other most well-known poems include "Mother to Son," "The Negro Speaks of Rivers," and "Theme for English B."

Because this chapter has focused on controversial and disturbing historical events that informed the environment in which Langston Hughes and Claude McKay worked—as well as providing some of their content—readers of this book might assume that all of Hughes's and McKay's poetry is overtly political. Both writers, however, wrote about many other topics, and some of their poems are quite joyful. They celebrate music and love and the community spirit that characterized Harlem during the 1920s. Hughes especially adopts stylistic devices from the blues and jazz; his poems are infused with that musical energy. Simultaneously, many of his poems rely on simple rhymes that can nevertheless surprise the reader and, especially, the listener. To these poems, the reader reacts with surprise and responds with delight. Claude McKay and Langston Hughes, in other words, used their talent and skills as writers to demand justice for people who experienced racism and other injustices, but they were whole people who also described happier occasions.

# IV

# *Cane*

## HISTORICAL BACKGROUND

*Cane* is an unusual book, comprising multiple genres—poetry, vignettes, short stories—that are usually published separately even if they are written by the same author. It is often called a novel because the separate sections comment on each other thematically, though sometimes it seems to be called a novel simply because it is an extended piece of (mostly) prose published between the same covers. Yet it does not exhibit the narrative arc most readers expect from novels, nor do the characters develop into the rounded figures typically found in novels. Nearly all of the individual pieces can stand alone; they benefit thematically from their context, but they don't depend on other sections or chapters for their sense. The unity in *Cane* is found in its lyricism and its motifs, but such unity often characterizes collections of poetry or shorter prose pieces, fiction or nonfiction. Another way of interpreting *Cane* is as a collection of linked stories that together create a world but that do not develop through the causal relationships typical of chapters in a novel. These generic labels—poem, story, novel—can be handy as efficient entry points into discussion of a book,

The original caption to this photograph in 1934 identifies Jean Toomer as a "colored author, essayist, and psychologist." Toomer's racial identification of himself shifted over the course of his life. (Bettmann/Corbis)

and they may even help us interpret a book since we have different expectations of different genres, but ultimately the question of genre in *Cane* is less interesting than many of the other questions we can ask about this particular piece of literature.

Jean Toomer himself did not consider *Cane* a novel, and he initially did not plan to publish the three major sections together as one book. He began writing the pieces that would form the first section on a train back to Washington, D.C., after he had spent a few months in Georgia. Experiencing life in the Deep South for the first time as a young man, he interpreted much that he saw mythically rather than, perhaps, realistically. He initially submitted only what now forms the first section of the book to publishers, but they found it too short to publish independently. In response, Toomer wrote the material that follows, set in the more urban Washington, D.C., and Chicago. The book is organized into three major sections, each one consisting of several shorter pieces. The first section occurs in Georgia and features female characters most prominently. The second section focuses more on relationships between men and women in urban spaces, while the third returns to the South but is more dispiriting in its attitude toward both the past and the future.

Several of the vignettes reveal the difficult positions women find themselves in, and they address the ramifications of sexual activity. Judged by others as shameful, the female characters tend to live in psychic isolation. Although the narrator often seems to perceive these characters as fulfilled through their sexuality, many readers interpret them as confined by definitions and expectations of gender. These characters are as often acted upon as permitted to act.

Published originally in 1923, *Cane* is one of the earliest major texts of the Harlem Renaissance. Claude McKay had published *Harlem Shadows* a year earlier, but most of the texts now thought to form the canon of this period had not yet been published, or even written. For this reason, *Cane* had a profound influence on other African American writers who could see hope for themselves in his success. Yet the book itself does not look ahead toward a gleaming postwar future but rather back toward a time and lifestyle that were fading into history. Yet the style is modernist, not only because different genres collide with each other, but also because of the disillusionment and alienation experienced by some of the characters and the fragmentation of consciousness revealed through Toomer's point of view choices. Especially when read against 19th-century literature, this book is impressively experimental.

Ironically, however, given its influence on other African American writers, *Cane* did not signal the beginning of an oeuvre centered on African American experience; rather, Toomer quickly turned toward other material. When others later attempted to define his work as African American, Toomer resisted, denying permission for poems from *Cane* to be included in an anthology of African American writing and eventually even denying, or at least questioning, his own African ancestry. Many writers and other artists resist classifications according to demographic factors, preferring to be known as a "poet," for example, rather than as a "woman poet" or "black poet" because the classification can seem to diminish the achievement, implying that the writing is not accomplished enough to be considered alongside all other work but only alongside a limited sample. On the other hand, this resistance can also stem from a writer's own internalized sexism or racism. Any potential relationship between those two motives is difficult to untangle, even for the writer himself or herself; such a task would be virtually impossible for a critic writing from a distance of decades. Contemporary readers may wish that Toomer had followed *Cane* with similar material, but ultimately this book succeeds regardless of what its author wrote after 1923.

Like many pieces of literature that later attain significant success, *Cane* received some positive critical attention when it was published, but it was not particularly popular among general readers. White readers found neither the stereotypic southern black minstrelsy with which they were familiar, nor the energy they associated voyeuristically with Harlem. A new edition was published in 1967, however, and since then Toomer has garnered substantial scholarly attention. His work appears in literary anthologies and on the syllabi of college courses. Many critics currently attend to Toomer's ambivalence toward a racialized identity, while others analyze his interests in spirituality. Not surprisingly given the focus of *Cane,* one of the most intriguing critical questions continues to be the development of female characters and Toomer's attitudes toward gender.

# ABOUT JEAN TOOMER

Jean Toomer was born in 1894 in Washington, D.C.; his given name was Nathan Pinchback Toomer. He was named after his father, Nathan Toomer, and given his mother's maiden name as his middle name. His father had been married twice before he married Nina Pinchback, over the objections of her family. Both the Pinchback and the Toomer families were racially mixed, with European and African American ancestry, and both families were economically advantaged. When Nathan Toomer abandoned his family soon after Jean Toomer was born, his mother moved with her son back to her family home. Toomer's maternal grandfather, angry at his son-in-law's behavior, insisted that his grandson be called something other than Nathan, so the family began calling him Eugene, which was his godfather's name. Eugene was shortened to Jean as a nickname, and it was this name that stuck. Toomer's mother remarried when he was still a boy, but she died in 1909, and he spent the remainder of his youth living with his maternal grandparents in Washington, D.C.

Because of his mixed-race ancestry, Jean Toomer's complexion was light, and many people assumed he was white. Scholars disagree about whether he intentionally passed as white or simply passively permitted others to think what they would. During his childhood, his family sometimes lived in a predominantly white neighborhood, and at other times in a predominantly black area; how his extended family members identified themselves racially is not always clear. In later life, Toomer attempted to identify himself as what he was—a person whose ancestry included several ethnicities, or in other words, an American—but most people nevertheless insisted on categorizing him as black. At that time, racial categories were more rigidly defined than they are today, and most Americans understood race according to binary systems—one could be either black or white, never both.

After graduating from the rigorous Dunbar High School, Toomer attended several colleges, but he never completed a degree. He also held several jobs, unable or unwilling to settle on a career. In terms of his literary career, a significant experience was a few months he spent as a school principal in Georgia, where he witnessed a style of racism he had not previously known. Much of this experience informs *Cane*. He read widely, however, and his reading seems to have influenced him more than many other aspects of his life. During his twenties, many of his friends were intellectuals and artists, most especially Waldo Frank, a well-known writer at the time who influenced the development of *Cane,* although the two men had a major falling out soon after the publication of Toomer's novel.

Both men, however, had become interested in the mystical philosophy of George I. Gurdjieff, and during the mid-1920s Toomer studied at the Gurdjieff Institute in France. Returning to the United States, he taught this philosophy to others, including Nella Larsen, whose work is the subject of the next chapter of this book.

Toomer married for the first time in 1931; his wife, Margery Latimer, also a writer, was white, and their marriage was controversial, even scandalous to some. Margery died a year later, giving birth to their daughter, whom Toomer named after his deceased wife. He remarried in 1934. His second wife was photographer Marjorie Content, also white; they remained married until Toomer's death. In 1940, the couple moved to Doylestown, Pennsylvania, where they joined the Religious Society of Friends (Quakers), though Toomer also continued his study of Gurdjieff and explored other spiritual and psychological ideas over much of his life.

Toomer had begun to publish poems and stories in periodicals as a comparatively young man. Ironically, perhaps, when Toomer submitted a story to *The Liberator* magazine, which was edited by Claude McKay, McKay

The original caption of this photograph, from March 26, 1932, identifies Jean Toomer as a "part-negro poet and psychologist, with his bride, the former Marjory Latimer." (Bettmann/Corbis)

rejected the work because he felt that it was unclear—but he also assumed that "Jean" was a woman. *Cane,* Toomer's only novel—if novel is what it is—was published in 1923, when Toomer was 29. After the publication of *Cane,* Toomer turned his attention away from African American subjects, though he continued to publish essays and plays and other shorter works. After *Cane,* however, Toomer found publication difficult, and his publication record does not adequately represent the writing he produced. His last published works were pamphlets addressing Quaker ideas. He stopped publishing during the 1940s, though he continued to write, especially autobiographical material that wasn't published until after his death. Much that Toomer wrote, in fact, has been posthumously collected and either published for the first time or reprinted. Aside from *Cane,* which was reprinted in 1969, most significant are probably his collected poems and his letters. Despite the fact that Toomer often resisted classification as an African American writer, most critical attention to his work focuses on its place within the Harlem Renaissance, and nearly all of it examines *Cane.*

Jean Toomer died in Doylestown, Pennsylvania, in 1967, just two months before Langston Hughes would die in New York. As is true with many writers, including Zora Neale Hurston whose work is discussed later in Chapter VI of this book, Toomer's posthumous reputation exceeds the respect he received during his lifetime. He was elected to the Georgia Hall of Fame in 2002, despite the fact that he lived there only briefly. Although his work isn't as popular as the poetry of Langston Hughes nor is *Cane* as well-known as *Their Eyes Were Watching God,* it is unlikely that Jean Toomer will disappear from public attention again anytime soon.

## HISTORICAL EXPLORATION: LYNCHING

"Lynching" is the term applied to a murder when the victim is overtaken by a mob and killed. Although lynchings are most often associated with hanging, victims of lynching were sometimes burned alive or shot; occasionally their bodies were burned after they had been hung. Victims were frequently tortured before they died; some descriptions that can be found in newspaper articles or other historical sources are disturbingly gruesome. Lynchings evoke such terror because the victim generally isn't permitted a trial but is often arbitrarily identified as a target (less commonly, a person who had been convicted of a crime is forcibly removed from a jail before he can be executed so that he can be lynched by vigilantes). In the United States, lynchings occurred most often in the South between 1880 and 1920, although some instances of lynching occurred even before the

Civil War, and they continued intermittently until the 1960s. And while most lynchings occurred in the South, several also occurred in northern states. African Americans were the most frequent victims; over 3,000 African Americans are known to have been lynched by groups of white people during this period. Yet some white people were also lynched.

The number of lynchings increased as whites in the South regained power. Immediately following the war, the Ku Klux Klan was involved in several hundred lynchings, but the Klan's activities diminished temporarily, only to rearise in the second decade of the 20th century. One political motive of lynching was to terrorize African Americans into relinquishing their determination to vote or exercise other rights as citizens. Despite the Constitutional Amendments that had been passed following the Civil War, many white people remained unwilling to perceive African Americans as equal citizens; they certainly were not willing to permit African Americans to hold political power over whites. While the legislatures of many southern states wrote laws that effectively disenfranchised African Americans, other individuals went further, accomplishing illegally what they could not entirely accomplish legally.

One of the most disturbing aspects of lynching was the public support they received, to the extent that it became a spectator sport. Crowds would gather to witness the spectacle as if it were a form of grotesque entertainment. Some took photographs and printed post cards as souvenirs; the publicity inspired further fear among potential victims.

The vigilantes involved in lynching generally claimed that the victim had committed a crime, and that the courts did not work effectively or swiftly enough to accomplish proper punishment. Since some lynchings occurred after a victim had been tried and sentenced, however, the claim of an ineffective judicial system is obviously false. Some mobs were simply determined to engage in direct vigilante violence. Most often, the purported crime was said to be rape of a white woman, stemming from firmly held stereotypes regarding the sexual proclivities of free black men. Claims that a rape or other form of sexual harassment had occurred were nearly always exaggerated and often entirely fabricated. Rumors of rape, however, evoked such rage and fear among some white people that they were willing, even eager, to suspend the law in their quest for their own version of justice.

Lynching as a characteristic of southern life is most prominent in the chapter called "Blood-Burning Moon" in the first section of *Cane* and to a lesser extent in the long chapter called "Kabnis" that comprises the third section of the book. "Blood-Burning Moon" features three central characters. Louisa, an African American woman, works in the kitchen of a white family. The youngest son of that family, Bob Stone, is in love with Louisa, and she reciprocates his love. However, Louisa is also loved by Tom Burwell, an African American man who works in the fields and so believes he's at a disadvantage since he can't easily communicate his love to Louisa. Tom is also less articulate than many others, so even when he can spend time with Louisa he can't speak his feelings very easily. Though she loves Bob, Louisa is aware that she might be better off giving her heart to an African American man. When Tom is working with a group of others boiling sugar cane, another man speculates about Louisa's relationship with Bob Stone, and Tom goes to Louisa for assurance that the rumors are untrue.

Bob Stone, though he is obsessed with Louisa, can't quite make sense of his desire and wishes that times had never changed, that he could still be the master of Louisa as his ancestors had been masters of others. He believes that as a white man, he should not need to negotiate with an African American person, male or female. When Louisa does not appear for their pre-arranged date, Bob goes looking for her and finds her with Tom. Bob attacks Tom, and when Tom defends himself, he kills Bob by slicing his throat with a knife. The African American witnesses go into hiding, turning out the lights in their homes because they know what is likely to happen—and if white people are intent on lynching, they don't want to be found.

A mob of white men captures Tom and ties him to a stake. They soak the ground with kerosene, and then they set Tom on fire. Toomer describes Tom's death graphically, as the mob swarms around him, relinquishing their humanity. Although many of the lyrical details in this story are very poetic, this scene is horrifying and consistent with descriptions of lynchings found in newspaper reports and other nonfiction sources.

In "Kabnis," a northern African American has gone South to teach. He initially believes that he is safe because he defines himself as a "gentleman," but his companion, Layman, warns him that white people don't recognize class distinctions among African Americans. Layman continues, describing occasions he's seen lynch mobs mutilate bodies long after the victims were dead. He describes a time when a mob brutally killed a pregnant woman and then ripped the still-living fetus from her in order to kill it because she had tried to hide her husband from the mob. Kabnis begins to fear for his own life, and he is soon forced to leave the school, though not primarily for fear of southern whites but because he has been drinking.

## Ida B. Wells

The first document below is taken from a speech and article by Ida B. Wells (1862–1931), who was the most prominent antilynching proponent at the turn of the 20th century. She had been born a slave during the Civil War; her parents died of yellow fever when she was a teenager. As a young adult, she worked as a journalist, often reporting on discrimination against African Americans. Her life changed on March 9, 1892, when she was 30 years old and three acquaintances were lynched in Memphis, Tennessee. After this, Wells devoted much of her life to publicizing lynching and its racist foundations. Her work was widely published and widely read. In the excerpt below, Wells asserts her belief that lynchings were not simply the impulsive acts of out-of-control mobs but were in fact an ingrained feature of American life designed to dominate and terrorize African Americans. She refers to an "unwritten law" that people seem to believe has the force and authority of written law, when in fact unwritten laws are not laws at all. She cites several specific incidents and highlights two major points: that lynchings violate the most fundamental principles upon which the United States was founded, and that most often a single innuendo or suggestion that a white woman has been attacked is sufficient for vigilantes to lynch a black man. This idea that white women are continually vulnerable to attacks by black men is a feature of nearly all responses to lynching.

## From Ida B. Wells, "Lynch Law in America," 1900

Our country's national crime is *lynching*. It is not the creature of an hour, the sudden outburst of uncontrolled fury, or the unspeakable brutality of an insane mob. It represents the cool, calculating deliberation of intelligent people who openly avow that there is an "unwritten law" that justifies them in putting human beings to death without complaint under oath, without trial by jury, without opportunity to make defense, and without right of appeal. . . .

No emergency called for lynch law. It asserted its sway in defiance of law and in favor of anarchy. There it has flourished ever since, marking the thirty years of its existence with the inhuman butchery of more than ten thousand men, women, and children by shooting, drowning,

As an antilynching crusader and the founder of the African American women's club movement and other civil rights organizations, Ida Wells-Barnett was one of the most influential African American women of the late 19th and early 20th centuries. (Getty Images)

hanging, and burning them alive. Not only this, but so potent is the force of example that the lynching mania has spread throughout the North and middle West. It is now no uncommon thing to read of lynchings north of Mason and Dixon's line, and those most responsible for this fashion gleefully point to these instances and assert that the North is no better than the South.

This is the work of the "unwritten law" about which so much is said, and in whose behest butchery is made a pastime and national savagery condoned. The first statute of this "unwritten law" was written in the blood of thousands of brave men who thought that a government that was good enough to create a citizenship was strong enough to protect it. Under the authority of a national law that gave every citizen the right to vote, the newly-made citizens chose to exercise their suffrage. But the reign of the national law was short-lived and illusionary. Hardly had the sentences dried upon the statute-books before one Southern State after another raised the cry against "negro domination" and proclaimed there was an "unwritten law" that justified any means to resist it. . . .

The alleged menace of universal suffrage having been avoided by the absolute suppression of the negro vote, the spirit of mob murder should have been satisfied and the butchery of negroes should have ceased. But men, women, and children were the victims of murder by individuals and murder by mobs, just as they had been when killed at the demands of the "unwritten law" to prevent "negro domination." Negroes were killed for disputing over terms of contracts with their employers. If a few barns were burned some colored man was killed to stop it. If a colored man resented the imposition of a white man and the two came to blows, the colored man had to die, either at the hands of the white man then and there or later at the hands of a mob that speedily gathered. If he showed a spirit of courageous manhood he was hanged for his pains, and the killing was justified by the declaration that he was a "saucy nigger." Colored women have been murdered because they refused to tell the mobs where relatives could be found for "lynching bees." Boys of fourteen years have been lynched by white representatives of American civilization. In fact, for all kinds of offenses—and, for no offenses—from murders to misdemeanors, men and women are put to death without judge or jury; so that, although the political excuse was no longer necessary, the wholesale murder of human beings went on just the same. A new name was given to the killings and a new excuse was invented for so doing.

Again the aid of the "unwritten law" is invoked, and again it comes to the rescue. During the last ten years a new statute has been added to the "unwritten law." This statute proclaims that for certain crimes or alleged crimes no negro shall be allowed a trial; that no white woman shall be compelled to charge an assault under oath or to submit any such charge to the investigation of a court of law. The result is that many men have been put to death whose innocence was afterward established; and today, under this reign of the "unwritten law," no colored man, no matter what his reputation, is safe from lynching if a white woman, no matter what her standing or motive, cares to charge him with insult or assault.

It is considered a sufficient excuse and reasonable justification to put a prisoner to death under this "unwritten law" for the frequently repeated charge that these lynching horrors are necessary to prevent crimes against women. The sentiment of the country has been appealed to, in describing the isolated condition of white families in thickly populated negro districts; and the charge is made that these homes are in as great danger as if they were surrounded by wild beasts. And the world has accepted this theory without let or hindrance. In many cases there has been open expression that the fate meted out to the victim was only what he deserved. In many other instances there has been a silence that says more forcibly than words can proclaim it that it is right and proper that a human being should be seized by a mob and burned to death upon the unsworn and the uncorroborated charge of his accuser. No matter that our laws presume every man innocent until he is proved guilty; no matter that it leaves a certain class of individuals completely at the mercy of another class; no matter that it encourages those criminally disposed to blacken their faces and commit any crime in the calendar so long as they can throw suspicion on some negro, as is frequently done, and then lead a mob to take his life; no matter that mobs make a farce of the law and a mockery of justice; no matter that hundreds of boys are being hardened in crime and schooled in vice by the repetition of such scenes before their eyes—if a white woman declares herself insulted or assaulted, some life must pay the penalty, with all the horrors of the Spanish Inquisition and all the barbarism of the Middle Ages. The world looks on and says it is well.

Not only are two hundred men and women put to death annually, on the average, in this country by mobs, but these lives are taken with the greatest publicity. In many instances the leading citizens aid and abet by their presence when they do not participate, and the leading journals inflame the public mind to the lynching point with scare-head articles and offers of rewards. Whenever a burning is advertised to take place, the railroads run excursions, photographs are taken, and the same jubilee is indulged in that characterized the public hangings of one hundred years ago. There is, however, this difference: in those old days the multitude that stood by was permitted only to guy or jeer. The 19th century lynching mob cuts off ears, toes, and fingers, strips off flesh, and distributes portions of the body as souvenirs among the crowd. If the leaders of the mob are so minded, coal-oil is poured over the body and the victim is then roasted to death. This has been done in Texarkana and Paris, Tex., in Bardswell, Ky., and in Newman, Ga. In Paris the officers of the law delivered the prisoner to the mob. The mayor gave the school children a holiday and the railroads ran excursion trains so that the people might see a human being burned to death. In Texarkana, the year before, men and boys amused themselves by cutting off strips of flesh and thrusting knives into their helpless victim. At Newman, Ga., of the present year, the mob tried every conceivable torture to compel the victim to cry out and confess, before they set fire to the faggots that burned him. But their trouble was all in vain—he never uttered a cry, and they could not make him confess. . . .

The negro has suffered far more from the commission of this crime [rape] against the women of his race by white men than the white race has ever suffered through *his* crimes. Very scant notice is taken of the matter when this is the condition of affairs. What becomes a crime deserving capital punishment when the tables are turned is a matter of small moment when the negro woman is the accusing party.

But since the world has accepted this false and unjust statement, and the burden of proof has been placed upon the negro to vindicate his race, he is taking steps to do so. The Anti-Lynching Bureau of the National Afro-American Council is arranging to have every lynching investigated and publish the facts to the world, as has been done in the case of Sam Hose, who was burned alive last April at Newman, Ga. The detective's report showed that Hose killed Cranford, his employer, in self-defense, and that, while a mob was organizing to hunt Hose to punish him for killing a white man, not till twenty-four hours after the murder was the charge of rape, embellished with psychological and physical impossibilities, circulated. That gave an impetus to the hunt, and the Atlanta *Constitution's* reward of $500 keyed the mob to the necessary burning and roasting pitch. Of five hundred newspaper clippings of that horrible affair, nine-tenths of them assumed Hose's guilt—simply because his murderers said so, and because it is the fashion to believe the negro peculiarly addicted to this species of crime. All the negro asks is justice—a fair and impartial trial in the courts of the country. That given, he will abide the result. . . .

*Source:* Wells, Ida B. "Lynch Law in America."
*Arena,* January 1900.

## Magazine Reports of Lynching

The next two documents are taken from popular magazines published close to the turn of the 20th century, after lynching had become undeniably common but decades before enough people with enough power would become outraged enough by the practice to stop it. The fact that this topic appeared in such periodicals indicates how widespread the practice must have been. The first document "Colored Men Protest" reports on and supports a protest rally against lynching in New York City. The article specifies that the rally featured both black and white speakers, confirming that any racial divide wasn't absolute—although the mobs tended to be composed of white men, many other white men objected to their actions. The author of this article also suggests that any disruptive activity protesting against lynching is well-earned disruption, for the crime is so barbaric as to require an outraged response. The second article also provides evidence that people supporting or opposing lynching cannot easily be divided into whites and blacks, or northerners and southerners. According to this article, several prominent southerners have spoken forcefully against lynching, including the governor of Georgia. If people want to take the law into their own hands, some of these men suggest, they should not expect representatives of the law to ignore their actions. Governor Atkinson even suggests that people have intentionally spread false rumors in order to incite a lynching so that others would murder their competitors; lynching, in other words, was sometimes simply a business decision. Again, this article describes some of the lynchings in graphic detail, but the context suggests that readers would likely have been familiar with such descriptions. Perhaps most importantly, the governor states that everyone in a community is responsible for the mores of that community, and when people keep silent, they permit the criminals to succeed.

## "Colored Men Protest," 1892

The mass meeting of colored citizens at Cooper Union on April 4th, to protest against lawless outrages upon their race in the South, was impressive in its numbers and earnestness. The speakers were of both races, but the addresses made by such colored leaders as Hon. John R. Lynch of Mississippi and Rev. W. B. Derrick gave a thoroughly representative character to the demonstration. The protest made against the continued barbarous treatment of the negroes in the Southern States should have its effect on public sentiment. The newspapers have contained many accounts of late of the lynching of black men under the most revolting circumstances. The same diabolic disposition manifested by the Texarkana mob that coolly burned their victim alive has been shown in numerous other Southern localities where colored men accused of crime have been brutally slaughtered by armed mobs without trial or hearing.

No intelligent colored man wants criminals of his own race to go unpunished. But every man in the country, black as well as white, is entitled to the protection of the law, and to a fair legal trial when charged with wrong doing. In many places in the South to-day law is only for the whites; the mob, the rope and the Winchester are for the negroes. And the very men who deny the benefits of the law to members of the colored race are themselves deliberate law breakers by their action in forcibly suppressing the negro's right to the franchise.

The rule of the minority through brute force in many Southern States, and the constant tendency to regard the negro as a being outside the pale of the law, is a disgrace to our civilization and a crime against nineteenth century enlightenment. These wrongs cannot continue without endangering the peace and security of every State in which they exist. They concern the whole nation; for the evil effects which they bring about injure the whole country, North and South alike.

The condemnation of Southern race outrages by the colored people of New York last night was not one whit too severe. The appeal which they made to public sentiment and American justice should not go unanswered.

*Source:* "Colored Men Protest." *The American Missionary* 46, no. 5 (1892): 145–46.

## "Southern Protests against Lynching," 1898

While the crime of lynching has not of late by any means been confined to our Southern States, certain well-known conditions have made it more frequent there. It is therefore interesting to note that from the South have lately come some of the most earnest protests against this disgrace to our civilization.

In an address delivered not long ago by Edward J. McDermott of Louisville, Kentucky, strong ground was taken against these outrages from the point of view of a lawyer and a statesman. The papers have recently printed a charge to the grand jury in Nashville, Tennessee, by Judge Anderson, in which he urged the enforcement of the law against those who take the law into their own hands. Said the judge: "An application of this law to a few mobbers will give them a respect for the law and a regard for the peace and order of the community that they never felt before. Whenever occasion arises," he added, "I intend to see, so far as I can, that it is enforced in all its provisions; and I am sure that you will not be found remiss in your duty in regard thereto. Let the law be promulgated, and the people understand that it will be enforced if violated, and then rarely, if ever, will occasion arise for the infliction of its penalties."

But the most important recent Southern deliverance on the subject which has come to our notice is that of Governor Atkinson of Georgia. His message to the General Assembly of the State on the 27th of October last discusses the whole subject with freedom and force. It seems that since November 1, 1894, there have been lynched in Georgia one negro woman, two white men, and nineteen black men—twenty-two in all. Nine of these, including one white man, were not charged with the revolting crime, or the attempt thereat, which occasions a majority of the lynchings in the Southern States.

The governor, in the course of his presentation of the subject, makes the startling statement that he believes that during his administration there have been several men lynched who were not guilty of the crimes with which they were charged. "How many cannot be known, for their tongues are hushed, and they are denied an opportunity to prove their innocence. I am informed," says the governor, "that one man whom the mob believed to be guilty was shot down. *A question then arose as to his identity,* and he was salted down like a hog, shipped to the location of the crime, and found to be the wrong man!" The governor calls attention to the fact that during the past year evidence has come to light in other States showing that victims of the mob have been innocent men. During this governor's term, one man who was rescued from the mob was afterward tried and proved innocent. Another fled from the mob to the executive office, obtained protection and a trial by jury, and he too was proved not guilty.

Again, it appears, as would naturally be expected in such circumstances, that false charges have been made against men with a view of bringing about their convenient removal by lynch law, though in the special instances cited without the complete success of the plot. In one case this was the means sought for the suppression of evidence against a violator of the prohibition law; in another case the object was to prevent the collection of a debt!

Governor Atkinson insists that lynch law tends to let the guilty escape; that it discourages investment, drives away immigration, advertises the State as lawless and half civilized, and degrades the character of the people. "This barbarous practice," he declares with patriotic indignation, "does not decrease, but increases, crime. Having stained their hands in blood, its perpetrators are more easily led again to violate law. Recently a man tried on the charge of murder and convicted of shooting a citizen through the window, as he sat by his own hearthstone at night, confessed also that he it was who tied the rope around the necks of the two men who were lynched in Columbus in 1896. I condemn it, and will not apologize for such lawlessness. To exterminate the practice, it must be made odious and dangerous. The penalty should be the scorn of the people and the punishment of the law."

The governor recommends stricter laws against the offense most often giving occasion to lynching, more prompt administration of justice, and also laws more effectually protecting prisoners in the charge of State officials; but, above all, he appeals to that public opinion which not only makes but enforces legislation. Responsibility for the crime of lynching, as the governor well says, rests not only upon the actors, but upon the community which permits and tolerates the crime. He declares truly that "it can and will be stopped when the better element who deprecate mob law aggressively condemn and determine to suppress the practice."

What is true of these infamous lynchings is true of all the other crying evils of our social and political system. If decent people would stand together, not only in condemning but in actually suppressing them, they would soon cease to tarnish the fair fame of the republic.

*Source:* "Southern Protests against Lynching."
*The Century* 55, no. 3 (1898): 476–77.

## Newspaper Reports on Lynching

The next three documents are articles from the *New York Times,* two letters to the editor and one news article. In the first letter, "Lynching in Georgia," a resident of Georgia has written to the *Times* in order to explain the people's preference for lynching rather than legal responses to crime. The author states that lynching is nearly always the people's response to one crime only, rape. In contrast to the authors of some of the other documents in this section, he assures readers of the *Times* that innocent people are never lynched. To explain the discrepancy between the number of white and black men who are lynched, he claims that black men are simply more prone to crime, particularly sexual crime. He even suggests that freedom following the Civil War is a factor, since the young men reputedly most guilty of this crime were all born after the war. If readers were to extend his argument, he clearly implies that a solution to the problem of lynching would be to reestablish slavery.

The next article reports the sentiments of a well-known southern woman, Mrs. W. H. Felton (who is also mentioned in the first article), the wife of a former congressman. She speaks vehemently in favor of lynching, arguing that not only should any black man guilty of rape be lynched, but that 1,000 black men should be lynched for each rape; obviously, what these men would be "guilty" of is simply being black. Because Mrs. Felton repeats this statement, readers will understand that her words were not simply the result of heated emotion that she might come to regret. Although these first two excerpts from the *Times* might seem to agree with each other, it is hard to reconcile Mrs. Felton's desire to lynch 1,000 men each time a single crime is committed with the previous author's claim that innocent men are never lynched.

The final excerpt from the *Times* is another letter to the editor, from Arthur A. Schomburg (1874–1938). Schomburg was originally from Puerto Rico; after he immigrated to New York, he advocated for Latin American and African American rights. He also began collecting African American literature and art; his collection was eventually purchased by the New York Public Library and became the foundation for the Arthur Schomburg Center for Research in Black Culture, located at the Harlem branch of the New York Public Library. He was a significant figure during the Harlem Renaissance, and so his letter to the *Times* carries more weight than a similar letter from a less well-known person might have. In his letter, he refers to a lynching that had recently occurred in Delaware, and he questions why Americans permit such activity. Lynching is so barbaric, he suggests at the end of his letter, that only cannibalism, a feast composed of the flesh of the burnt victim, could be more savage.

# "Lynching in Georgia," 1897

Public Sentiment Favors It as Punishment for the Single Crime That Brings It About

*To the Editor of the New York Times:*

The *Times* has always been a fair paper, and, while decided in its convictions, has always been willing to do justice to the South. It has seen the unmixed folly of exciting on the part of its readers antipathy to a class of their fellow-countrymen whose prosperity they shared and whose adversity affected them seriously. To misstate the individual facts has been less a habit on the part of the Northern press than to misplace them and to draw conclusions from them which are not true. That our reporters, in their desire to make a sensation, are largely responsible for this misreading is doubtless true, but still much of it arises from a want of acquaintance with all the circumstances.

Many persons, from reading the accounts of our own dailies, and especially as these statements of theirs are reproduced with comments in the Northern press, would draw a conclusion that in Georgia we were a race of lawless savages, and, naturally, the law-abiding will avoid our State in seeking for homes.

It is useless to deny much that is said to be true, but there is so much that is true that is not told that I think perhaps there might be a different verdict if these untold facts were known.

I am free to admit that any man of any race who assaults a woman with vile intent will likely be hanged by the mob without bringing him into court or giving him a legal trial.

I admit as candidly that the men who do this lynching are never arrested, nor is their act considered by the people generally as criminal.

It is useless for our papers to say that public sentiment is against lynching for rape. The lawyers are opposed to it, the daily press opposes it, and the preachers condemn it, but the masses of the people approve it, and say, "When brutes cease to rape helpless women men will cease to hang the brutes. Till then, not."

It is also true that it is a rare thing for a white man or a mulatto to be lynched. The victims are generally black negroes of the lowest order.

For other crimes than rape there is not often any lynching. Dr. Ryder, a white man, whose case has excited great attention, who had shot and killed a beautiful and accomplished young lady in a fit of jealous rage, and who had been found guilty by a jury, and a negro who shot at his wife and killed another woman, and then killed in cold blood a prominent merchant, are the only cases I now recall.

For other crimes than rape the law takes its tedious way.

Tom Woolfolk murdered his whole family to get the estate. No man doubted his guilt, the jury convicted him before leaving the box, but it took two years and two jury trials and an expenditure of $20,000 to get him to the gallows.

A negro killed an old man in cold blood near Macon for a few dollars' worth of supplies and after a long delay was hanged by the Sheriff.

A negro killed his wife coolly and brutally. It took two years and two trials to hang him when he was hanged by the Sheriff, but a negro assaulted a few weeks ago a little girl of six years, and nearly killed the child. He was hung by the mob. A negro assaulted a fair young lady of one of our best families, and she barely escaped with her life. He was hanged by the mob.

A white man assaulted a young woman who was afterward found to be a woman of doubtful reputation. The jail was broken open by the mob and he was hanged.

I merely mention these cases because they came almost under my own eye, and were in one section of the State.

The reason the negroes are generally the victims of lynch law is because the negro is generally the criminal. It is not hostility to the race, else he would be lynched for other crimes, but it is because he seems particularly given to this odious crime. Nearly all our thieves and burglars and house-burners are negroes, but for these crimes they are never punished save by regular legal processes, and as we said above, lynching is generally done for one crime alone, and is rarely done, for that crime is not common. It is almost always committed by negroes, and negroes of the lowest order. Among the hundreds of thousands of this race in Georgia there are but few who have been charged with this crime. When it is committed the utmost care is taken to identify the criminal and only when his identity is beyond question is the execution ordered. It is done in a quiet, decided way as a general thing, although in cases of great atrocity sometimes the criminal is shot as well as hanged.

I am not defending this extra judicial process of punishing crime, but it is not more cruel than a long confinement in a close dungeon, and a halter in a jail yard at the end of it. The only ground of objection to this mode of dealing with these criminals is the fear that the innocent might suffer. As the most careful precautions are taken against this result it is not a likely thing lest the wrong man is executed.

Before the law, all are equal; juries have no respect to color in making their verdicts. A rich planter left $400,000 to a negro woman, said to be his child. The kinspeople tried to break the will, but it was sustained in every court; but, while all this is true, a man who assaults a woman, black or white, will be hanged.

Mrs. Felton, who defended the unwritten law, spoke the sentiment of the people. It is well enough to admit it. Our people say: We would like to have the good opinion of our Northern friends, but we can get along without it if it is to be secured by falsehood. The Northern people are not here. If they were, the first time one of their daughters was assaulted they would head the mob. The Northern people could help to remedy this evil. If those who have given the negroes so much money and so great sympathy would simply say, "This thing must stop; if your people commit these crimes they ought to die, and you need not expect sympathy from us," then the preachers and teachers who are their beneficiaries would speak out, and there would be a change of sentiment, which would be a great blessing to those who make it.

Our daily press denounces lynching, our governor denounces it, our preachers denounce it, but it is simply falsehood to say that the people are with them. It may be a sad truth, but I am sure that the people are fixed as destiny, and there is, as far as I can see, only one remedy for it, and that is to stop the crime. It was almost unknown before the negro was freed. It is now always committed by young negroes, who have been born in freedom. They are not ignorant; they are simply vile, and they must know the inexorableness of the doom.

I do not think the people who condone the offense of the lynchers like lynch law, no more than those who resisted the fugitive slave law liked the rebellion against the United States government, nor those who managed the underground railroad were glad to be habitual lawbreakers. They simply recognize the fact that there are extraordinary measures demanded by extraordinary occasions.

The number of those who commit these crimes are not many, and the dread of those who have never lived in the south of violence to their families is not well founded.

The daily papers make the most of every case, and seem to delight in magnifying the evil. One would suppose, who was not well-informed, that his family would be in peril because of the presence of these savages, and judging from the fact that so many negroes are criminals he might come to the conclusion that the whole race was debauched. The fact is, we are not a law-breaking people, in the main, neither white men nor negroes—but the fact is that while we have a great many law-abiding negroes, a great many good citizens among them, nearly all our criminals come from that class. The people who compose your criminal classes do not come this way, and our white people are generally law-abiding, and so the robberies, burglaries, assaults in our land come generally from the negroes. They do not often murder white men, for difficulties between these two races are rare. They murder each other. They have their own dives kept by people of their own color, and this is where the gambling and drinking goes on, and where the blood is generally shed.

It may seem strange to those who think this is a land of cut-throats to say that in no land is there a morality more Puritanic than in Georgia. A glass of soda water may not be sold on Sunday. A fruit stand may not be opened. A freight train is not permitted to turn a wheel; in 100 counties no whiskey is sold; $1,000,000 a year is spent on the common schools.

A Republican is as highly esteemed as a Democrat. If our individual States are not competent to manage these local troubles, they cannot be managed, and it is not the wisest course for those who are far removed from the scene of danger to decide positively what might or might not to be done.

I have not attempted to defend the lynchers, no more than to defend the Vigilance committee or committee of safety, but simply to state the case as I am sure it really is.

GEORGIA.

*Source:* "Lynching in Georgia." *The New York Times,* September 16, 1897.

# "Woman Advocates Lynching," 1898

Wife of Ex-Congressman Felton of Georgia Advocates for Vengeance upon Negro Assailants

ATLANTA, Ga, Nov. 15—Mrs. W.H. Felton, wife of ex-Congressman W.H. Felton, declared to-day, a thousand negroes should be lynched every week, if this was necessary to protect women of the South, and that the negro race should be destroyed if assaults upon white women continued. Mrs. Felton said:

"I repeat what I said at Tybee one year ago, and I reaffirm the same. Addressing farmers then, I said the crying need of women on farms is security in their lives and homes. It is a disgrace in a free country when violence is a public reproach and those who compose the best part of God's creation are trembling and are afraid to be left alone in their homes.

"With due respect to your politics, I say that when you take the negro into your embraces on election day to control his vote, and use liquor to befuddle his understanding and make him believe he is your brother; when you 'honey-snuggle' at the polls and make him familiar with your tricks in politics, so long will lynching prevail, because the cause will grow and increase with every election.

"When there is not enough religion in the pulpit to organize a crusade against this sin nor justice in the Court House to punish this crime, nor manhood in the Nation enough to put a sheltering arm around innocence and virtue, if it requires lynching to protect women's dearest possession from drunken human brutes—then I say lynch a thousand a week if it is necessary! The race will be destroyed by the whites in self-defense unless law and order prevail.

"I place the blame where it should be, in politics. Such politics will ruin the prosperity of the South and destroy the negro race at last."

Mrs. Felton declared that Manley, the Wilmington negro editor, should be made to fear the lynching rope rather than occupy a place in the New York newspapers.

Source: "Woman Advocates Lynching." The New York Times, November 16, 1898.

## Arthur A. Schomburg, "Lynching a Savage Relic," 1903

To the Editor of the New York Times:

The letter on "The Law's Delay," published by you on June 24, seems to have been written while the mind was under some heavy emotional impulses. The statement that the mob who lynched and burned a negro murderer at Wilmington, Del., was "composed of average American citizens, of men just like us," may be true, so far as appearances are concerned. The law-abiding citizens who have implicit confidence in the supremacy of law and order will never condescend to take any part in lynching nor burning a "black wild beast" to satisfy the savage instinct which, according to some scientists, is still under our veneer of civilization, developed in some people to better advantage than in others.

While nobody regrets that the negro murderer paid with life for his dastardly and terrible crime, there is a feeling among Christian people when an outcast has committed a horrible murder that the majesty of the law ought to be allowed to punish him with the severest penalty. This is preferable to having "men like the rest of us" take the law in their hands, usurp established justice and create in its place the partial administration of justice and the punishment of culprits to the satisfaction of mob rule. So when the excitement has abated, those who are distant listeners cannot help expressing doubt in the equitable and the just administration of the laws in such States.

I venture to answer that "justice according to law" would have been meted out to the negro murderer swiftly and surely. The fact that he had been placed within the prison was evidence that the wheels of justice would have ground slow and true in his case. To have paraded the negro murderer through the machinery of justice is disgraceful to Judges who hold such positions on their honor, and to pronounce sentence of death under like conditions amid the excited vociferations of the mob would have been timid and appalling.

Now we come to the next phase. Why is it that a civilized community will permit negroes to be burned at the stake? Are we retrograding to a primitive condition of life, that the passions must be satisfied by deeds that were in existence centuries past? There only remain to be seen at some future lynching and burning the eating of the roasted victim, and then we shall have reached the fin de siècle, the zenith of civilization.

I began with the letter and will end with it. Those who took part in the Wilmington (Del.) lynching "constitute a representative American community," says the letter, but the moral reasoning is weak; for what is the use of fixed principles of right and wrong if they are to be treated as mere abstractions and not as the practical guide of conduct?

Arthur A. Schomburg
New York, June 25, 1903.

*Source:* Schomburg, Arthur A. "Lynching a Savage Relic." *The New York Times,* June 25, 1903.

## The Dyer Anti-Lynching Bill

The final document in this section is the "Dyer Anti-Lynching Bill." It is called a bill rather than a law because it failed to garner a passing vote in Congress. The bill was introduced by Representative Leonidas C. Dyer, representing Missouri, in 1918. He was responding to earlier race riots in

St. Louis as well as to the lynchings of African Americans in the South. This bill easily passed in the House of Representatives, but southern senators filibustered on three separate occasions, in 1922, 1923, and 1924 in order to prevent the Senate from voting on the bill. President Harding had earlier announced his support for the bill, so if it had passed Congress, it would have become law. This bill would have made lynching a federal crime, granting federal courts jurisdiction in prosecuting lynching cases. Guilty verdicts might have been more likely in federal courts than in the more local state courts, where many jury members were perceived to be sympathetic to the agenda of the defendants. In addition, and perhaps most controversially, the bill also mandated criminal charges for officials, like sheriffs or police officers, who were required to protect criminals until their execution. If a mob demanded that a prisoner be turned over to them and the sheriff complied, the sheriff could be charged under this bill as well as those who committed the actual lynching. Fines paid by those found guilty would have been used to support the families of lynching victims. The failure of this bill to pass despite its repeated introduction in Congress suggests how deeply embedded lynching was as a cultural practice in some parts of the United States.

---

## Dyer Anti-Lynching Bill, 1922

An Act to assure to persons within the jurisdiction of every State the equal protection of the laws, and to punish the crime of lynching.

Be it enacted by the Senate and House of Representatives of the United States of America in Congress assembled, That the phrase "mob or riotous assemblage," when used in this act, shall mean an assemblage composed of three or more persons acting in concert for the purpose of depriving any person of his life without authority of law as a punishment for or to prevent the commission of some actual or supposed public offense.

Sec. 2. That if any State or governmental subdivision thereof fails, neglects, or refuses to provide and maintain protection to the life of any person within its jurisdiction against a mob of riotous assemblage, such State shall by reason of such failure, neglect, or refusal be deemed to have denied to such person the equal protection of the laws of the State, and to the end that such protection as is guaranteed to the citizens of the United States by its Constitution may be secured it is provided:

Sec. 3. That any State or municipal officer charged with the duty or who possesses the power or authority as such officer to protect the life of any person that may be put to death by any mob or riotous assemblage, or who has any such person in his charge as a prisoner, who fails, neglects, or refuses to make all reasonable efforts to prevent such person from being so put to death, or any State or municipal officer charged with the duty of apprehending or prosecuting any person participating in such mob or riotous assemblage who fails, neglects, or refuses to make all reasonable efforts to perform his duty in apprehending or prosecuting to final judgment under the laws of such State all persons so participating except such, if any, as are to have been held to answer for such participation in any district court of the United States, as herein provided, shall be guilty of a felony, and upon conviction thereof shall be punished by imprisonment not exceeding five years or by a fine of not exceeding $5,000, or by both such fine and imprisonment.

Any State or municipal officer, acting as such officer under authority of State law, having in his custody or control a prisoner, who shall conspire, combine, or confederate with any person to put such prisoner to death without authority of law as a punishment for some alleged public offense, or who shall conspire, combine, or confederate with any person to suffer such prisoner to be taken or obtained from his custody or control for the purpose of being put to death without authority of law as a punishment for an alleged public offense, shall be guilty of a felony, and those who so conspire, combine, or confederate with such officer shall likewise be guilty of a felony. On conviction the parties participating therein shall be punished by imprisonment for life or not less than five years.

Sec. 4. That the district court of the judicial district wherein a person is put to death by a mob or riotous assemblage shall have jurisdiction to try and punish, in accordance with the laws of the State where the homicide is committed, those who participate therein: Provided, That it shall be charged in the indictment that by reason of the failure, neglect, or refusal of the officers of the State charged with the duty of prosecuting such offense under the laws of the State to proceed with due diligence to apprehend and prosecute such participants the State has denied to its citizens the equal protection of the laws. It shall not be necessary that the jurisdictional allegations herein required shall be proven beyond a reasonable doubt, and it shall be sufficient if such allegations are sustained by a preponderance of the evidence.

Sec. 5. That any county in which a person is put to death by a mob or riotous assemblage shall, if it is alleged and proven that the officers of the State charged with the duty of prosecuting criminally such offense under the laws of the State have failed, neglected, or refused to proceed with due diligence to apprehend and prosecute the participants in the mob or riotous assemblage, forfeit $10,000, which sum may be recovered by an action therefor in the name of the United States against any such county for the use of the family, if any, of the person so put to death; if he had no family, then to his dependent parents, if any; otherwise for the use of the United States. Such action shall be brought and prosecuted by the district attorney of the United States of the district in which such county is situated in any court of the United States having jurisdiction therein. If such forfeiture is not paid upon recovery of a judgment therefor, such court shall have jurisdiction to enforce payment thereof by levy of execution upon any property of the county, or may compel the levy and collection of a tax, therefor, or may otherwise compel payment thereof by mandamus or other appropriate process; and any officer of such county or other person who disobeys or fails to comply with any lawful order of the court in the premises shall be liable to punishment as for contempt and to any other penalty provided by law therefor.

Sec. 6. That in the event that any person so put to death shall have been transported by such mob or riotous assemblage from one county to another county during the time intervening between his capture and putting to death, the county in which he is seized and the county in which he is put to death shall be jointly and severally liable to pay the forfeiture herein provided.

Sec. 7. That any act committed in any State or Territory of the United States in violation of the rights of a citizen or subject of a foreign country secured to such citizen or subject by treaty between the United States and such foreign country, which act constitutes a crime under the laws of such State or Territory, shall constitute a like crime against the peace and dignity of the United States, punishable in like manner as in the courts of said State or Territory, and within the period limited by the laws of such State or Territory, and may be prosecuted in the courts of the United States, and upon conviction the sentence executed in like manner as sentences upon convictions for crimes under the laws of the United States.

Sec. 8. That in construing and applying this act the District of Columbia shall be deemed a county, as shall each of the parishes of the State of Louisiana.

That if any section or provision of this act shall be held by any court to be invalid, the balance of the act shall not for that reason be held invalid.

*Source:* The Dyer Anti-Lynching Bill.
United States Congress, July 28, 1922.

## Discussion Questions

1. Read any of the following other pieces of literature: *The Autobiography of an Ex-Colored Man* by James Weldon Johnson, *Light in August* by William Faulkner, "Between the World and Me" by Richard Wright, "Lynchsong" by Lorraine Hansberry, "The Swimmers" by Alan Tate, "The Vigilante" by John Steinbeck, or "A Little Talk about Mobs" by O. Henry. Compare the representation of lynching in that text with the description of it in *Cane.*

2. Read another book that is composed of pieces in multiple genres and compare that book with *Cane.* How do the different genres affect your interpretation of the text? Some examples include *Bad Indians* by Deborah Miranda, *Ceremony* and *Storyteller* by Leslie Marmon Silko, and *House Made of Dawn* by N. Scott Momaday.

3. Read "Blood-Burning Moon" alongside several of the poems included in *Cane.* In a class discussion or essay, analyze how the different content or tonal distinctions among the pieces influences your understanding of each individual piece.

4. Write an essay describing an occasion when you witnessed or participated in an act of violence. How did this event affect you, other participants, witnesses, and your community at large?

5. Write a story, poem, or play that includes a violent episode in order to critique violence. Be careful not to sensationalize the violence.

6. Write an essay describing any unwritten rules within your own social group. What are people expected to do, permitted to do, or forbidden from doing—even if those actions are never explicitly discussed?

7. Write an essay or have a class discussion about the rules or laws that can be broken without consequence in your school or community. What factors contribute to authority figures failing to enforce the rules? How does this attitude affect the atmosphere in your school or community?

8. Research the history of Reconstruction following the Civil War and trace the correlation of political changes in the South with the incidence of lynchings.

9. When Supreme Court Justice Clarence Thomas was nominated, his confirmation hearings were particularly controversial. Research this event, paying particular attention to his use of the phrase "high-tech lynching." Hold a debate in your class about whether this was an ethically appropriate use of the term. Should "lynching" be used as a metaphor?

10. Look up the origins of the expression "strange fruit." Read the original poem and listen to one or more musicians performing the song. How do these artistic interpretations affect your understanding of lynching?

11. Read any of the articles in this section and write an analysis of the article's rhetorical strategies. Concentrate not simply on what the article is attempting to persuade the reader to believe but on *how* the author attempts to persuade the reader. That is, what does the author do with language? Does the author appeal primarily to logic, emotions, or ethics? What types of evidence does the author present to support his or her view?

12. Reenact a debate on the Dyer Anti-Lynching Bill. What reasons might senators provide for opposing it? Is support of the bill as self-evident as it might seem to readers in the 21st century?

13. Research any specific case of lynching. Are the details of that case consistent with the descriptions of lynchings presented in the documents above?

14. Many jurisdictions in the United States now have a category of crime designated as a "hate crime." Research what this means, which crimes the term may apply to, and why it was created.

15. Research the life of Ida B. Wells or of another person dedicated to a cause of justice. What did this person do to create changes in his or her society? How effective were his or her actions?

16. Write a letter to the editor of a newspaper objecting to a practice of injustice that disturbs you. Be sure to include specific evidence of that injustice.
17. Research an episode of racialized violence that occurred within the last 20 or 30 years. What similarities does this event have with lynchings at the turn of the 20th century? How are the events different?

## Suggested Readings

Alexandre, Sandy. "Out on a Limb: The Spatial Politics of Lynching Photography." *Mississippi Quarterly* 62, no. 1–2 (2008–2009): 71–112.

Allen, James, John Lewis, Leon F. Litwack, and Hilton Als. *Without Sanctuary: Lynching Photography in America*. Santa Fe, NM: Twin Palms Publishers, 2000.

Apel, Dora and Shawn Michelle Smith. *Lynching Photographs*. Oakland: University of California Press, 2008.

Armstrong, Julie Buckner. *Mary Turner and the Memory of Lynching*. Athens: University of Georgia Press, 2011.

Arnold-Lourie, Christine. "'A Madman's Deed, A Maniac's Hand': Gender and Justice in Three Maryland Lynchings." *Journal of Southern History* 41, no. 4 (2008): 1031–45.

Bailey, Amy Kate and Karen A. Snedker. "Practicing What They Preach? Lynching and Religion in the American South, 1890–1929." *American Journal of Sociology* 117, no. 3 (2011): 844–87.

Baker, Bruce E. "Lynch Law Reversed: The Rape of Lula Sherman, the Lynching of Manse Waldrop, and the Debate over Lynching in the 1880s." *American Nineteenth Century History* 6, no. 3 (2005): 273–93.

Banks, Kimberly. "'Like a Violin for the Wind to Play': Lyrical Approaches to Lynching by Hughes, Du Bois, and Toomer." *African American Review* 38, no. 3 (2004): 451–65.

Berg, Manfred. *Popular Justice: A History of Lynching in America*. Chicago: Ivan R. Dee, 2011.

Brown, Mary Jane. "Advocates in the Age of Jazz: Women in the Campaign for the Dyer Anti-Lynching Bill." *Peace & Change* 28, no. 3 (2003): 378–419.

Brundage, W. Fitzhugh. *Lynchings in the New South: Georgia and Virginia, 1880–1930*. Urbana: University of Illinois Press, 1993.

Burns, Adam. "Without Due Process: Adam E. Pillsbury and the Hoar Anti-Lynching Bill." *American Nineteenth Century History* 11, no. 2 (2010): 233–52.

Capeci, Dominic J., Jr. *The Lynching of Cleo Wright.* Lexington: University Press of Kentucky, 1998.

Carr, Cynthia. *Our Town: A Heartland Lynching, a Haunted Town, and the Hidden History of White America.* New York: Broadway Books, 2007.

Cone, James H. *The Cross and the Lynching Tree.* Maryknoll, NY: Orbis Books, 2011.

Cooks, Bridget R. "Confronting Terrorism: Teaching the History of Lynching through Photography." *Pedagogy* 8, no. 1 (2008): 134–45.

Curriden, Mark and Leroy Phillips. *Contempt of Court: The Turn-of-the-Century Lynching That Launched a Hundred Years of Federalism.* New York: Anchor Books, 2001.

Davis, David A. "Not Only War Is Hell: World War I and African American Lynching Narratives." *African American Review* 42, no. 3–4 (2008): 477–91.

Decosta-Willis, Miriam, Ed. *The Memphis Diary of Ida B. Wells.* Boston: Beacon Press, 1995.

Dray, Philip. *At the Hands of Persons Unknown: The Lynching of Black America.* New York: Modern Library Edition, 2003.

Edmunds, Susan. "The Race Question and the 'Question of the Home': Revisiting the Lynching Plot in Jean Toomer's *Cane.*" *American Literature: A Journal of Literary History, Criticism, and Bibliography* 75, no. 1 (2003): 141–68.

Fabre, Genevieve and Michael Feith, eds. *Jean Toomer and the Harlem Renaissance.* New Brunswick, NJ: Rutgers University Press, 2001.

Feimster, Crystal N. *Southern Horrors: Women and the Politics of Rape and Lynching.* Cambridge, MA: Harvard University Press, 2011.

Finnegan, Terence. *A Deed So Accursed: Lynching in Mississippi and South Carolina, 1881–1940.* Charlottesville: University of Virginia Press, 2013.

Foley, Barbara. "'In the Land of Cotton': Economics and Violence in Jean Toomer's *Cane.*" *African American Review* 32, no. 2 (1998): 181–98.

Frisken, Amanda K. "'A Song Without Words': Anti-Lynching Imagery in the African American Press, 1889–1898." *Journal of African American History* 97, no. 3 (2012): 240–69.

Giddings, Paula J. *Ida: A Sword Among Lions: Ida B. Wells and the Campaign Against Lynching.* New York: Harper, 2009.

Goldsby, Jacqueline. *A Spectacular Secret: Lynching in American Life and Literature.* Chicago: University of Chicago Press, 2006.

Gonzales-Day, Ken. *Lynching in the West: 1850–1935.* Durham, NC: Duke University Press, 2006.

Ifill, Sherrilyn. *On the Courthouse Lawn: Confronting the Legacy of Lynching in the Twenty-first Century.* Boston: Beacon Press, 2007.

Jack, Jordynn and Lucy Massagee. "Ladies and Lynching: Southern Women, Civil Rights, and the Rhetoric of Interracial Cooperation." *Rhetoric & Public Affairs* 14, no. 3 (2011): 493–510.

Jean, Susan. "'Warranted' Lynchings: Narratives of Mob Violence in White Southern Newspapers, 1880–1940." *American Nineteenth Century History* 6, no. 3 (2005): 351–72.

Jett, Brandon. "Paris Is Burning: Lynching and Racial Violence in Lamar County, 1890–1920." *East Texas Historical Journal* 51, no. 2 (2013): 40–64.

Loewen, James W. *Sundown Towns: A Hidden Dimension of American Racism.* New York: The New Press, 2005.

Lovett, Christopher C. "A Public Burning: Race, Sex, and the Lynching of Fred Alexander." *Kansas History* 33, no. 2 (2010): 94–115.

Lutes, Jean M. "Lynching Coverage and the American Reporter-Novelist." *American Literary History* 19, no. 2 (2007): 456–81.

Madison, James H. *A Lynching in the Heartland: Race and Memory in America.* New York: Palgrave Macmillan, 2003.

Mathews, Donald G. "The Southern Rite of Human Sacrifice: Lynching in the American South." *Mississippi Quarterly* 62, no. 1–2 (2009): 27–70.

McGovern, James R. *Anatomy of a Lynching: The Killing of Claude Neal.* Baton Rouge: Louisiana State University Press, 1992.

Metress, Christopher. *The Lynching of Emmett Till: A Documentary Narrative.* Charlottesville: University of Virginia Press, 2002.

Meyers, Christopher G. "'Killing Them by the Wholesale': A Lynching Rampage in South Georgia. *Georgia Historical Quarterly* 90, no. 2 (2006): 214–35.

Mikkelsen, Vincent P. "Fighting for Sergeant Caldwell: The NAACP Campaign against 'Legal' Lynching after World War I." *Journal of African American History* 94, no. 4 (2009): 464–86.

Mitchell, Koritha. *Living with Lynching: African American Lynching Plays, Performance, and Citizenship, 1890–1930.* Urbana: University of Illinois Press, 2012.

Nevels, Cynthia Skove. *Lynching to Belong: Claiming Whiteness through Racial Violence.* College Station: Texas A & M University Press, 2007.

Newkirk, Vann R. *Lynching in North Carolina: A History 1865–1941.* Jefferson, NC: McFarland, 2014.

Perkins, Kathy A. and Judith L. Stephens, eds. *Strange Fruit: Plays on Lynching by American Women.* Bloomington: Indiana University Press, 1998.

Pfeifer, Michael J., ed. *Lynching Beyond Dixie: American Mob Violence Outside the South.* Urbana: University of Illinois Press, 2013.

Rice, Anne P. *Witnessing Lynching: American Writers Respond.* New Brunswick, NJ: Rutgers University Press, 2003.

Rushdy, Ashraf H. A. *The End of American Lynching.* New Brunswick, NJ: Rutgers University Press, 2012.

Scruggs, Charles and Lee VanDemarr. *Jean Toomer and the Terrors of American History.* Philadelphia: University of Pennsylvania Press, 1998.

Simien, Evelyn M., ed. *Gender and Lynching: The Politics of Memory.* New York: Palgrave Macmillan, 2011.

Stephens, Judith L. "Art, Activism, and Uncompromising Attitude in Georgia Douglas Johnson's Lynching Plays." *African American Review* 39, no. 1–2 (2005): 87–102.

Stovel, Katherine. "Local Sequential Patterns: The Structure of Lynching in the Deep South, 1882–1930." *Social Forces* 79, no. 3 (2001): 843–80.

Tolnay, Stewart E. and E. M. Beck. *A Festival of Violence: An Analysis of Southern Lynchings, 1882–1930.* Urbana: University of Illinois Press, 1995.

Waldrep, Christopher. *Lynching in America: A History in Documents.* New York: New York University Press, 2006.

Waligora-Davis, Nicole A. "Dunbar and the Science of Lynching." *African American Review* 41, no. 2 (2007): 303–11.

Webb, Jeff. "Literature and Lynching: Identity in Jean Toomer's *Cane.*" *ELH* 67, no. 1 (2000): 205–28.

Wells, Ida B. *Crusade for Justice: The Autobiography of Ida B. Wells,* edited by Alfreda M. Duster. Chicago: University of Chicago Press, 1970.

Wells, Ida B. and Jacqueline Jones Royster. *Southern Horrors and Other Writing: The Anti-Lynching Campaign of Ida B. Wells, 1892–1900.* Boston: Bedford/St. Martin's, 1997.

Wells-Barnett, Ida B. *On Lynchings.* Amherst, NY: Humanity Books, 2002.

West, Benjamin S. *Crowd Violence in American Modernist Fiction: Lynchings, Riots, and the Individual under Assault.* Jefferson, NC: McFarland, 2013.

Wexler, Laura. *Fire in a Canebrake: The Last Mass Lynching in America.* New York: Scribner, 2004.

Williams, Kidada E. "Resolving the Paradox of Our Lynching Fixation: Reconsidering Racialized Violence in the American South after Slavery." *American Nineteenth Century History* 6, no. 3 (2005): 323–50.

Wood, Amy Louise. *Lynching and Spectacle: Witnessing Racial Violence in America, 1890–1940.* Chapel Hill: University of North Carolina Press, 2011.

Zecker, Robert M. "'Let Each Reader Judge': Lynching, Race, and Immigrant Newspapers." *Journal of American Ethnic History* 29, no. 1 (2009): 31–66.

## HISTORICAL EXPLORATION: PROHIBITION

Most often, Americans associate Prohibition with the decade of the 1920s, when the Eighteenth Amendment to the U.S. Constitution was in effect—despite the fact that the 1920s are also known as the Jazz Age and the Roaring Twenties. This impression is accurate as far as it goes, but it is important to recognize that objections to alcohol use and abuse had long preceded this amendment. Like most amendments to the Constitution (though not all, as discussion of the Twenty-First Amendment below will indicate), the Eighteenth Amendment underwent much discussion and was opposed by many. During the 19th century, "temperance"—or abstention from alcohol use—arose as a popular social cause. Many people who supported the abolition of slavery and the right of women to vote also supported temperance. At that time, temperance was, in other words, a liberal cause, although it may seem like a conservative choice today. Many people who opposed the Nineteenth Amendment, the women's suffrage

Following police orders, prohibition officers pour wine down the drain in New York ca. 1920. When prohibition began, government officials were often challenged by the quantities of alcohol that had already been produced, since it could no longer be sold. (Bettmann/Corbis)

amendment which guaranteed women the right to vote, did so because they feared that once women began to vote, prohibition would become the law of the land because so many women would vote for it. Ironically, although the two amendments were passed in close proximity to each other, prohibition went into effect before women were able to vote.

One of the primary rationales for the temperance movement was the effect on families when a husband and father (and it was usually the male head of a household rather than a mother or wife who was assumed to abuse alcohol) spent the family income on alcohol. Women and children went hungry and often suffered physical abuse at the hands of a drunk husband or father. Several political organizations developed, the most prominent of which was the Women's Christian Temperance Union, to create popular and political support for the prohibition of alcohol.

When the proposed Eighteenth Amendment finally passed Congress, however, its adoption by the states was swift. In August 1917, the U.S. Senate passed a resolution supporting a prohibition amendment. By December of that year, the House of Representatives and the Senate had reached an agreement on the language of that resolution. The proposed amendment was then forwarded to the states. For an amendment to the Constitution to be passed, three-fourths of the states must pass it. A little more than a year later, a sufficient number of states had passed the amendment; in all, 46 states passed the amendment by January 16, 1919. The amendment would go into effect one year later, on January 17, 1920. Meanwhile, Congress had also passed the Volstead Act, a much more detailed law that outlined how the amendment would be enforced. This law was passed on October 29, 1919, despite the fact that President Woodrow Wilson vetoed it.

Within a short time, however, serious unintended consequences of prohibition emerged. Organized crime established a secure foothold in American culture by developing a system to distribute alcohol illegally, through the operation of secret stills, smuggling of alcohol into the country from Canada and other countries, and the development of speakeasies and other social clubs where alcohol would be served. The United States has never since been able to control organized crime, despite the revocation of the Eighteenth Amendment several years later. In addition, the government spent an enormous amount of its budget attempting to enforce the amendment; this expenditure was in addition to tax revenue lost because alcohol was no longer legally sold. The budgetary strains became unsustainable, especially as the United States entered the Great Depression.

A little more than a decade after the Prohibition Amendment went into effect, it was repealed through the Twenty-First Amendment to the U.S.

Constitution. This amendment was ratified on December 5, 1933. Currently, many localities remain "dry," though in most parts of the United States, anyone who is 21 years old or older may legally purchase and use alcohol.

The issue of Prohibition is most prominent in *Cane* in a short piece called "Seventh Street" that opens section two and in "Kabnis" in the final section. "Seventh Street" consists of four lines of poetry at the beginning and end, framing a paragraph of prose. It is set in Washington, D.C., and illustrates the conflict between Prohibition and a postwar desire for freedom and celebration coupled with money available for spending—for many people associate celebration with alcohol use. The piece refers to "Bootleggers" driving Cadillacs, men who supplied alcohol illegally and seemed to live a flashy extravagant lifestyle. They made crime, in other words, look appealing. Yet with its frequent references to blood, "Seventh Street" also suggests that bootlegging and alcohol use at this time are dangerous and potentially violent. They are simultaneously compelling and daring and also fearsome and harmful.

In "Kabnis," the central character, Kabnis, resents his employer's insistence that he abstain from alcohol use. In violation of his employment agreement, he drinks corn liquor, presumably homemade, and he argues that he's doing nothing wrong as long as he doesn't drink in public. (The Volstead Act had specified that people could drink alcohol in their own homes.) Yet he is nevertheless fired when his drinking is discovered. This story illustrates some of the motives behind prohibition, as Kabnis is expected to be a role model for his students, inspiring them to a life of success through responsibility.

### Temperance Songs

The first three documents below are temperance songs, a genre of music that became popular as the temperance movement gained force. Because of their entertainment value, these songs could influence people more subtly than overt political arguments might. Many of these songs were composed and performed, and temperance themes also emerged in other forms of entertainment, including stories and plays. The first song below, "The Drunkard and His Family," clearly illustrates the concerns of many in the temperance movement, focusing on the effects of alcohol abuse on the family. The wife is represented as virtuous, even forgiving her husband his neglect of their family. The "drunkard," though, also suffers, as he dies alone and unmourned. So the song is a cautionary tale on many levels. The next song, by famed composer Stephen G. Foster, approaches temperance from a different perspective, that of a man whose friends are indulging in alcohol. The speaker in the lyrics declines to join in. Though the point of view in this song is different from that of "The Drunkard and His Family," the theme is consistent, as the speaker also is concerned about his mother—so again alcohol use, abuse, and its consequences are gendered. The third song, "The Temperance Army," presents yet another perspective. Here, temperance supporters are presented as militant, and the tone is aggressive rather than sentimental. This song resembles other marching songs with political themes.

## Mary Lantz, "The Drunkard and His Family," 1854

**1**

He turned aside and staggered in,
As oft he did before,
And to the landlord faltering said
Do give me one glass more,
Do give me one glass more,
Do give me one glass more,
And to the landlord faltering said
Do give me one glass more.

**2**

The glass was giv'n his purple lips,
Now pressed the poisonous bowl,
He drinks while wife and children starve,
And ruins his poor soul,
And ruins his poor soul,
And ruins his poor soul,
He drinks while wife and children starve,
And ruins his poor soul.

**3**

I saw him at the close of day,
Before the tavern door,
His eyes were sunk, his lips were parched,
I viewed him o'er and o'er,

I viewed him o'er and o'er,
I viewed him o'er and o'er,
His eyes were sunk, his lips were parched,
I viewed him o'er and o'er.

## 4

His infant boy stood by his side
And lisping to him said,
Father go home, mother is sick,
And sister cries for bread,
And sister cries for bread,
And sister cries for bread,
Father go home, mother is sick,
And sister cries for bread.

## 5

O God forgive my husband dear,
The dying woman said,
Though he has been unkind to me,
And children cry for bread,
And children cry for bread,
And children cry for bread,
Though he has been unkind to me,
And children cry for bread.

## 6

One year elapsed, I passed that way,
A crowd stood 'round the door,
I asked the cause, some one replied,
The drunkard is no more.
The drunkard is no more.
The drunkard is no more.
I asked the cause, some one replied,
The drunkard is no more.

## 7

I saw his fun'ral passing by,
No wife nor child was there,

They too had joined their mother earth,
And left this world of care,
And left this world of care,
And left this world of care.
They too had joined their mother earth,
And left this world of care.

*Source:* Lantz, Mary. "The Drunkard and His Family."
Dansville, NY: J. G. Sprague, 1854.

## Stephen G. Foster, "Comrades, Fill No Glass for Me," 1855

**1**

Oh! comrades, fill no glass for me
To drown my soul in liquid flame.
For if I drank, the toast should be
To blighted fortune, health and fame.
Yet, though I long to quell the strife,
That passion holds against my life.
Still, boon companions may ye be,
But comrades, fill no glass for me.
Still, boon companions may ye be,
But comrades, fill no glass for me.

**2**

I know a breast that once was light
Whose patient sufferings need my care,
I know a hearth that once was bright,
But drooping hopes have nestled there.
Then while the tear drops nightly steal
From wounded hearts that I should heal,
Though boon companions ye may be—
Oh! comrades, fill no glass for me.

**3**

When I was young I felt the tide
Of aspirations undefiled.
But manhood's years have wronged the pride
My parents centered in their child.
Then, by a mother's sacred tear,
By all that memory should revere,
Though boon companions ye may be—
Oh! comrades, fill no glass for me.

*Source*: Foster, Stephen G. "Comrades, Fill No Glass for Me."
Baltimore: Miller and Beacham, 1855.

## J. M. Kieffer, "The Temperance Army," 1874

**1**

Now the temp'rance army's marching,
with the Christian's armor on;
Love our motto, Christian Captain,
Prohibition is our song!
Chorus:
Yes, the temp'rance army's marching,
And will march forevermore,
And our triumph shall be sounded,
Round the world from shore to shore,
Marching on, Marching on forevermore,
And our triumph shall be sounded,
Round the world from shore to shore.

**2**

Now the temp'rance army's marching,
Firm and steady in our tread;
See! the mothers they are leading,
Marching boldly at the head.
Chorus

**3**

Now the temp'rance army's marching,
Wives and Sisters in the throng;
Shouting, "Total Prohibition,"
As we bravely march along.
Chorus.

*Source:* Kieffer, J. M. "The Temperance Army."
Cleveland: Brainard's Sons, 1874.

## Legal Documents Addressing Prohibition

The next three documents are the three primary legal texts addressing pro-hibition. The first, the Eighteenth Amendment to the U.S. Constitution, is brief and straightforward. The most pertinent statements are in section one, which specifies the activities that cannot be performed regarding alcohol. It cannot be produced or sold, but the amendment does not forbid the consumption of alco-hol. It also specifically addresses the use of alcohol as a beverage, not its use for other purposes.

Following the Eighteenth Amendment is an excerpt from the Volstead Act, a much more detailed law describing how the Eighteenth Amendment could be enforced. It is very specific, both in its definitions and its other sec-tions, as an attempt to prevent loopholes. This law permits alco-hol to be used for sacramental purposes, that is, in churches cel-ebrating communion. However, only a clergy member or another officially appointed person could purchase wine for this reason. Ordinary people, therefore, could not purchase alcohol by claiming

A member of The Crusaders, a national organization opposed to Prohibition, holds a banner in 1930 supporting the repeal of the Eighteenth Amendment, which made alcohol illegal. After years of controversy, Prohibition ended in 1933 with the passage of the Twenty-first Amendment. (Library of Congress)

it would be used by their church or synagogue. The law also permits doctors, under limited circumstances, to prescribe alcohol as part of medical treatment, provided they abide by strict regulations in terms of record keeping. In later sections, the law provides for civil penalties if anyone is injured or killed as a result of someone else using alcohol. The last section states that mere possession of alcohol in violation of the Eighteenth Amendment is sufficient evidence that the alcohol would be used for illegal purposes.

Following the Volstead Act is the Twenty-First Amendment to the U.S. Constitution, which repealed the Eighteenth Amendment. Although prohibition may have solved some problems, it created many others, some of which were worse than the alcohol abuse that occurred before 1920. The Twenty-First Amendment does not state that alcohol use will be legal anywhere in the country, only that the previous amendment would be repealed. If individual states or towns wished to pass laws prohibiting alcohol, those jurisdictions were free to do so. The federal government, however, would no longer forbid the manufacture or distribution of alcohol.

## Eighteenth Amendment to the U.S. Constitution, 1919

### Section 1

After one year from the ratification of this article the manufacture, sale, or transportation of intoxicating liquors within, the importation thereof into, or the exportation thereof from the United States and all territory subject to the jurisdiction thereof for beverage purposes is hereby prohibited.

### Section 2

The Congress and the several States shall have concurrent power to enforce this article by appropriate legislation.

### Section 3

This article shall be inoperative unless it shall have been ratified as an amendment to the Constitution by the legislatures of the several

States, as provided in the Constitution, within seven years from the date of the submission hereof to the States by the Congress.

*Source:* The Eighteenth Amendment (Amendment XVIII) of the Unites States Constitution, 1919.

# From the Volstead Act, 1920

An Act to prohibit intoxicating beverages, and to regulate the manufacture, production, use, and sale of high-proof spirits for other than beverage purposes, and to insure an ample supply of alcohol and promote its use in scientific research and in the development of fuel, dye, and other lawful industries.

Be it enacted by the Senate and House of Representatives of the United States of America in Congress assembled, That the short title of this Act shall be the "National Prohibition Act."

## Title II

Prohibition of Intoxicating Beverages.

Sec. 1. When used in Title II and Title III of this Act (1) The word "liquor" or the phrase "intoxicating liquor" shall be construed to include alcohol, brandy, whisky, rum, gin, beer, ale, porter, and wine, and in addition thereto any spirituous, vinous, malt or fermented liquor, liquids, and compounds, whether medicated, proprietary, patented, or not, and by whatever name called, containing one-half of 1 per centum or more of alcohol by volume which are fit for use for beverage purposes: Provided, That the foregoing definition shall not extend to dealcoholized wine nor to any beverage or liquid produced by the process by which beer, ale, porter or wine is produced, if it contains less than one-half of 1 per centum of alcohol by volume, and is made as prescribed in section 37 of this title, and is otherwise denominated than as beer, ale, or porter, and is contained and sold in, or from, such sealed and labeled bottles, casks, or containers as the commissioner may by regulation prescribe. . . .

Sec. 3. No person shall on or after the date when the eighteenth amendment to the Constitution of the United States goes into effect, manufacture, sell, barter, transport, import, export, deliver, furnish or possess any intoxicating liquor except as authorized in this Act, and all the provisions of this Act shall be liberally construed to the end that the use of intoxicating liquor as a beverage may be prevented.

Liquor for nonbeverage purposes and wine for sacramental purposes may be manufactured, purchased, sold, bartered, transported, imported, exported, delivered, furnished and possessed, but only as herein provided, and the commissioner may, upon application, issue permits therefor . . .

Sec. 4. The articles enumerated in this section shall not, after having been manufactured and prepared for the market, be subject to the provisions of this Act if they correspond with the following descriptions and limitations, namely:

(a) Denatured alcohol or denatured rum produced and used as provided by laws and regulations now or hereafter in force.
(b) Medicinal preparations manufactured in accordance with formulas prescribed by the United States Pharmacopoeia, National Formulary or the American Institute of Homeopathy that are unfit for use for beverage purposes.
(c) Patented, patent, and proprietary medicines that are unfit for use for beverage purposes.
(d) Toilet, medicinal, and antiseptic preparations and solutions that are unfit for use for beverage purposes.
(e) Flavoring extracts and sirups that are unfit for use as a beverage, or for intoxicating beverage purposes.
(f) Venegar and preserved sweet cider.

A person who manufactures any of the articles mentioned in this section may purchase and possess liquor for that purpose, but he shall secure permits to manufacture such articles and to purchase such liquor, give the bonds, keep the records, and make the reports specified in this Act and as directed by the commissioner. No such manufacturer shall sell, use, or dispose of any liquor otherwise than as an ingredient of the articles authorized to be manufactured therefrom. No more alcohol shall be used in the manufacture of any extract, sirup, or the articles named in paragraphs b, c, and d of this section which may be used for beverage purposes than the quantity necessary for extraction or solution of the elements contained therein and for the preservation of the article. . . .

Sec. 6. No one shall manufacture, sell, purchase, transport, or prescribe any liquor without first obtaining a permit from the commissioner so to do, except that a person may, without a permit, purchase and use liquor for medicinal purposes when prescribed by a physician as herein provided, and except that any person who in the opinion of the commissioner is conducting a bona fide hospital or sanatorium engaged in the treatment of persons suffering from alcoholism, may, under such rules, regulations, and conditions as the commissioner shall prescribe, purchase and use, in accordance with the methods in use in such institution, liquor, to be administered to the patients of such institution under the direction of a duly qualified physician employed by such institution. . . .

Nothing in this title shall be held to apply to the manufacture, sale, transportation, importation, possession, or distribution of wine for sacramental purposes, or like religious rites, except section 6 (save as the same requires a permit to purchase) and section 10 hereof, and the provisions of this Act prescribing penalties for the violation of either of said sections. No person to whom a permit may be issued to manufacture, transport, import, or sell wines for sacramental purposes or like religious rites shall sell, barter, exchange, or furnish any such to any person not a rabbi, minister of the gospel, priest, or any officer duly authorized for the purpose by any church or congregation, nor to any such except upon an application duly subscribed by him, which application, authenticated as regulations may prescribe, shall be filed and preserved by the seller. The head of any conference or diocese or other ecclesiastical jurisdiction may designate any rabbi, minister, or priest to supervise the manufacture of wine to be used for the purposes and rites in this section mentioned, and the person so designated may, in the discretion of the commissioner, be granted a permit to supervise such manufacture.

Sec. 7. No one but a physician holding a permit to prescribe liquor shall issue any prescription for liquor. And no physician shall prescribe liquor unless after careful physical examination of the person for whom such prescription is sought, or if such examination is found impracticable, then upon the best information obtainable, he in good faith believes that the use of such liquor as a medicine by such person is necessary and will afford relief to him from some known ailment. Not more than a pint of spirituous liquor to be taken internally shall be prescribed for use by the same person within any period of ten days and no prescription shall be filled more than once. Any pharmacist filling a prescription shall at the time indorse upon it over his own signature the word "canceled," together with the date when the liquor was delivered, and then make the same a part of the record that he is required to keep as herein provided.

Every physician who issues a prescription for liquor shall keep a record, alphabetically arranged in a book prescribed by the commissioner, which shall show the date of issue, amount prescribed, to whom issued, the purpose or ailment for which it is to be used and directions for use, stating the amount and frequency of the dose.

Sec. 8. The commissioner shall cause to be printed blanks for the prescriptions herein required, and he shall furnish the same, free of cost, to physicians holding permits to prescribe. The prescription blanks shall be printed in a book form and shall be numbered consecutively from one to one hundred, and each book shall be given a number, and the stubs in each book shall carry the same numbers as and be copies of the prescriptions. The books containing such stubs shall be returned to the commissioner when the prescription blanks have been used, or sooner, if directed by the commissioner. All unused, mutilated, or defaced blanks shall be returned with the book. No physician shall prescribe and no pharmacist shall fill any prescription for liquor except on blanks so provided, except in cases of emergency, in which event a record and report shall be made and kept as in other cases. . . .

Sec. 12. All persons manufacturing liquor for sale under the provisions of this title shall securely and permanently attach to every container thereof, as the same is manufactured, a label stating name of manufacturer, kind and quantity of liquor contained therein, and the date of its manufacture, together with the number of the permit authorizing the manufacture thereof; and all persons possessing such liquor in wholesale quantities shall securely keep and maintain such label therein; and all persons selling at wholesale shall attach to every package of liquor, when sold, a label setting for the kind and quantity of liquor contained therein, by whom manufactured, the date of sale, and the person to whom sold; which label shall likewise be kept and maintained thereon until the liquor is used for the purpose for which such sale was authorized. . . .

Sec. 17. It shall be unlawful to advertise anywhere, or by any means or method, liquor, or the manufacture, sale, keeping for sale or furnishing of the same, or where, how, from whom, or at what price the same may be obtained. No one shall permit any sign or billboard containing such advertisement to remain upon one's premises. But nothing herein shall prohibit manufacturers and wholesale druggists holding permits to sell liquor from furnishing price lists, with description of liquor for sale, to persons permitted to purchase liquor, or from advertising alcohol in business publications or trade journals circulating generally among manufacturers of lawful alcoholic perfumes, toilet preparations, flavoring extracts, medicinal preparations, and like articles. . . .

Sec. 18. It shall be unlawful to advertise, manufacture, sell, or possess for sale any utensil, contrivance, machine, preparation, compound, tablet, substance, formula direction, or recipe advertised, designed, or intended for use in the unlawful manufacture of intoxicating liquor. . . .

Sec. 20. Any person who shall be injured in person, property, means of support, or otherwise by any intoxicated person, or by reason of the intoxication of any person, whether resulting in his death or not, shall have a right of action against any person who shall, by unlawfully selling to or unlawfully assisting in procuring liquor for such intoxicated person, have caused or contributed to such intoxication, and in any such action such person shall have a right to recover actual and exemplary damages. In case of the death of either party, the action or right of action given by this section shall survive to or against his or her executor or administrator, and the amount so recovered by either wife or child shall be his or her sole and separate property. Such action may be brought in any court of competent jurisdiction. In any case where parents shall be entitled to such damages, either the father or mother may sue alone therefor, but recovery by one of such parties shall be a bar to suit brought by the other.

Sec. 21. Any room, house, building, boat, vehicle, structure, or place where intoxicating liquor is manufactured, sold, kept, or bartered in violation of this title, and all intoxicating liquor and property kept and used in maintaining the same, is hereby declared to be a common nuisance, and any person who maintains such a common nuisance shall be guilty of a misdemeanor and upon conviction thereof shall be fined not more than $1,000 or be imprisoned for not more than one year, or both. If a person has knowledge or reason to believe that this room, house, building, boat, vehicle, structure, or place is occupied or used for the manufacture or sale of liquor contrary to the provision of this title, and suffers the same to be so occupied or used, such room, house, building, boat, vehicle, structure, or place shall be subject to a lien for and may be sold to pay all fines and costs assessed against the person guilty of such nuisance for such violation, and any such lien may be enforced by action in any court having jurisdiction. . . .

Sec. 29. Any person who manufactures or sells liquor in violation of this title shall for a first offense be fined not more than $1,000, or imprisoned not exceeding six months, and for a second or subsequent offense shall be fined not less than $200 nor more than $2,000 and be imprisoned not less than one month nor more than five years. . . .

Sec. 33. After February 1, 1920, the possession of liquors by any person not legally permitted under this title to possess liquor shall be a prima facie evidence that such liquor is kept for the purpose of being sold, bartered, exchanged, given away, furnished, or otherwise disposed of in violation of the provisions of this title. Every person legally permitted under this title to have liquor shall report to the commissioner within ten days after the date when the eighteenth amendment of the Constitution of the United States goes into effect, the kind and amount of intoxicating liquors in his possession. But it shall not be unlawful to possess liquors in one's private dwelling while the same is occupied and used by him as his dwelling only and such liquor need not be reported, provided such liquors are for use only for the personal consumption of the owner thereof and his family residing in such dwelling and of his bona fide guests when entertained by him therein; and the burden of proof shall be upon the possessor in any action concerning the same to prove that such liquor was lawfully acquired, possessed, and used. . . .

*Source:* The Volstead Act. Public Law 66–66. 83, 41 *U.S. Statutes at Large* 305–323 (1920).

# The Twenty-First Amendment to the Constitution of the United States, 1933

## Section 1

The eighteenth article of amendment to the Constitution of the United States is hereby repealed.

## Section 2

The transportation or importation into any State, Territory, or possession of the United States for delivery or use therein of intoxicating liquors, in violation of the laws thereof, is hereby prohibited.

## Section 3

This article shall be inoperative unless it shall have been ratified as an amendment to the Constitution by conventions in the several States, as provided in the Constitution, within seven years from the date of the submission hereof to the States by the Congress.

*Source:* The Twenty-First Amendment (Amendment XXI) to the United States Constitution, 1933.

## Newspaper Articles Reporting on Prohibition

The last two documents in this chapter are newspaper articles covering the passage of the Eighteenth Amendment to the U.S. Constitution. These articles contain several statistics that illustrate how profound a change prohibition would create in American culture. Hundreds of distilleries and breweries had existed in the country, as well as hundreds of thousands of bars, saloons, and pubs. These businesses would all be closed, resulting in the loss of hundreds of thousands of jobs. The federal government, as well as state and local governments, would lose substantial tax revenue. These articles also trace the history of prohibition, from a time when most people considered the proposition impossible, even ludicrous, to its passage into law. Because many people had believed prohibition had no chance of becoming reality, pro-alcohol forces did not pay much attention to the issue until prohibition had already gathered substantial support from many ordinary Americans. By then, it was too late to prevent. By the time the amendment was ratified, much liquor had been stockpiled in the United States; much of that might be smuggled from one part of the country to another, but authorities estimated that even that would be entirely used up within a few years. The tone of these articles suggests that the writers believed the amendment would be permanent; they did not seem to anticipate any efforts to repeal it, certainly not as quickly as those efforts emerged.

# From "Whole Country Goes Dry," 1919

Nebraska, Last State Needed, Ratified Prohibition Amendment Today.

Nation Will Be Bone Dry Within Year from Today.

One year from today the United States goes "dry."

Prohibition has become part of the basic law of the nation.

Ratification today of the federal dry amendment by the legislature of Nebraska makes that measure the eighteenth amendment to the Federal Constitution.

All but half a dozen of the forty-eight States are expected to adopt the amendment in the next few weeks, but the action of Nebraska today gives the ratification of three-fourths of the States, the number necessary to administer John Barleycorn the knock-out punch.

### War Prohibition July 1

One year from today every saloon, brewery, distillery, and wine press in the land must close its doors unless—as now seems likely—they are already closed at that time by war prohibition, which goes into effect next July 1, and stays until completion of demobilization. . . .

The amendment at one stroke wiped out 236 distilleries, 992 breweries, and over 300,000 saloons and wholesale liquor establishments.

It cuts from employees of these institutions an annual income of more than $70,000,000 in pre-war times.

### $1,000,000,000 Revenue Lost

It cuts off from the United States $1,000,000,000 in revenue proposed under the new revenue bill.

It removes the liquor question from national, State, and city politics and helps decrease city, State, and federal expense by decreasing law violations.

The fight on liquor, triumphant today, is an old one.

It raised its head early in the nineteenth century and was looked upon as "another crank notion." But it gathered strength. Churches took it up, doctors followed, and then came the organization of anti-liquor societies, the W.C.T.U., the Anti-Saloon League, and others.

In the middle of the nineteenth century, Maine went dry. Kansas followed.

### Carrie Nation Arises

The militant Carrie Nation, of Kansas, rose up in 1900, and proved to be one of the most picturesque figures the fight has developed.

Ten years later the movement swept the country. Another constitutional amendment was offered—the eighteenth addition to the Constitution.

Distilleries propose a fight on the amendment in the courts on the grounds that it was not adopted by two-thirds of the whole Congress, and that the seven-year limitation invalidated the measure.

"Dry" leaders say that they are confident that neither of these contentions will hold, and on their side are preparing legislation carrying heavy penalties for violating prohibition. A special agency in the internal revenue bureau probably will be asked. . . .

*Source:* "Whole Country Goes Dry." *Washington Times,*
January 16, 1919: 1.

# From "Nation-Wide Prohibition Ends Fight of 112 Years," 1920

War on John Barleycorn Begun by Women in Little Ohio Town Finally Caused Abolishment of Strong Drink for Entire Nation.

National prohibition in the United States, under a specific constitutional provision, is the fruition of a movement which had its beginning in America 112 years ago. Efforts to check the use of ardent spirits were started in this country in 1808. It grew steadily, evolving into a demand for prohibition rather than regulation as far back as 1847. The question was taken into politics through the organization of the Prohibition party in convention at Chicago, September 1, 1869.

The war of women on liquor began with the organization of the Women's Christian Temperance Union in Ohio during the "crusade" during 1873 and 1874.

Maine was the first state to declare for prohibition. It went "dry" in 1851. Prohibition was made a part of its constitution in 1884. Kansas was the second state to embrace prohibition. That was in 1880. North Dakota was third, in 1889.

But the prohibition wave which has swept the liquor business entirely out of the country began with the action of the Georgia State Legislature in 1907. By their own acts, in a steady procession, thirty-three states followed suit. In twenty-one prohibition was decreed by popular vote and in twelve by act of the legislatures.

### Webb-Kenyon Act

Prohibition made its first big advance nationally when Congress passed on March 1, 1913, the Webb-Kenyon law forbidding the shipment of liquor from "wet" to "dry" territory. . . .

The [18th] amendment was submitted by the House, 28 to 128, and by the Senate, 65 to 20.

When Congress submitted the amendment, December 18, 1917, it attempted a restriction, limiting the time for ratification to seven years. Instead, the necessary thirty-six states ratified Constitutional prohibition within thirteen months, the thirty-sixth registering its approval January 16, 1919. The last state to ratify was Pennsylvania, and the next to last New York. . . .

### Liquor Men Too Confident

Except for starting small and easily handled backfires the liquor people made no effort to counter the progress of prohibition until the passage of the Webb-Kenyon law. The only movement within the trade to meet some of the most potent arguments of the "Drys" was represented by the Model License League, an organization that received comparatively little support from the saloon interests, which never for a moment believed that their power in politics could be entirely overborne.

That this attitude has persisted to the last is indicated by the fact that the liquor interests hoisted prices to almost prohibitive altitudes last July, and retained huge stocks in warehouses. These same stocks, which now constitute a problem for the government officials, who must guard them in bonded warehouses until some means are found for disposing of them, without violating the law which forbids export, import and possession of liquor anywhere but in private homes.

Millions of gallons were held, in spite of the fact that other millions were exports, apparently in anticipation of a time when a reaction from absolute prohibition would afford an outlet at huge profits. The hoped-for reaction failed to materialize during the period of war-time prohibition, and under the rigid provisions of the constitutional amendment modification is all the more difficult, though the liquor interests are hoping now that the government, to solve the problem of the stored liquor, will agree to buy it.

### Proclaimed on January 29, 1919

The prohibition amendment was proclaimed January 29, 1919, the proclamation fixing January 16, 1920, twelve months after ratification by the thirty-sixth state, as the date for its going into effect.

Congress went to work on enforcement legislation, and the law produced is regarded as drastic enough to dry up all reserve sources of liquor, according to official estimates, in five or six years. By 1925, it is stated, the United States will be a desert with entirely exhausted cellars.

The United States not only loses a revenue of $500,000,000 a year through prohibition, but will require millions, during the first years at least, to enforce the provisions of the law putting the amendment into effect.

Daniel C. Roper, Commissioner of Internal Revenue, has delegated enforcement to a special prohibition bureau under John F. Kremer, of Mansfield, Ohio. Mr. Kremer has divided the country into nine districts, each with a supervisor. Each state has a director, and the bureau will have at hand a large corps of enforcement agents who will be shifted from state to state at periods frequent enough to prevent the forming of friendships or alliances and consequent interference with the administration of the law in letter as well as in spirit.

*Source:* "Nation-Wide Prohibition Ends Fight of 112 Years." *New York Tribune,* January 17, 1920: 3.

## Discussion Questions

1. Write a song or produce a music video addressing a political or social cause you support. Be sure the song is entertaining as well as educational.

2. Write an essay comparing any one of the temperance songs included above to other folk songs. You might consider songs that address slavery and abolition, the dust bowl, civil rights, or military recruitment.

3. Create a series of campaign posters, slogans, bumper stickers, etc. supporting or opposing prohibition.

4. Write an essay describing someone you know who has abused alcohol or another drug. Include a discussion of that person's behavior on his or her family and friends.

5. Watch several television programs throughout a week. Keep track of references to alcohol, including how many times characters are shown drinking. Also keep track of advertisements for beer, wine coolers, or other forms of alcohol. What does this data reveal about the place of alcohol in American culture?

6. Read another novel published during the 1920s. How is alcohol use portrayed in this novel? Is Prohibition referred to by the characters or narrator? You might consider *The Sun Also Rises* or *A Farewell to Arms* by Ernest Hemingway, *The Great Gatsby* by F. Scott Fitzgerald, or *Babbitt* by Sinclair Lewis.

7. Research a significant individual or organization that supported prohibition. You might consider the WCTU, the Anti-Saloon League, Carrie Nation, or Billy Sunday.

8. Research addictions treatment programs in your area.

9. Research a specific effect of alcohol abuse on society, for example, medical treatment, affiliated crime, domestic abuse or neglect, lost wages, or other problems.

10. Write a White Paper identifying a specific problem related to alcohol or other drug use and then proposing the best solution to that problem.

11. Organize a discussion in your class about how alcohol and other drugs should be regulated by the government. Consider such topics as advertising, taxation, age limits for consumption, limits on the number of liquor licenses in a given locality, and any other related issues you believe are important.

12. Research a dry town or county. What is its rationale for local prohibition? Or research the history of alcohol regulation in your town or state. Aside from the Prohibition era, was it ever dry? Has the legal age for alcohol use ever changed?

13. Look up newspaper articles following the passage of the Twenty-First Amendment to the U.S. Constitution. Do they cite similar statistics as those articles referring to the Eighteenth Amendment? What rationales are provided for the repeal of the Eighteenth Amendment?
14. Imagine that you are living in 1919. Hold a debate in your class addressing prohibition. You might assign historical roles to your classmates, including for example a leader of the Women's Christian Temperance Union, a saloon owner, a church pastor, a woman whose husband drinks excessively, a man who drinks frequently but responsibly, etc.
15. Research laws and practices regarding alcohol use in another country and compare your findings to similar laws and practices in the United States.
16. Conduct a survey of your classmates regarding their use of alcohol, exposure to alcohol, attitudes toward alcohol use, etc. If you can find national data for your age group, compare the data you receive from your classmates to national statistics.
17. Interview a police officer, judge, social worker, or lawyer about the role of alcohol or other drugs in the lives of people they interact with as part of their job.
18. Research the differences in alcohol use among different racial or ethnic groups. Consider not only rates of alcohol use overall, but also types of alcohol consumed, rates of alcoholism, attitudes toward use, etc.

## Suggested Readings

Asbridge, Mark and Swarna Weerasinghe. "Homicide in Chicago from 1890–1930: Prohibition and Its Impact on Alcohol- and Non-Alcohol-Related Homicides." *Addiction* 104, no. 3 (2009): 355–64.

Augst, Thomas. "Temperance, Mass Culture, and the Romance of Experience." *American Literary History* 19, no. 2 (2007): 297–323.

Bader, Robert Smith. *Prohibition in Kansas: A History.* Lawrence: University of Kansas Press, 1986.

Bailey, Frankie Y. and Alice P. Green. *Wicked Albany: Lawlessness and Liquor in the Prohibition Era.* Charleston, SC: The History Press, 2009.

Bauer, Bryce T. *Gentlemen Bootleggers: The True Story of Templeton Rye, Prohibition, and a Small Town in Cahoots.* Chicago: Chicago Review Press, 2014.

Behr, Edward. *Prohibition: Thirteen Years That Changed America.* New York: Arcade Publishing, 2011.

Bordin, Ruth Birgitta Anderson. *Women and Temperance: The Quest for Power and Liberty, 1873–1900.* Philadelphia: Temple University Press, 1981.

Clark, Norman H. *Deliver Us from Evil: An Interpretation of American Prohibition.* New York: W.W. Norton, 1976.

Dannenbaum, Jed. *Drink and Disorder: Temperance Reform in Cincinnati from the Washingtonian Revival to the WCTU.* Urbana: University of Illinois Press, 1984.

Davis, Marni. *Jews and Booze: Becoming American in the Age of Prohibition.* New York: New York University Press, 2014.

Endersby, James W. "Prohibition and Repeal: Voting on Statewide Liquor Referenda in Texas." *Social Science Journal* 49, no. 4 (2012): 503–12.

Fahey, David M. *Temperance and Racism: John Bull, Johnny Reb, and the Good Templars.* Lexington: University Press of Kentucky, 1996.

Fahey, David M. "Why Some Black Lodges Prospered and Others Failed: The Good Templars and the True Reformers." *Ethnic & Racial Studies* 36, no. 2 (2013): 337–52.

Frendreis, John and Loyol Raymond Tatalovich. "'A Hundred Miles of Dry': Religion and the Persistence of Prohibition in the U.S. States." *State Politics and Policy Quarterly* 10, no. 3 (2010): 302–19.

Funderberg, J. Anne. *Bootleggers and Beer Barons of the Prohibition Era.* Jefferson, NC: McFarland, 2014.

Gusfield, Joseph R. *Symbolic Crusade: Status Politics and the American Temperance Movement.* Urbana: University of Illinois Press, 1986.

Guthrie, John Jr. *Keepers of the Spirits: The Judicial Response to Prohibition Enforcement in Florida, 1885–1935.* Westport, CT: Praeger, 1998.

Hamm, Richard F. *Shaping the Eighteenth Amendment: Temperance Reform, Legal Culture, and the Polity, 1880–1920.* Chapel Hill: University of North Carolina Press, 1995.

Johanneck, Elizabeth. *Twin Cities Prohibition: Minnesota Blind Pigs and Bootleggers.* Charleston, SC: The History Press, 2011.

Kobler, John. *Ardent Spirits: The Rise and Fall of Prohibition.* New York: Putnam, 1973.

Lamme, Meg Opdycke. "Shining a Calcium Light: The WCTU and Public Relations History." *Journalism and Mass Communication Quarterly* 88, no. 2 (2011): 245–66.

Lantzer, Jason S. *"Prohibition Is Here to Stay": The Reverend Edward S. Shumaker and the Dry Crusade in America.* Notre Dame, IN: University of Notre Dame Press, 2009.

Lerner, Michael A. *Dry Manhattan: Prohibition in New York City.* Cambridge, MA: Harvard University Press, 2009.

Lewis, Michael. "Access to Saloons, Wet Voter Turnout, and Statewide Prohibition Referenda, 1907–1919." *Social Science History* 32, no. 3 (2008): 373–404.

Linderoth, Matthew R. *Prohibition on the North Jersey Shore: Gangsters on Vacation.* Charleston, SC: The History Press, 2010.

Mappen, Mark. *Prohibition Gangsters: The Rise and Fall of a Bad Generation.* New Brunswick, NJ: Rutgers University Press, 2013.

Mason, Philip P. *Rum Running and the Roaring Twenties: Prohibition on the Michigan-Ontario Waterway.* Detroit: Wayne State University Press, 1995.

Murdach, Allison D. "The Temperance Movement and Social Work." *Social Work* 54, no. 1 (2009): 56–62.

Okrent, Daniel. *Last Call: The Rise and Fall of Prohibition.* New York: Scribners, 2011.

Peck, Garrett. *The Prohibition Hangover: Alcohol in America from Demon Rum to Cult Cabernet.* New Brunswick, NJ: Rutgers University Press, 2009.

Rumbarger, John J. *Profits, Power, and Prohibition: Alcohol Reform and the Industrializing of America, 1800–1930.* Albany: State University of New York Press, 1989.

Schrad, Mark Lawrence. "Constitutional Blemishes: American Alcohol Prohibition and Repeal as Policy Punctuation." *Policy Studies Journal* 35, no. 3 (2007): 437–63.

Spinelli, Lawrence. *Dry Diplomacy: The United States, Great Britain, and Prohibition.* Lanham, MD: Rowman and Littlefield, 2008.

Stewart, Bruce E. "Select Men of Sober and Industrious Habits: Alcohol Reform and Social Conflict in Antebellum Appalachia." *Journal of Southern History* 73, no. 2 (2007): 289–322.

Sweet, Julie Anne. "'That Cursed Evil Rum': The Trustees' Prohibition Policy in Colonial Georgia." *Georgia Historical Quarterly* 94, no. 1 (2010): 1–29.

Thomas, Michael D., Diana W. Thomas, and Nicholas A. Snow. "Rational Irrationality and the Political Process of Repeal: The Women's Organization for National Prohibition Reform and the 21st Amendment." *Kyklos* 66, no. 1 (2013): 130–52.

Tracy, Sarah W. *Alcoholism in America: From Reconstruction to Prohibition.* Baltimore: Johns Hopkins University Press, 2005.

Tyrrell, Ian. *Woman's World/Woman's Empire: The Woman's Christian Temperance Union in International Perspective. 1880–1930.* Chapel Hill: University of North Carolina Press, 1991.

Tyrrell, Ian R. *Sobering Up: From Temperance to Prohibition in Antebellum America, 1800–1860.* Westport, CT: Praeger, 1979.

Unrau, William E. *White Man's Wicked Water: The Alcohol Trade and Prohibition in Indian Country, 1802–1892*. Lawrence: University of Kansas Press, 1996.

Wagner, Michael A. "'As Gold Is Tried in the Fire, So Hearts Must Be Tried by Pain': The Temperance Movement in Georgia and the Local Option Law of 1885." *Georgia Historical Quarterly* 93, no. 1 (2009): 30–54.

Warner, Jessica. "Temperance, Alcohol, and the American Evangelical: A Reassessment." *Addiction* 104, no. 7 (2009): 1075–84.

Wasserman, Ira M. "Prohibition and Ethnocultural Conflict: The Missouri Prohibition Referendum of 1918." *Social Science Quarterly* 70, no. 4 (1981): 886–901.

Whayne, Jeanne M. "Caging the Blind Tiger: Race, Class, and Family in the Battle for Prohibition in Small Town Arkansas." *Arkansas Historical Quarterly* 71, no. 1 (2012): 44–60.

Wood, Darryl S. and Paul J. Gruenewald. "Local Alcohol Prohibition, Police Presence and Serious Injury in Isolated Alaska Native Villages." *Addiction* 101, no. 3 (2006): 393–403.

## WHY WE READ *CANE* TODAY

Because of its unusual approach to genre, material from *Cane* is often read today as individual pieces, perhaps more often than the book is read as a whole. Nearly all of the poems can stand alone—for just as readers often encounter the poetry of Langston Hughes or Claude McKay in anthologies before they seek out full collections, readers may also discover "Georgia Dusk" or "Beehive" or "Harvest Song" in an edited collection of American poetry or African American poetry before they have read *Cane*. Similarly, many of the prose pieces can be read and understood independently of their context in *Cane*. So why read the full book?

Despite the juxtaposition of the multiple genres and the tonal shifts from one section of the book to another, Jean Toomer structured this book carefully. The first section contains several short poems and stories that describe and celebrate southern agrarian life, even as they also refer to racial discrimination and the simmering violence implicit in all southern life during this period. Section two also consists of several short pieces, but they are set in northern and more urban environments. Section three consists only of one extended story, "Kabnis," itself divided into six sections, whose central character is an African American man who has come from the North to a southern school. Yet although the pieces all make sense individually, they gain significance when read in the context of each other. The fear of lynching in "Kabnis," for example, is more concretely persuasive and more emotionally resonant to those who have already read "Blood-Burning Moon." The romanticized descriptions of Georgia in some of the poems are subverted by the violence and threats of violence in some of the stories. When the entire book is read, each piece provides a foundation for those that follow and a commentary on those that have preceded it.

In contrast to some of the other writers considered in this book, Jean Toomer's later work was not particularly well received and is not widely read today, so his reputation rests almost exclusively on *Cane*. Although many writers are best known for one or two of their books even if they published several, the work of those more prolific writers often benefits from readers' interest in the author as much as in an individual text. Because readers often seek out further work of an author after they've enjoyed one book, multiple books gain exposure from the success of one. Such is not the case with Toomer. Aside from *Cane*, only a few books by him are currently in print, and some of these include material also found in *Cane*. However, many well-respected writers ultimately produced a small oeuvre—quality and quantity being distinct measures.

Contemporary readers continue to find *Cane* compelling for several reasons, most related to its mixed genre nature and its place within a modernist canon. The poems often address universalized topics—romance and nature—but successfully particularize those topics to early 20th-century settings. Modern readers are therefore both comfortably situated in and dislocated from the poems. The poems are generally accessible, yet they also describe experiences most 21st-century readers would not have direct experience with. "Song of the Sun," for example, mentions slavery as if it were a recent memory, and "Cotton Song" suggests that harvesting the crop depends much more on physical labor than current mechanized processes demand. Similarly, "Reapers" describes workers who rely on scythes and horses. On the other hand, pastoral poems like "Nullo" and "Evening Song" which rely so extensively on concrete imagery to convey their meaning could have been written much more recently. Although these poems reward repeated readings, they also provide a firm enough basis in material reality that even most readers inexperienced in poetry can appreciate them.

Many of the stories are also accessible, especially the character studies in section one. Some of the stories are more stylistically challenging and illustrate the disjointed characteristics common to modernist writing. The narrators will make more leaps, demanding an intellectual engagement from readers rather than overtly explaining connections among many of the plot points. This style can be initially disorienting, though once readers become fully immersed in the stories, the links between characters and events become clearer. Like many modernist texts, *Cane* is sometimes more fruitfully reread than read. In lesser novels, these demands on the reader would be simply frustrating rather than rewarding. Fortunately, however, the lyrical language in *Cane* is sufficiently inviting, so many readers will respond patiently to the more difficult sections.

This lyrical language is one of the factors that prevent the book from becoming a merely documentary text, useful for its anthropological or ethnographical insights into an earlier time but not otherwise compelling a century after its composition. Reading *Cane* today, we do discover details about the lives of people during the early 20th century—and one benefit of reading fiction generally is access to the lives of people unlike ourselves. But we also discover that those lives are not so unlike our own after all. People continue to appreciate nature and engage in romance. People still long for transcendence while immersed in the quotidian details of their day-to-day lives. People still long for a better day.

Most significantly, perhaps, *Cane* continues to speak to Americans because we still live in a culture characterized by racialized violence. The lynchings that terrorized many African Americans, as well as members of some other vulnerable groups, occur very rarely in the United States today. But other forms of violence have become increasingly common. An updated revision of *Cane* would not likely include the same types of scenes that occur in "Blood-Burning Moon," but it would nevertheless describe other forms of violence. Technologies of violence have changed in the near-century since *Cane* was originally published, but the structure of violence upon which the United States has developed remains firmly in place. The book continues to speak to modern audiences, therefore, because readers emotionally grasp the implications of fear that many of the characters experience.

*Cane* is not an overwhelmingly violent book. Neither is it simply a romanticized portrait of rural life. It reveals the paradoxical nature of American culture which celebrates both violence and serenity, threat and security. This paradox perhaps provides that most unequivocal link across the centuries of American identity.

V

# *Passing* and *Quicksand*

## HISTORICAL BACKGROUND

The two novels considered in this chapter were published in close proximity to each other at the height of the Harlem Renaissance, first *Quicksand* in 1928 and then *Passing* in 1929. Together, they address many of the social issues that had become prominent during this period, including most significantly racial categories and identity, and how those identities are inflected by class and gender. The novels implicitly—and sometimes explicitly—interrogate how that cluster of identity categories affects citizenship and membership in a nation. Some types of institutionalized violence are less prominent in Larsen's work than in the poems and stories of the male writers addressed in Chapters III and IV, but the climax of *Passing* suggests that interpersonal violence, even intimate violence, also sometimes results from the American obsession with race.

In *Quicksand,* the protagonist, Helga Crane, is an often impulsive young woman who seems unable to settle into any one identity or role. The details of her background mirror much of Larsen's biography—Helga Crane's mother is Danish while her father is Caribbean; Helga Crane is employed

123

Harmon awards at the Zion church. Miss Harmon, daughter of founder William E. Harmon, congratulates winners of awards: Nella Larsen, Channing H. Tobins, James Weldon Johnson proxy of Claude McKay, and Dr. George Haynes, secretary of committee on race relations, circa 1929. (Bettmann/Corbis)

at a southern educational institution focused on racial uplift; Helga Crane leaves Chicago for Harlem and eventually the United States for Denmark. In the novel, Helga's dissatisfaction with her situation is often understandable, though the pattern she develops of repeatedly and entirely rejecting one life for another, and then another, suggests that her personality is unstable, and she therefore becomes less sympathetic as a character. Readers, that is, don't always understand her motives or the rationale for her choices and so sometimes not only fail to identify with her but also become less likely to empathize with her.

In Denmark, Helga is received as an exotic, desired as a Negro more than as an individual. Although she is not discriminated against as she would be in the United States, she is nevertheless perceived as a representative of a category rather than a person. Although Denmark opens up pleasant possibilities for her, in other words, it does so primarily because of race awareness. Danish society is no more colorblind than any other. Complicating this question of the exotic is the tendency in American literature to present African American women as sexualized exotic others, a trend African American female authors such are Larsen attempt to counteract.

Throughout the novel, Helga establishes a series of alignments with men who, though are dramatically different from one another, are nevertheless all inappropriate for her. She leaves a fiancé in the American South because, in part, he is too conventional in his upwardly mobile striving. In Denmark, she is courted by a prominent artist, but he is motivated by assumptions that she will enhance his public image and perhaps perform more thrillingly as a lover than European women he's known. When Helga returns to the United States, she makes what is perhaps her most bizarre decision, marrying a traditional southern minister, eventually subsuming her identity entirely in his as she bears him multiple children. The novel concludes with the suggestion that Helga dies, like many women before her, as a result of childbirth. The climax, therefore, critiques gender roles more overtly than it does racial identity.

The central character in *Passing,* Irene Redfield, is another mixed-race woman, one who can pass as white if she wishes to. She passes when it is convenient for her, as in the opening scene, but she is married to an African American man, and she lives with him and their son in Harlem. In contrast to *Quicksand, Passing* is set to a much greater extent in Harlem, and of all the novels discussed in this book, *Passing* most prominently features Harlem (the poetry of Langston Hughes also frequently describes Harlem, as the material in Chapter III reveals). In the first section of the novel, however, Irene coincidentally encounters an old friend, Clare Kendry, who lives as a white woman married to a white man, although she too is mixed race. Clare's husband is violently and crudely racist, so Clare must carefully guard her past, compartmentalizing her acquaintances into those who will protect her secret and those who cannot know it. Clare's tolerance of her husband's racism disturbs Irene and can also disturb the reader, but it also reveals Clare's fundamental contempt for her husband. As the novel progresses, Clare engages in increasingly risky behavior, partly for the thrill, partly because she's unduly confident, and partly because she misses the social ease she felt with African Americans.

The novel turns on the shifting alliances among Irene, Clare, Irene's husband, and Clare's husband. All of the relationships exhibit an unease throughout the novel, and the two marriages reveal the compromises spouses sometimes make contrary to their better judgment. Some of these compromises, even when made for the good of the marriage, end up breeding resentment and distrust. Both Irene's marriage and Clare's marriage are troubled and grow more troubled as the novel develops. Clare's death at the end both resolves and confirms some of the tensions among the characters—for the climax invites speculation. Several equally plausible scenarios could explain Clare's death—did she fall? jump? was she pushed? by whom—her husband? Irene? Although most readers will favor one or another explanation, their interpretations will inevitably be suggestive rather than conclusive.

Both *Quicksand* and *Passing* were received favorably by critics when they were published. Yet neither remained in the public eye for long, and neither received substantial interest from readers, especially outside of New York. As the Harlem Renaissance waned over the next decade and as Nella Larsen herself disappeared from public view, literary attention turned to other writers. During the last quarter of the 20th century, however, Larsen's work garnered renewed attention as critics, teachers, and readers developed greater interest in both African American and women's writing. For a time, psychoanalytic critics found the novels particularly fruitful. As attitudes shift not only about race generally in the United States, but also specifically about mixed or multirace identity, it will be interesting to trace responses to these novels. Currently, both novels are excerpted in major literary anthologies. *Quicksand* and *Passing* are frequently read together, though *Passing* has been the more popular of the two recently.

The two novels are easily paired, not only because they were composed by the same author or because they were published only a year apart, but also because their thematic interests are so similar. Both feature a female character as protagonist, one who achieves or attempts to achieve a substantial part of her identity through her alliance with a male character, her husband or romantic partner. Both novels reveal the restricted options available to women in the 1920s, especially African American women striving toward middle-class stability. Both interrogate definitions of race, and both ironize, even taunt, characters—and hence also readers—who assume that seeing is believing. And finally, both suggest that "race," a word most people believe they could define, is frustratingly complicated and perhaps in the end indefinable.

## ABOUT NELLA LARSEN

Nella Larsen's background is both intriguing and confusing. Some of the basic facts of her life are harder to substantiate than they are for the other authors discussed in this book. Much of the mystery is due to Larsen's own reticence and obfuscation. Although she at times claimed 1893 as her birth year, she was in fact born in Chicago on April 13, 1891, and her birth certificate lists her as "colored." Her parents were listed as Mary Hanson Walker and Peter Walker. Larsen herself stated that her mother was Danish and her father had been born in the West Indies. She stated that her father died when she was two years old, and that subsequently her mother married Peter Larson, who was Danish like her mother. In her biography of Larsen, however, Thadious M. Davis speculates that Peter Larson and Peter Walker might have been the same man; if they were, Walker would have passed from "colored" to white as he simultaneously passed from Walker to Larson. If Davis is correct, Nella Larsen would have been the only member of the family whose appearance made her African ancestry obvious, and this could

Nella Larsen, novelist of the Harlem Renaissance (1891–1964). (Library of Congress)

also explain some of the gaps in the historic record of her childhood. Unfortunately, although none of the available facts contradict Davis's theory, none of them absolutely confirm it either. Nevertheless, these details of her early life reveal the autobiographical influences on her novels.

Larsen spent some portions of her childhood in Denmark and also attended public schools in Chicago until she was 16, when she enrolled at Fisk University's Normal School, a historically black college in Nashville, Tennessee. Her interactions with her family of origin became increasingly infrequent as she entered adulthood. She later completed a course in nursing in New York City and then worked at the Tuskegee Institute before returning to New York in 1916. She met her husband, Elmer Imes, in New York; they were married in 1919 and lived in Harlem in order to participate in its cultural vibrancy. Through her husband, she met many influential and prestigious people, circulating among the wealthy and well-known. She socialized with many of the writers who remain the most prominent figures of the Harlem Renaissance. However, just as she failed to fit in fully with her own family due to the visible racial distinctions among the members, so too she failed to fit comfortably with her husband's social circle due to differences of class and education.

Larsen began writing soon after her marriage and began publishing short stories. She published the two novels that will be discussed further in this chapter, *Quicksand* and *Passing,* in 1928 and 1929, respectively. Although she completed a third novel, it was never published. She also won a Guggenheim Fellowship, the first African American woman to do so, which permitted her to travel throughout Europe. Her career as a writer was brought to an abrupt end, however, shortly after *Passing* was published. Larsen published a short story called "Sanctuary" and was accused of plagiarizing it from another writer. Larsen denied the charges, but the similarities between the two stories seemed too substantial for many readers. Critics currently disagree about the significance of the similarities between the two stories, although no one can plausibly argue that those similarities are entirely coincidental. Larsen published nothing else (although she may have continued writing) and withdrew from the public eye. Although her writing to this point had made her a prominent figure in the Harlem Renaissance, she did not maintain the relationships she had developed through her literary activity. Despite the fact that Larsen's novels began to receive renewed critical interest at the end of the 20th century and into the 21st, her time as an active writer formed only a brief portion of her life, slightly more than one decade of her more than 70 years.

In 1933, she divorced her husband and cut her ties with most of her social acquaintances, moving out of Harlem and again supporting herself as a nurse. Although she lived for 30 more years, her work fell out of favor. As she aged, she lived an increasingly isolated life and experienced periods of significant depression. Her exact death date is unknown, for she died alone in her New York apartment, apparently of heart failure. Her body was discovered by her landlord on March 30, 1964. She is buried in Cypress Hills Cemetery in Brooklyn.

## HISTORICAL EXPLORATION: RACIAL DEFINITIONS AND PASSING

"Race" is an idea most people believe they understand and could define. Yet common definitions are often contradictory. For example, is race determined by appearance, ancestry, or both (or neither)? How many races are there? If our definition depends on ancestry, do we simply ascribe each race to a continent? Are Egyptians the same race as Kenyans? What about Pakistanis and Vietnamese? Or Spaniards and Irish? If our definition depends on appearance, which physical features do we rely on to determine race? Why those features and not others? For example, is height a characteristic that is aligned with race? What is the difference between race and ethnicity? Is race behavioral? If not, why are people accused of "acting white" or "acting black"?

These questions are important because we understand race to be something that is real. Many laws in the United States, even so foundational a document as the U.S. Constitution, classify people according to race and assume that race is a biological as well as a legal form of identity. Yet even the legal definitions of race have been inconsistent. A person with very little African ancestry, perhaps 1/32 (having one great great great grandparent), would often be defined as "Negro." Yet persons with 1/8 Native American ancestry would not be defined as Native American. Some of these inconsistencies result from treaties that the U.S. government observes with Native Americans that do not apply to other racial groups, but the fact of inconsistency reveals that race is difficult to define, even for legislators passing laws addressing race.

Until the year 2000, the U.S. census permitted Americans to identify as members of one race only, under the assumption that races could not mix legally, even if they in fact did socially and sexually. Therefore, everyone had *a* race that they "really" were, even if they identified themselves differently. The assumption that a person is "really" one race is crucial to the question of passing. Because passing is an activity defined as misrepresentation, as presenting oneself as something one is not, there must be something that one really is—even if one's appearance permits confusion. Estimates of how many people have passed from one race to another—most often but not always from black to white—in the United States vary widely; someone who passed successfully would not, of course, be known to have passed. At the very least, thousands of people have passed as white when the law would have defined them as nonwhite; more likely, this number would reach hundreds of thousands. The benefits of passing as white are obvious—especially during the Jim Crow era, white people had access to better jobs, better housing, and better education. White people were also relieved of the daily humiliations of discrimination and prejudice. Yet a decision to pass into another race also required a person to sever all ties with his or her past, including relationships with parents and siblings as well as close friends—relationships with anyone who could, intentionally or not, reveal the secret of race.

As we would expect, the topic of passing is most prominent in the novel *Passing*. The two central characters, because of their similar appearances, have similar options, yet they reach different decisions. Clare Kendry has decided to pass actively and fully—she presents herself as a white woman, marrying a white man and circulating in white society. Yet, when the opportunity arises, she also decides to reintroduce herself to African American society, at great risk to her reputation, and eventually, to her life. Her longing for both the privileges of whiteness and the familiar acceptance of black culture reveals the perpetual ambivalence involved in a decision to pass. Irene Redfield, on the other hand, passes passively—she permits others to assume she is white without actually stating anything about her race. She takes advantage, therefore, of white privilege, while risking only embarrassment if her deception is discovered. Although this risk creates some anxiety for her, she is unlikely to suffer the dramatic consequences that Clare opens for herself.

The novel obviously critiques a decision to pass racially, but it also interrogates "race" as a definable category. If the complexions and other physical features of both Irene and Clare suggest that they are white, why are they classified as black? The book also extends questions of passing to include categories beyond race, including sexuality. Many critics contend that the friendship between Clare and Irene is characterized by sexual tension; each woman's sexual relationship with her husband is undeniably unsatisfying. The idea of passing, therefore, becomes more complex as the novel progresses.

### Definitions of Race

The first two documents below attempt to define race, for if laws distinguish among people of various races, representatives of the law must be able to determine an individual's race. The first document excerpts definitions of "Caucasian" and "Negro" from the *Dictionary of Races or People* that was prepared by and for the Immigration Commission. Current readers may find this document puzzling, for the authors consider language as a factor in race; presumably, cultures whose languages are related would share common origins and hence also be related by race. It also states that "Caucasian" applies to people outside of Europe but doesn't apply entirely to everyone native to Europe. The understanding of race according to this document doesn't appear to be objective in any scientific sense but instead sometimes appears to be quite subjective. Similarly, the excerpt reveals that while many anthropologists agree that the race of "Negro" exists, they don't agree about which people should be considered "Negro." By creating so many subcategories of the "grand division" of races, the document seems to subvert its own purpose, for many readers will eventually wonder whether the categories lose their usefulness. Obviously, whether a category is useful or not depends on its purpose. This document was created by the Immigration Commission because the United States at that time regulated immigration by country of origin, which is not identical to race but often correlates with race. An immigration law that would be passed in the following decade, the Johnson–Reed Act, would establish specific quotas for immigrants from every country in an attempt to maintain the racial composition of the United States at that time.

In the following documents, Georgia state laws defining race and pre-scribing certain types of behavior based on race, is much more straight-forward. Although laws from only the state of Georgia are included here, similar laws were passed in many other states and remained in effect for decades. It declares that people with any nonwhite "blood" will not be considered white. All birth certificates required newborns to be identified by race; these birth certificates would later be used to regulate marriage. White people were permitted to marry only other white people, as testi-fied to by their birth certificates; violation of these laws brought a penalty of imprisonment. Unlike the *Dictionary of Races or People,* these Georgia laws do not concern themselves with multiple subcategories but primarily with distinctions between white people and people of color. This concern suggests that the insistent opposition to "race mixing" was limited to the "purity" of only one race—white. These laws also reveal that governmen-tal interest in racial identity nearly always corresponded with the govern-ment's interest in regulating marriage, a topic that will be discussed in more detail in the next section of this chapter.

# From Reports of the Immigration Commission, 1911

CAUCASIAN, CAUCASIC, EUROPEAN, EURAFRICAN, or WHITE race. . . . The name given . . . to the white race or grand divi-sion of mankind as distinguished from the Ethiopian, Mongolian, American, and Malay races. . . . The term is now defined more suit-ably for our purposes in a broader sense . . . namely, to include all races, which, although dark in color or aberrant in other directions, are, when considered from all points of view, felt to be more like the white race, than like any of the four other races just mentioned. Thus the dark Gallas of eastern Africa are included, partly on linguistic grounds, partly because they have the regular features of the Caucasian; the Berbers of northern Africa because of the markedly blond and regular features found amongst them; the dark Hindus and other peoples of India still more emphatically because of their possessing an Aryan speech, relating them still more closely to the white race, as well as because of their physical type; and possibly the Polynesians, Indonesians, and Ainos of the Pacific because of their physical characteristics, although in this discussion these will be excluded from the definition. . . . The general opinion is that the Dravidians and Veddahs, south of the Aryan Hindus in India, are not Caucasian. They do not possess an Aryan tongue; and physically they more nearly approach the Negro.

It will be seen from the above that the Caucasian race was by no means originally confined to Europe. It has long covered the northern third of Africa and practically all of southern Asia to the borders of Farther India. Although called the "European" race, it more likely had its origin in Asia or even in Africa than in Europe. . . . It does not even now fill certain large sections of Europe. The Mongolian race not only occupies the most of eastern and northern Russia but northern Scandinavia and the greater part of Finland, while the dominant races of Turkey, of Roumania, and even of Hungary are Mongolian in origin.

Although the white race would be supposed to be the one best understood, it is really the one about which there is the most fundamental and sometimes violent discussion. The word "Caucasian," for instance is in nearly as bad repute as "Aryan" at the present time amongst etymologists. . . . While the word "Caucasian" has reference mainly to physical characters, "Aryan" will be used here as applying strictly to linguistic groupings . . . such use is general and practically unavoidable in immigration statistics and in European censuses. The English seldom use the word "Caucasian" in the narrower sense as designating only the peoples of the Caucasus Mountains. . . .

The Caucasian is the only grand division of mankind which possesses inflected languages. . . .

Passing now from the classification found most convenient in immigration topics, other schemes . . . should be referred to here.

Forty years ago Huxley replaced the word "Caucasian" by two terms: "Xanthochroi," meaning the blond race, and "Melanochroi," or the brunette portion of the Caucasian race. Ripley has summed up in a masterful manner all the physical classifications made since that of Huxley. He shows that the great consensus of opinion thus far favors the distinction of three great races in Europe, which he calls the "Teutonic," the "Alpine," and the "Mediterranean." . . . Ripley's classification is impracticable in immigration statistics and in censuses of races. . . . Moreover, it appears probable that his classification must be largely modified by the studies of Deniker, now in progress. The latter has added to the three classical races of Europe the "Atlanto-Mediterranean," the "Oriental," and the "Adriatic," with possibly three or four other "subraces." Ripley has practically admitted the existence of the Adriatic as a distinct race. . . . Deniker has wisely given as an alternative classification to that of his physical types a classification of "peoples" based on linguistic grounds. . . .

NEGRO, NEGROID, AFRICAN, BLACK, ETHIOPIAN, or AUSTAFRICAN. That grand division of mankind distinguished by its black color and, generally speaking, by its woolly hair. While the black, like the white and yellow races, is accepted by practically all ethnologists as a primary division of mankind, there is the greatest difference of opinion as to what should be included in it. Some would put the Hottentots and Bushmen of South Africa into a separate grand division. Still more would set apart the "Oceanic Negroes"—that is, the Negritos of Malaysia and the Papuans of New Guinea, and especially the Australians. Some call these doubtful branches "Negroid," a name applied by Huxley to all Negroes excepting the Australians.

In simple classification for Emigration purposes it is preferable to include all the above under the term "Negroes." They are alike in inhabiting hot countries and in belonging to the lowest division of mankind from an evolutionary standpoint. While the Australians do not have the kind of hair of the African Negroes, they are still lower in civilization. Only the Negrillos or dwarf Negroes of Africa and the Negritos of Malaysia equal them in this respect. The definition must exclude, however, the dark, almost black, Veddahs and Dravidian tribes of India, and especially the dark Hamites and Semites of northern and northeastern Africa. . . . The two latter groups belong to the Caucasian stocks of southwestern Asia, linguistically, as well as, to a certain extent, in temperament, civilization, and regularity of features. They inhabit nearly one-third of Africa, including Abyssinia. The so-called "Ethiopic" language and old form of Christianity are found in the latter country, and not in the misnamed "Ethiopian" race.

The only Negroes to whom practically all ethnologists are willing to apply the term are those inhabiting the central and western third of Africa, excluding even the Bantus, who occupy practically all Africa south of the Equator. The Bantus, well typified by the Zulu subdivision, are lighter in color than the true Negroes, never sooty black, but of a reddish-brown. From the Negroes proper of the Sudan have descended most American Negroes.

To some extent the northern Negro stock has become intermixed with the African Caucasian, already mentioned, especially about the upper Nile, in Abyssinia, and in Gallaland and Somali land farther east. . . .

There is a bewildering confusion in the terms used to indicate the different mixtures of white and dark races in America. Thus, all natives of Cuba, whether dark or white, are called "Creoles," as this word is loosely used in the United States; but Creole, as more strictly defined, applies only to those who are native-born but of pure European descent. This is the use of the word in Mexico. In Brazil and Peru, on the contrary, it is applied to those possessing colored blood in some proportion, in Brazil to Xejrroes of pure descent, in Peru to the issue of whites and mestizos. "Mestizo" is the Spanish word applied to half-breeds (white and Indian).

Immigration statistics count as Negro, or "African (black)" "aliens whose appearance indicates an admixture of Negro blood, . . . whether coming from Cuba or other islands of the West Indies, North or South America, Europe, or Africa." Only American-born immigrants of pure European blood are counted as Cuban. . . . All these "natives of the Western hemisphere," together with American Indians and Negroes, are included with the Magyar, Turkish, and Armenian races in the term "All others," the sixth grand division of immigrant races as classified by the Bureau of Immigration.

*Source:* Reports of the Immigration Commission. *Dictionary of Races or People.* Washington, DC: Government Printing Office, 1911: 30–32, 100–101.

# From Georgia Laws on Race and Color, 1927

Georgia

### Definition of "Negro" and "White"

§79–103. (2177) Persons of color who are.—All Negroes, mulattoes, mestizos and their descendants, having any ascertainable trace of either Negro or African, or West Indian, or Asiatic Indian blood in their veins, and all descendants of any person having either Negro or African, West Indian, or Asiatic Indian blood in his or her veins shall be known in this State as persons of color. [Acts 1865–6, p. 239; 1927, p. 272]

§53–312. "White person" defined—The term "White person" shall include only persons of the white or Caucasian race, who have no ascertainable trace of either Negro, African, West Indian, Asiatic Indian, Mongolian, Japanese, or Chinese blood in their veins. No person, any one of whose ancestors has been duly registered within the State Bureau of Vital Statistics as a colored person or person of color, shall be deemed to be a white person. [Acts 1927, p. 277] . . .

§53–307. Marriage license, form of application for, provided.— [Applicants for marriage license are required to give race and color of each applicant and race and color of each parent.] [Acts 1927, p. 274; 1933, p. 12]

§53–314. Birth of legitimate child of white parent and colored parent, report of, and prosecution.—When any birth certificate, showing the legitimate birth of any child to parents one of whom is white and one of whom is colored, shall be forwarded to the Bureau of Vital Statistics, it shall be the duty of the State Board of Health to report the same to the Attorney General of the State, with full information concerning the same. Thereupon it shall be the duty of the Attorney General to institute criminal proceedings against the parents of such child for any violations of the provisions of this Chapter which may have been violated. [Acts 1927, p. 278; 1933, p. 12] . . .

§53–106. (2941) Miscegenation prohibited.—It shall be unlawful for a white person to marry anyone except a white person. Any marriage in violation of this section shall be void. [Acts 1927, p. 277] . . .

§53–9903. Miscegenation; penalty.—Any person, white or colored, who shall marry or go through a marriage ceremony in violation of the provision of Sec. 53–106 shall be guilty of a felony, and shall be punished by imprisonment in the penitentiary for not less than one (1) year and not more than two (2) years. [Acts 1927, p. 277] (90, 113–114)

*Source:* Georgia State Laws, 1927. Reprinted in Pauli Murray, ed. *States Laws on Race and Color.* Athens: University of Georgia Press, 1997.

## Court Case Regarding Interracial Adoption

This next document depends on the kind of information in the previous two in order to make any sense. A child, Jacqueline Ann Henley, had been born to a white mother, but the child's race was debatable. Her birth certificate stated that she was white, but her appearance suggested that her father might have been black. Because her mother had died, she could not be called upon to clarify Jacqueline's paternity. After her mother's death, Jacqueline had lived with her aunt, who was also white, but the aunt had eventually refused to continue raising her because she believed Jacqueline's father was black. The Department of Welfare had placed the child with an African American family who desired to adopt her, but because Jacqueline's birth certificate stated that she was white, this adoption was not permitted. The prospective adoptive father, Robert Green, had sued to have Jacqueline's birth certificate changed. The anthropologist who testified as an expert could not specify the child's race with scientific certainty, but it is interesting to note the physical characteristics he focused on, once again revealing the detail social scientists considered relative to race. The court opted not to permit a change in the record because the judges determined that there should be absolutely no doubt as to the child's race before permitting the change.

For modern readers, this case raises several interesting points. First, just as interracial marriage was proscribed by law, so was interracial adoption. Rather than challenge that law, however, Robert Green attempted to "prove" that Jacqueline should be classified as black, perhaps because changing an individual birth certificate might be more possible than changing a law that implicated entire cultural practices. Additionally, the judges who ruled in the majority believed that ascribing a nonwhite identity to a child would create such an onerous burden that it could only be done if they had no doubt at all. Ordinarily, civil court cases demand only a pre-ponderance of the evidence, that is, a majority of the evidence, to find in favor of the plaintiff. Even criminal cases demand only that the jury con-clude beyond a "reasonable" doubt. Here, though, the judges would not permit any doubt at all; implicitly, then, racial identity is more significant than a heinous violent crime. Although this case could seem to affect only a few people directly, it reveals the profound seriousness racial identity had for Americans as recently as 1956.

## *Robert Green v. City of New Orleans*, 1956

Burton G. Klein, New Orleans, for plaintiff-appellant.

Henry B. Curtis and John F. Connolly, New Orleans, for City of New Orleans, defendant-appellee.

Frank J. Stich, Jr. New Orleans, curator ad hoc.

REGAN, Judge.

Plaintiff, Robert Green, a colored adoptive applicant, instituted this suit against the defendant, City of New Orleans, Bureau of Vital Statistics, endeavoring to obtain a writ of mandamus compelling the defendant to change the race, as revealed in the birth certificate of Jacqueline Ann Henley, age about four and a half years, from white to colored or to show cause why such change should not be made; plaintiff then requested that a curator ad hoc be appointed by the court to represent the interest of the minor child.

No answer appears in the record on behalf of the Bureau of Vital Statistics, however, Frank J. Stich, Jr., the curator ad hoc answered and generally denied the pertinent allegations of the plaintiff's petition.

From a judgment in favor of defendant dismissing plaintiff's suit, he has prosecuted this appeal.

The chronological facts are relatively simple. On November 2nd, 1950, Ruby Henly Preuc, a white woman gave birth to a female child, Jacqueline Ann Henley while confined in the Charity Hospital of New Orleans. Three weeks after the birth of the child Ruby Preuc brought it to the home of her sister, Mrs. Harold McBride. The identity of the child's father was never revealed to anyone by its mother and, there-fore, he is, at present, unknown. On October 11, 1952, Ruby Preuc died of a brain tumor in the Home for Incurables, where she had been confined since shortly after the birth of her child. On August 1, 1952, Mrs. McBride visited the Department of Welfare and requested it to accept the child as she felt it was a Negro and she could no longer permit her to remain in her home, since the neighbors were beginning to comment about the medium brown color of the child's skin. In order to facilitate this request proceedings were initiated wherein the child was declared abandoned by the Juvenile Court for the Parish of Orleans and, on October 1, 1952, it was placed in a Negro foster home where she has remained.

Plaintiff endeavored to adopt the child through the use of the facilities of the Department of Welfare, which approved his application, but an examination of the child's birth certificate disclosed an impediment in that she was registered as white in the Bureau of Vital Statistics, and that agency refused to change the designation of the race of the child to colored. Hence this suit.

The only question posed for our consideration is one of fact and that is whether Jacqueline Ann Henley has been proved to be a member of the Negro race?

Plaintiff contends that the lower court erred in its judgment, for the reason that sufficient evidence was offered during the trial hereof to prove that the child was a Negro. On the other hand, the curator ad hoc insists that the evidence adduced at the trial was not sufficient to compel the Bureau of Vital Statistics to change the birth certificate of the child from white to that of a colored person.

We feel compelled to remark at the inception of this opinion that we were completely fascinated by the novel-like tenor of this record. The trial judge, apparently in order to afford the plaintiff the benefit of every doubt and an unimpeded opportunity to prove his case with that legal certainty which the law requires, most liberally relaxed the rules of evidence, therefore, much of the testimony that we shall refer to or quote hereinafter, insofar as plaintiff's case is concerned, will, we believe, be predicated, to a large extent, on hearsay, inferences and presumptions of fact.

Counsel for plaintiff in order to sustain his client's contention that sufficient evidence was adduced in the trial court to prove that the child was, at least, part Negro, points to the testimony of Herbert Stanton, a Negro laborer, who related that Ruby Preuc was employed as a barmaid in a Negro saloon, a fact which everyone seems to have conceded. He further asserted that he corresponded with Ruby Preuc when she was visiting her sister in Detroit, Michigan. A letter was offered in evidence written, during this time, by Stanton to Ruby Preuc and it contained such phrases as "but you know that I'll always love you"; "I wish you was home I miss you so" and "with love, Rock." On Direct and cross examination he further related that he had never "gone out" with her nor had he been "intimate with her" and upon being interrogated "Did you ever meet her after work?", he responded "her boss used to bring her home . . . a white man."

Counsel conceded in oral argument that the testimony of Stanton and the letter were not offered to prove parentage, but merely to show Ruby Preuc's close association with Negroes.

Plaintiff offered in evidence the testimony of Mrs. Emma Smith, who related that birth certificates were her special assignment and that it was she who had prepared the child's birth record. Upon being interrogated "The color and race of the father, do you ask that question?", she responded, "No, if she is a white mother. We do not ask if her husband is white, we take it for granted he is white." The certificate that Mrs. Smith prepares ultimately becomes the actual birth record and for that purpose it is forwarded to the Department of Public Health, a fact which was admitted by Mrs. Naomi Drake, Deputy Registrar of the Bureau of Vital statistics for the City of New Orleans.

Mrs. Harold McBride, sister of Ruby Preuc, testified that three weeks after the birth of the baby, Ruby Preuc and the child came to her home, wherein Ruby resided until she was removed to the Home for Incurables, where she subsequently died. Sometime after Ruby Preuc was confined in the Home for Incurables and about two months before she died, Mrs. McBride visited the Department of Public Welfare and requested it to accept the child because "she didn't fit in my family, she was too dark . . . I told Mrs. Oberholtzer there had been remarks passed that the child was possibly a nigger." However, Mrs. McBride, both on direct and cross examination, related that she had never seen her sister consort with Negroes "outside of work" and that she did not actually know if the child was part Negro.

Mrs. Catherine Oberholtzer testified that Mrs. McBride, when she visited her, stated that "she would like the agency to make plans for the child since she felt that she was a Negro and she could no longer keep her in the house; the child was growing darker day by day."

Charles Collins testified that when Mrs. McBride visited his office she informed him that ". . . she lived in an all white neighborhood and that it would sooner or later be embarrassing . . . to have the child in her household . . . because of its color."

The only expert witness offered to enlighten the court appeared on behalf of the plaintiff and it is on his testimony that plaintiff rests his case. Dr. Arden R. King stated that he was a professor of Anthropology at Tulane University and had done graduate work in physical anthropology and archeology. He related that the child was four and a half years of age at the time of his examination to determine if there was any possibility that she was part Negro. He testified at great length on two occasions and, in the final analysis, more briefly summarized what he had previously asserted:

"There are three characteristics which are distinctly Negro in this child. One is the lip seam, the division between the integumental lip, the skin lip above here, and the mucous lip, is clearly marked, the little ridge; and secondly, the distinctly small, delicate ears; and third, perhaps the most indicative of all, there are concentrations of pigments in diagnostic positions of the anatomy.

"While I could get these three characteristics occurring in an individual who had no Negro ancestry, it would be so rare—we have records of it—it would be so rare as not to be considered at all probable."

Upon being interrogated ". . . could you say positively there was some degree of Negro blood less than one-fourth, no matter how small?", he responded ". . . you ask me to not be scientific, and I can not. I won't go beyond saying extremely probable." Dr. King concluded by asserting that if this child was nine or ten years old he would then be in a more advantageous position to determine its race.

The curator ad hoc insists that the foregoing evidence is not sufficient to compel the Bureau of Vital statistics to change the birth certificate of the child from white to that of a colored person and, therefore, requests that the judgment refusing the writ of mandamus be affirmed.

The trial judge obviously was of the opinion that the plaintiff had failed to prove his case with that legal certainty which the law requires in cases of this nature and our examination of the record fails to disclose any error in his factual or legal conclusions. The testimony of Stanton was not offered by plaintiff to prove parentage, but merely to show Ruby Preuc's close association with a Negro or Negroes. The inference, of course, which plaintiff desired to create by virtue of Stanton's testimony was intimacy sufficient to create a presumption of fatherhood.

The testimony of Mrs. Emma Smith likewise was not offered to prove parentage, but to create a presumption of negligence in the Charity Hospital in failing to diligently endeavor to ascertain the race of the newborn infant before issuance of the birth certificate to the Bureau of Vital Statistics, which accepts it as such at face value.

Mrs. McBride's opinion of the race of the child, unsupported by evidence other than appears herein, certainly was not proof thereof.

As we have related hereinabove, in the last analysis, plaintiff rests his case on the testimony of Dr. Arden R. King, who qualified as an expert in the field of anthropology, which the record informs us is the science of man in relation to physical character, distribution, origin, classification and relationship of races. As we have seen, the very utmost that Dr. King could say with respect to this child being part Negro was that "this was an extreme probability."

It is well recognized that anthropology is an inexact science and, therefore, Dr. King could not say with certainty that the child was part Negro and that this uncertainty was accentuated by the tender age of the child. We believe that it is also well recognized that all the methods presently in use to determine race are precarious and that their provisional findings must be accepted with the utmost caution.

The general rule that a civil case need not be proven beyond a reasonable doubt is conceded, but we know of no case wherein the courts have applied this general rule when the purpose was to change the race of a person as disclosed in a birth or death certificate.

In the relatively recent case of State ex rel. Treadaway v. Louisiana State Board of Health, on rehearing, La. App. 1952, 56 So. 2d 249, 250, we said "there must be no doubt at all," and the following extract therefrom serves to point up the reason for this assertion:

"In Villa v. Lacoste, 213 La. 654, 35 So. 2d 419, 421, the Supreme Court, in discussing the effect of a certificate issued by the State Board of Health, said clearly that such certificates constitute only prima facie proof of the correctness of the statements contained therein and held that such evidence as was introduced had been 'ample to overcome the prima facie case' made by the certificates themselves.

"We wondered whether we had accorded too great an effect to the certificate under attack here.

"In Sunseri v. Cassagne, 191 La. 209, 185 So. 1, 5, the Supreme Court, in another somewhat similar matter, held that a person who has been commonly accepted as being of the Caucasian race should not be held to be of the colored race *'unless all the evidence adduced leaves no room for doubt that such is the case.'*

"The Supreme Court remanded the matter in order that further evidence might be adduced and finally *held that there was no doubt,* and maintained the correctness of the certificates which were there involved and which showed the defendant to be colored.

"We wondered whether the evidence here left no room for doubt.

"Thoroughly aware of the transcendent importance of our conclusion to those involved and to others affected though not parties, we diligently endeavored to convince ourselves that there might be room for doubt.

"We interpret the language used in the Sunseri case and quoted above as indicating that the proof in such case should be even more convincing than that which is necessary in such cases and must be proved 'beyond a reasonable doubt.' *We feel that the language used by the Supreme Court means that there must be no doubt at all.*

"However, as the Supreme Court found itself compelled to do when the Sunseri case was presented to it finally, Sunseri v. Cassagne, 195 La. 19, 196 So. 7, 9, we must hold that the evidence here leaves no room for doubt and that the certificate under attack should not be changed." (italics ours)

The Supreme Court granted a writ of certiorani in the foregoing case, 221 La. 1048, 61 So. 2d 735, 739, and having satisfied themselves that this court's conclusions with respect to the facts and the law were correct, adopted the opinion of this court and, in the concluding paragraph of its opinion, asserted:

"Relator must show that he has a clear legal right to have the correction made. The legal certainty of the proof submitted must be such as to compel the Registrar of Vital Statistics to perform the ministerial duty of changing the recordation from 'Colored' to 'White.' The proof of record falls far short of any such assumption. As the name indicates, the records kept by the Registrar are vital to the general public welfare. *The registration of a birthright must be given as much sanctity in the law as the registration of a property right.*"

In view of the unequivocal rationale expressed in the foregoing cases we must entertain the opinion that the evidence adduced herein is not sufficient to compel the Bureau of Vital Statistics to change the birth certificate of the child from white to Negro at the present time. The final cause of law is the welfare of society. The rule that misses this aim cannot permanently justify its existence. The above jurisprudence is predicated on that major premise.

We notice that the trial court inadvertently dismissed plaintiff's suit. We believe that plaintiff should have been nonsuited by virtue of the fact that the testimony of the expert Dr. King revealed that when the child was more developed and mature, he would then occupy an excellent position to testify with greater certainty as to its race.

For the reasons assigned the judgment appealed from is amended by dismissing the plaintiff's case as of non-suit and, as thus amended, it is affirmed.

Amended and affirmed.

JANVIER, Judge (dissenting).

I do not retract one syllable of what was said in State ex rel. Tread away v. State Board of Health, La. App., 56, So. 2d 249, 250, and I agree that, as we said there, the language used by the Supreme Court in Sunseri v. Cassagne, 191 La. 209, 185 So. 1, should be interpreted as meaning that in practically all such cases vital statistics records should not be ordered changed unless there is "no doubt at all" of the incorrectness of those records. Nor do I to any extent criticize my associates who feel that the record here leaves some possible doubt on the question of whether the little girl is a Negress.

There is a vast distinction between the facts of this case and the facts found in practically all other cases in which an effort has been made to force a change in such records. The distinction lies in the fact that here, at the very outset of our investigation, we find that the entry showing the race was made as the result of a presumption and not because of a stated fact.

In practically all cases the information as to the race, etc., is given by a member of the family and is based on knowledge or at least on a well founded belief as to the race of the parents. Here the record shows that no one gave any information as to the race of the father of the child and its race was stated as white merely because of the custom in the hospital that where a white mother gives birth to a child and there is no knowledge as to who is the father it is "presumed" that the father is white. The entry on the record of the Board of Health was made from information given by the hospital, which information was not based on knowledge but merely on the referred to presumption.

We know that the father was not white or Caucasian because on that point the anthropologist to whom I shall later refer says that he has no doubt at all. His only possible doubt was as to whether the race of the father might be something other than Negro though, as I will show hereafter, he found Negro characteristics and did not find any other characteristics. We start then with a record which we know is incorrect. I myself feel that there is no doubt at all and, being without doubt that the father was a Negro, I cannot permit myself to consent to a decree which must have a most harmful effect on the welfare of the little girl and to some extent on the public welfare as well.

There is no doubt in my mind that every person who has come into contact with this record really has no doubt at all that the little girl in question is a Negress. First of all, we notice that the aunt of the little girl (the sister of the mother) found it necessary to give up the custody of the child because she fully realized that it was a Negress. She so stated to at least two persons. Then the Welfare Association had no doubt at all of the race of the child and made arrangements for its adoption by a Negro family and only then discovered that its race had been registered as "white."

We come to the adoptive family and find that there is no doubt at all as to the race and this is evidenced by the attempt to force a change of the records so that it might be adopted as a Negro.

In my opinion there is no doubt in the mind of Dr. King, the Professor of Anthropology at Tulane University. He said that the father of the child was of other than the white race and that the only characteristics other than Caucasian which he could possibly identify were those of the Negro race, and that in his opinion the father was of the Negro race, but, when pressed as to whether he could positively say that there was no doubt at all, he merely said that personally he believed it, but that as a scientist he realized that there was the possibility of error from a scientific point of view and that therefore he could not say that, from that point of view, there was no doubt at all.

A person of the Negro race has as much right to have such records correctly made as a person of the white race. And I cannot condemn this little girl to the humiliation and embarrassment which must ensue if this incorrect entry is to stand even for the five or six years suggested by my associates. There is no assurance that after the lapse of those five or six years another effort will be made to effect the necessary correction, and there will result the most unfortunate situation that the little girl registered as white will continue to associate with Negroes and that her social life will be only with Negroes and yet she will be unable to marry a Negro since, being registered as a white person, miscegenation laws will make such a marriage impossible. In fact, during the five or six years suggested by my associates she will labor under the embarrassment of associating socially only with Negroes who will no doubt taunt her with being registered as "white."

The record convinces me that she is of the Negro race and that we should so declare.

I respectfully dissent.

*Source: Robert Green v. City of New Orleans.* 88 So.2d 76 (1956).
Department of Public Health. Court of Appeal of Louisiana,
Orleans. June 11, 1956. Rehearing Denied June 27,
1956. Writ of Certiorari Denied September 28, 1956.

## Autobiographies Discussing Racial Passing

The final two documents in this section present the experiences of individuals who briefly passed as members of another race. *Running a Thousand Miles for Freedom* is a slave narrative composed by William Craft that describes how he and his wife, Ellen, escaped slavery. Because Ellen's complexion was light, she could pass for white, so she disguised herself as a white man who would pose as the owner of William. Given the social practices at the time, it was easier for Ellen to disguise herself as a white man than it would have been for the two to travel together if Ellen had attempted to pass as a white woman. Ellen's passing was successful; the couple did escape slavery. Her goal, however, was not to live as a white person permanently but simply to pass for the few days it took her and William to reach northern free states. Even so, her disguise was elaborate and demanded quick thinking on her part.

The next document describes how John Howard Griffin disguised himself as a black man in order to discover what being black meant during the middle of the 20th century. Although Griffin's motive was to conduct research that could not be accomplished any other way, some white people did pass as black at other points in American history, often because the person they wished to marry was black. Since racial identity is often equivocal, it is hypothetically as possible—though much less expected—for a white person to pass as black as it is for a black person to pass as white. However, in practical terms, it is often harder for a member of a dominant group to pass as a member of a subordinate group because dominant people tend to pay much less attention to the details of the lives of their subordinates than subordinates are forced to pay to their superiors.

## From William Craft, *Running a Thousand Miles for Freedom: The Escape of William and Ellen Craft from Slavery*, 1860

My wife's first master was her father, and her mother his slave, and the latter is still the slave of his widow.

Notwithstanding my wife being of African extraction on her mother's side, she is almost white—in fact, she is so nearly so that the tyrannical old lady to whom she first belonged became so annoyed, at finding her frequently mistaken for a child of the family, that she gave her when eleven years of age to a daughter, as a wedding present. This separated my wife from her mother, and also from several other dear friends. But the incessant cruelty of her old mistress made the change of owners or treatment so desirable, that she did not grumble much at this cruel separation.

It may be remembered that slavery in America is not at all confined to persons of any particular complexion; but as the evidence of a slave is not admitted in court against a free white person, it is almost impossible for a white child, after having been kidnapped and sold into or reduced to slavery, in a part of the country where it is not known (as often is the case), ever to recover its freedom. . . .

We were married, and prayed and toiled on till December, 1848, at which time (as I have stated) a plan suggested itself that proved quite successful, and in eight days after it was first thought of we were free from the horrible trammels of slavery, and glorifying God who had brought us safely out of a land of bondage.

Knowing that slaveholders have the privilege of taking their slaves to any part of the country they think proper, it occurred to me that, as my wife was nearly white, I might get her to disguise herself as an invalid gentleman, and assume to be my master, while I could attend as his slave, and that in this manner we might effect our escape. After I thought of the plan, I suggested it to my wife, but at first she shrank from the idea. She thought it was almost impossible for her to assume that disguise, and travel a distance of 1,000 miles across the slave States. However, on the other hand, she also thought of her condition. She saw that the laws under which we lived did not recognize her to be a woman, but a mere chattel, to be bought and sold, or otherwise dealt with as her owner might see fit. Therefore the more she contemplated her helpless condition, the more anxious she was to escape from it. So she said, "I think it is almost too much for us to undertake; however, I feel that God is on our side, and with his assistance, notwithstanding all the difficulties, we shall be able to succeed. Therefore, if you will purchase the disguise, I will try to carry out the plan." . . .

Some of the best slaveholders will sometimes give their favourite slaves a few days' holiday at Christmas time; so, after no little amount of perseverance on my wife's part, she obtained a pass from her mistress, allowing her to be away for a few days. The cabinet-maker with whom I worked gave me a similar paper, but said that he needed my services very much, and wished me to return as soon as the time granted was up. I thanked him kindly; but somehow I have not been able to make it convenient to return yet; and, as the free air of good old England agrees so well with my wife and our dear little ones, as well as with myself, it is not at all likely we shall return at present to the "peculiar institution" of chains and stripes.

On reaching my wife's cottage she handed me her pass, and I showed mine, but at that time neither of us were able to read them.

It is not only unlawful for slaves to be taught to read, but in some of the States there are heavy penalties attached, such as fines and imprisonment, which will be vigorously enforced upon anyone who is humane enough to violate the so-called law. . . .

However, at first, we were highly delighted at the idea of having gained permission to be absent for a few days; but when the thought flashed across my wife's mind that it was customary for travellers to register their names in the visitors' book at hotels, as well as in the clearance or Custom-house book at Charleston, South Carolina—it made our spirits droop within us.

So, while sitting in our little room upon the verge of despair, all at once my wife raised her head, and with a smile upon her face, which was a moment before bathed in tears, said, "I think I have it!" I asked what it was. She said, "I think I can make a poultice and bind up my right hand in a sling, and with propriety ask the officers to register my name for me." I thought that would do.

It then occurred to her that the smoothness of her face might betray her; so she decided to make another poultice, and put it in a white handkerchief to be worn under the chin, up the cheeks, and to tie over the head. This nearly hid the expression of the countenance, as well as the beardless chin. . . .

My wife, knowing that she would be thrown a good deal into the company of gentlemen, fancied that she could get on better if she had something to go over the eyes; so I went to a shop and bought a pair of green spectacles. This was in the evening.

We sat up all night discussing the plan and making preparations. Just before the time arrived, in the morning, for us to leave, I cut off my wife's hair square at the back of the head, and got her to dress in the disguise and stand out on the floor. I found that she made a most respectable looking gentleman.

My wife had not ambition whatever to assume this disguise, and would not have done so had it been possible to have obtained our liberty by more simple means; but we knew it was not customary in the South for ladies to travel with male servants; and therefore, not-withstanding my wife's fair complexion, it would have been a very difficult task for her to have come off as a free white lady, with me as her slave; in fact, her not being able to write would have made this quite impossible. We knew that no public conveyance would take us, or any other slave, as a passenger, without our master's consent. This consent could never be obtained to pass into a free State. My wife's being muffled in the poultices, &c., furnished a plausible excuse for avoiding general conversation, of which most Yankee travellers are passionately fond. . . .

I took the nearest possible way to the train, for fear I should be recognized by someone, and got into the negro car in which I knew I should have to ride; but my *master* (as I will now call my wife) took a longer way round, and only arrived there with the bulk of the passengers. He obtained a ticket for himself and one for his slave to Savannah, the first port, which was about two hundred miles off. My master then had the luggage stowed away, and stepped into one of the best carriages.

But just before the train moved off I peeped through the window, and, to my great astonishment, I saw the cabinet-maker with whom I had worked so long, on the platform. He stepped up to the ticket-seller and asked some questions, and then commenced looking rapidly through the passengers, and into the carriages. Fully believing that we were caught, I shrank into a corner, turned my face from the door, and expected in a moment to be dragged out. The cabinet-maker looked into my master's carriage, but did not know him in his new attire, and, as God would have it, before he reached mine the bell rang, and the train moved off. . . .

As soon as the train had left the platform, my master looked round in the carriage, and was terror-stricken to find a Mr. Cray—an old friend of my wife's master, who dined with the family the day before, and knew my wife from childhood—sitting on the same seat.

The doors of the American railway carriages are at the ends. The passengers walk up the aisle, and take seats on either side; and as my master was engaged in looking out of the window, he did not see who came in.

My master's first impression, after seeing Mr. Cray, was that he was there for the purpose of securing him. However, my master thought it was not wise to give any information respecting himself, and for fear that Mr. Cray might draw him into conversation and recognize his voice, my master resolved to feign deafness as the only means of self-defense.

After a little while, Mr. Cray said to my master, "It is a very fine morning, sir." The latter took no notice, but kept looking out of the window. Mr. Cray soon repeated this remark, in a little louder tone, but my master remained as before. This indifference attracted the attention of the passengers near, one of whom laughed out. This, I suppose, annoyed the old gentleman; so he said, "I will make him hear"; and in a loud tone of voice repeated, "It is a very fine morning, sir."

My master turned his head, and with a polite bow said, "Yes," and commenced looking out of the window again.

One of the gentlemen remarked that it was a very great deprivation to be deaf. "Yes," replied Mr. Cray, "and I shall not trouble that fellow any more."

*Source:* Craft, William. *Running a Thousand Miles for Freedom: The Escape of William and Ellen Craft from Slavery.* London: William Tweedie, 1860: 3–4, 16–19, 22–23.

# From John Howard Griffin, *Black Like Me,* 1960

I had my last visit with the doctor. . . . The treatment had not worked as rapidly or completely as we had hoped, but I had a dark undercoating of pigment which I could touch up perfectly with stain. We decided I would shave my head, since I had no curl. The dosage was established and the darkness would increase as time passed. . . .

. . . I fixed myself a bite of supper . . ., putting off the moment when I would shave my head, grind in the stain and walk out into the New Orleans night as a negro.

. . . Finally I began to cut my hair and shave my head. . . . I applied coat after coat of stain, wiping each coat off. Then I showered to wash off all the excess. . . .

The transformation was total and shocking. I had expected to see myself disguised, but this was something else. I was imprisoned in the flesh of an utter stranger, an unsympathetic one with whom I felt no kinship. All traces of the John Griffin I had been were wiped from existence. . . .

The completeness of this transformation appalled me. . . . I became two men, the observing one and the one who panicked, who felt Negroid even into the depths of his entrails.

I felt the beginnings of a great loneliness, not because I was a Negro but because the man I had been, the self I knew, was hidden in the flesh of another. . . .

The worst of it was that I could feel no companionship with this new person. I did not like the way he looked. . . . For a few weeks I must be this aging, bald Negro; I must walk through a land hostile to my color, hostile to my skin.

*Source:* Griffin, John Howard. *Black Like Me.* New York: Signet, 1960: 14–16. Copyright © 1960, 1961, 1977 by John Howard Griffin. Reprinted with the permission of New American Library, a division of Penguin Putnam, Inc.

## Discussion Questions

1. Compare the biographies of Nella Larsen and Zora Neale Hurston. How do you account for the similarities and differences?

2. Compare the types of violence in Larsen's work with violence in Hurston, Hughes, McKay, and Toomer. Based on this comparison, can you draw any conclusions about the concern of writers of the Harlem Renaissance about the nature of violence?

3. Research changes in childbearing practices since 1900. How has childbearing become more medicalized? How has safety for both mother and child improved? How can the "safety" of childbirth be applied metaphorically to the practice of passing?

4. Compare and contrast the settings of *Quicksand* and *Passing.* How do the settings influence the plots of the novels? What types of activity can or cannot occur in particular settings?

5. Watch a movie that focuses on the practice of passing. How do movies correspond with novels? Some examples include *Imitation of Life* (1934 and 1959), *The Jazz Singer* (1927, 1952, 1980), *Showboat* (1936), *Veiled Aristocrats* (1932), *God's Stepchildren* (1938), *Pinky* (1949), and *The Human Stain* (2003).

6. Write an essay describing a time when you pretended to be something you were not (do not choose an occasion when the point was masquerade, like a Halloween party; choose an occasion when you

sincerely hoped others would misinterpret your identity). How successful were you? What were your motives? How did you feel about yourself afterward?

7. Write an essay describing a secret you're keeping. What would happen if that secret were revealed?

8. In your class, try to come to a consensus on the definition of "race." Is it dependent on appearance, ancestry, or something else? What about adopted children—are they the same "race" as their adoptive parents? How is race different from ethnicity? How does a person know what race he or she is? How many races are there?

9. Research the term "scientific racism." What does it mean? Analyze the logic of its practitioners. Does the logic make sense to you? Why or why not?

10. Examine a current questionnaire from the U.S. Census Bureau. How does it classify race? Research how racial data collected from the census is used; what are the practical effects of gathering this information?

11. Nobel Prize–winning author Toni Morrison once referred to Bill Clinton as America's first black president. Look up the context of her remarks to decide what she meant. Based on this statement, how is race defined?

12. Read one or more additional slave narratives and compare the experiences of the authors with the experience of William and Ellen Craft. Do other slaves describe altering their appearance in order to escape?

13. Read a history book or watch a documentary focused on the history of race in America, Jim Crow laws and practices, or another topic related to segregation and discrimination and compare the presentation of that topic in that nonfiction source to how it is portrayed in Nella Larsen's fiction.

14. Choose a social issue you are interested in and research the laws related to that issue in your state. If you wanted to change those laws, what would you have to do? Would it be more effective to work toward legislative change, or to address the issue through the court system?

## Suggested Readings

Bayor, Ronald H. *Race and Ethnicity in America: A Concise History.* New York: Columbia University Press, 2003.

Belluscio, Stephen J. *To Be Suddenly White: Literary Realism and Racial Passing.* Columbia: University of Missouri Press, 2006.

Brody, Jennifer DeVere. "Clare Kendry's 'True' Colors: Race and Class Conflict in Nella Larsen's *Passing.*" *Callaloo* 15, no. 4 (1992): 1053–65.

Broyard, Bliss. *One Drop: My Father's Hidden Life—A Story of Race and Family Secrets.* New York: Little, Brown and Company, 2008.

Caughie, Pamela. "'Not Entirely Strange, . . . Not Entirely Friendly': Passing and Pedagogy." *College English* 54, no. 7 (1992): 775–93.

Chesnutt, Charles W. *The House behind the Cedars.* New York: Houghton Mifflin, 1900.

Dagbovie-Mullins, Sika. *Crossing-Black: Mixed Race Identity in Modern American Fiction and Culture.* Knoxville: University of Tennessee Press, 2013.

Davis, F. James. *Who Is Black? One Nation's Definition.* College Park, PA: Penn State University Press, 2001.

Davis, Thadious M. *Nella Larsen: Novelist of the Harlem Renaissance: A Woman's Life Unveiled.* Baton Rouge: Louisiana State University Press, 1994.

Dawahare, Anthony. "The Gold Standard of Racial Identity in Nella Larsen's *Quicksand* and *Passing.*" *Twentieth Century Literature* 52, no. 1 (2006): 22–41.

Dawkins, Marcia Alesan. *Clearly Invisible: Racial Passing and the Color of Cultural Identity.* Waco, TX: Baylor University Press, 2012.

Dreisinger, Baz. *Near Black: White-to-Black Passing in American Culture.* Amherst: University of Massachusetts Press, 2008.

Eubanks, W. Ralph. "Color Lines: How DNA Ancestry Testing Can Turn Our Notions of Race and Ethnicity Upside Down." *American Scholar* 82, no. 2 (2013): 20–28.

Gehlawat, Ajay. "The Strange Case of the Princess and the Frog: Passing and the Elision of Race." *Journal of African American Studies* 14, no. 4 (2010): 417–31.

Ginsberg, Elaine K. *Passing and the Fictions of Identity.* Durham, NC: Duke University Press, 1996.

Goldsmith, Meredith. "Shopping to Pass, Passing to Shop: Consumer Self-Fashioning in the Fiction of Nella Larsen." In *Middlebrow Moderns: Popular American Women Writers of the 1920,* edited by Lisa Botshon, Meredith Goldsmith, and Joan Shelley Rubin, 263–90. Boston: Northeastern University Press, 2003.

Gordon-Reed, Annette. *Race on Trial: Law and Justice in American History.* New York: Oxford University Press, 2002.

Griffith, John. *Black Like Me.* 50th Anniversary edition. New York: Signet, 2010.

Haizlip, Shirlee Taylor. *Finding Grace: Two Sisters and the Search for Meaning beyond the Color Line.* New York: The Free Press, 2004.

Hannaford, Ivan. *Race: The History of an Idea in the West.* Baltimore: Johns Hopkins University Press, 1996.

Harper, Phillip Brian. "Passing for What? Racial Masquerade and the Demands of Upward Mobility." *Callaloo* 21, no. 2 (1998): 380–97.

Higginbotham, F. Michael. *Race Law: Cases, Commentary, and Questions.* Durham, NC: Carolina Academic Press, 2010.

Hobbs, Allyson. *A Chosen Exile: A History of Racial Passing.* Cambridge, MA: Harvard University Press, 2014.

Jenkins, Candice M. "Decoding Essentialism: Cultural Authenticity and the Black Bourgeoisie in Nella Larsen's *Passing.*" *MELUS* 30, no. 3 (2005): 129–54.

Johnson, James Weldon. *The Autobiography of an Ex-Colored Man.* New York: Penguin, 1990.

Khanna, Nikki and Cathryn Johnson. "Passing as Black: Racial Identity Work among Biracial Americans." *Social Psychology Quarterly* 73, no. 4 (2010): 380–97.

Larson, Charles R. *Invisible Darkness: Jean Toomer and Nella Larsen.* Iowa City: University of Iowa Press, 1993.

Lewis, Vashti Crutcher. "Nella Larsen's Use of the Near-White Female in *Passing* and *Quicksand.*" In *Perspectives on Black Popular Culture,* edited by Harry B. Shaw, 36–45. Bowling Green, OH: Popular Press, 1990.

Little, Jonathan. "Nella Larsen's *Passing:* Irony and the Critics." *African American Review* 26, no. 1 (1992): 173–82.

Lopez, Ian Haney. *White by Law: The Legal Construction of Race.* 10th Anniversary edition. New York: New York University Press, 2006.

Lutes, Jean Marie. "Making up Race: Jessie Fauset, Nella Larsen, and the African American Cosmetics Industry." *Arizona Quarterly: A Journal of American Literature, Culture, and Theory* 58, no. 1 (2002): 77–108.

McIntire, Gabrielle. "Toward a Narratology of Passing: Epistemology, Race, and Misrecognition in Nella Larsen's *Passing.*" *Callaloo* 35, no. 3 (2012): 778–94.

Molina, Natalia. *How Race Is Made in America: Immigration, Citizenship, and the Historical Power of Racial Scripts.* Berkeley: University of California Press, 2013.

O'Toole, James M. *Passing for White: Race, Religion, and the Healy Family, 1820–1920.* Amherst: University of Massachusetts Press, 2002.

Pfeiffer, Kathleen. *Race Passing and American Individualism.* Amherst: University of Massachusetts Press, 2003.

Ramon, Donovan L. "'You're Neither One Thing (N)or the Other': Nella Larsen, Philip Roth, and the Passing Trope." *Philip Roth Studies* 8, no. 1 (2012): 45–61.

Retman, Sonnet. "Langston Hughes's 'Rejuvenation through Joy': Passing, Racial Performance, and the Marketplace." *African American Review* 45, no. 4 (2012): 593–602.

Rottenberg, Catherine. "Passing: Race, Identification, and Desire." *Criticism* 45, no. 4 (2003): 435–52.

Sanchez, Maria C. and Linda Schlossberg, eds. *Passing: Identity and Interpretation in Sexuality, Race, and Religion.* New York: New York University Press, 2001.

Sandweiss, Martha A. *Passing Strange: A Guilded Age Tale of Love and Deception across the Color Line.* New York: Penguin, 2009.

Scharfstein, Daniel J. *The Invisible Line: A Secret History of Race in America.* New York: Penguin, 2012.

Scott, Ellen. "More Than a 'Passing' Sophistication: Dress, Film Regulation, and the Color Line in 1930s American Films." *Women's Studies Quarterly* 41, no. 1–2 (2013): 60–86.

Sheehy, John. "The Mirror and the Veil: The Passing Novel and the Quest for American Racial Identity." *African American Review* 33, no. 3 (1999): 401–15.

Sherrard-Johnson, Cherene. "'A Plea for Color': Nella Larsen's Iconography of the Mulatta." *American Literature: A Journal of Literature, History, and Bibliography* 76, no. 4 (2004): 833–69.

Smedley, Audrey and Brian D. Smedley. *Race in North America: Origin and Evolution of a Worldview.* Boulder, CO: Westview Press, 2012.

Sullivan, Nell. "Nella Larsen's *Passing* and the Fading Subject." *African American Review* 32, no. 3 (1998): 373–86.

Toth, Josh. "Deauthenticating Community: The Passing Intrusion of Clare Kendry in Nella Larsen's *Passing*." *MELUS* 33, no. 1 (2008): 55–73.

Twain, Mark. *Pudd'nhead Wilson and Those Extraordinary Twins.* New York: Penguin, 1986.

Van Thompson, Carlyle. "Makin a Way Outta No Way: The Dangerous Business of Racial Masquerade in Nella Larsen's *Passing*." *Women & Performance: A Journal of Feminist Theory* 15, no. 1 (2005): 79–104.

Vogel, Andrew. "Blurring the Color Line: Race and the American Dream in *The Autobiography of an Ex-Colored Man, Passing,* and *Cane*." In *The American Dream*, edited by Keith Newlin, 146–67. Ipswich, MA: Salem Press, 2013.

Wald, Gayle. *Crossing the Line: Racial Passing in Twentieth-Century U.S. Literature and Culture.* Durham, NC: Duke University Press, 2000.

Watson, Reginald. "The Tragic Mulatto Image in Charles Chesnutt's *The House behind the Cedars* and Nella Larsen's *Passing.*" *CLA Journal* 46, no. 1 (2002): 48–71.

Williams, Vernon J., Jr. *Rethinking Race: Franz Boas and His Contemporaries.* Lexington: University Press of Kentucky, 1996.

Wilson, Mary. "'Working Like a Colored Person': Race, Service, and Identity in Nella Larsen's *Passing.*" *Women's Studies* 42, no. 8 (2013): 979–1009.

Zackodnik, Teresa. "Passing Transgressions and Authentic Identity in Jessie Fauset's *Plum Bun* and Nella Larsen's *Passing.*" In *Literature and Racial Ambiguity*, edited by Teresa Hubel and Nell Brooks, 45–69. Amsterdam, Netherlands: Rodopi, 2002.

# HISTORICAL EXPLORATION: INTERRACIAL MARRIAGE

Interracial marriage laws have a long history in the United States. The first such laws were passed in 1660, in fact, long before the American Revolution, and they remained in effect in several states for three centuries. Most of these laws originally forbade marriage between white people and African Americans, but many eventually expanded to include a ban on marriage between whites and Native Americans and Asians. Although such laws had been on the books for two centuries before the Civil War, enforcement became much more rigorous as anxieties about white supremacy and racial purity heightened following the abolition of slavery. Antimiscegenation laws formed only one component of the widespread and deeply engrained Jim Crow practices during the late 19th and early 20th centuries, of course, but because marriage is such a personal and intimate decision, these laws could be particularly frustrating. Only in 1967 did the Supreme Court declare that such laws are unconstitutional.

The only states that never passed antimiscegenation laws are Minnesota, Wisconsin, New York, New Jersey, Connecticut, Vermont, New Hampshire, Alaska, and Hawaii. Several states repealed their antimiscegenation laws shortly after the Civil War, and many others repealed theirs during the mid-20th century. All of the states that had formed the Confederacy as well as all the border states except Maryland enforced these laws until the Supreme Court declared them unconstitutional. Some states also had laws forbidding any sexual activity between people of different races, but more laws focused on marriage itself due to the legal, economic, and social benefits granted to married people.

Both of Nella Larsen's novels feature interracial relationships, though the contexts are dramatically different. In *Passing,* Clare—as long as she is defined as black—is married to a man of a different race, though he, of course, doesn't realize that. Clare's marriage illustrates the reason for much of the anxiety related to racial categories at this time. Because her physical features permit her to pass as white, her husband can't know her "true" race unless she tells him. States that recorded a person's race on birth certificates and required submission of birth certificates before marriage licenses would be issued were seeking to avoid this type of deception. When Clare's husband begins to suspect her deception, he becomes enraged, even murderous—not sim-

WHAT MISCEGENATION IS!

—AND—

WHAT WE ARE TO EXPECT

Now that Mr. Lincoln is Re-elected.

**Title page of book against the mixing of races, published in 1864. Despite the numbers of people of mixed race background in the United States, the suggestion that individuals of different races would interact provoked anxiety among many. (Corbis)**

ply because his wife has been dishonest but because he has consequently been intimate with a member of a race he despises. Because Clare and her husband reside in New York, the legal status of their marriage is not affected, but as the climax of the novel demonstrates, other dangers await her.

In *Quicksand,* however, Helga's identity as a visibly mixed-race woman becomes an asset of sorts when she travels to Europe. Interracial relationships are not considered scandalous in Denmark, and she is pursued by Axel Olsen, a prominent artist. Yet he treats her as an exotic and propositions her disrespectfully, less due to any racism he feels than due to a more pervasive sexism. Despite her attempts to flee the discrimination she experiences in the United States, Helga fails to discover the freedom she seeks in the less racially restrictive Denmark. When she returns to the United States, she eventually surrenders to a conventional marriage to a black minister, a marriage that is doomed to disappoint her for many reasons.

## Legal Cases Addressing Interracial Marriage

The first two documents below are taken from court cases that address the issue of interracial marriage. The first, *Pace v. Alabama*, questions the legality of an Alabama law forbidding interracial marriage and condemning anyone found guilty to significant punishments. The plaintiff, Tony Pace, argued that the law was discriminatory and violated the Fourteenth Amendment to the U.S. Constitution because it stipulated punishment of interracial couples that did not apply to couples of the same race. The court found that the law was constitutional because both parties in a given interracial marriage would be punished similarly. That is, the white and black members of the couple were treated equally. Implicitly, the law would have been considered unconstitutional only if one member of the couple were found guilty and punished. This logic was applied to several similar court cases in other states until the middle of the 20th century.

The second document is taken from the decision of the case that overturned antimiscegenation laws, *Loving v. Virginia*. Because the state of Virginia did not permit interracial marriage, Mildred and Richard Loving were married in Washington, D.C., where they subsequently resided. After they moved back to Virginia, they were arrested. When the Lovings initiated a lawsuit to overturn Virginia's law on constitutional grounds, the state courts upheld the law based on the same logic that had been described

**Mr. and Mrs. Richard Perry Loving, an interracial couple, fought Virginia's law against interracial marriages in 1967. This landmark Supreme Court case established that state bans on interracial marriages are unconstitutional. (Bettmann/Corbis)**

in *Pace v. Alabama*. The Supreme Court of the United States, however, declared that such laws did in fact violate the Fourteenth Amendment. As of 1967, therefore, states were no longer permitted to enforce such laws.

# From *Pace v. Alabama*, 1883

U.S. Supreme Court

Section 4189 of the Code of Alabama, prohibiting a white person and a negro from living with each other in adultery or fornication, is not in conflict with the Constitution of the United States, although it prescribes penalties more severe than those to which the parties would be subject, were they of the same race and color.

Section 4184 of the Code of Alabama provides that

"If any man and woman live together in adultery or fornication, each of them must, on the first conviction of the offense, be fined not less than one hundred dollars, and may also be imprisoned in the county jail or sentenced to hard labor for the county for not more than six months. On the second conviction for the offense with the same person, the offender must be fined not less than three hundred dollars, and may be imprisoned in the county jail, or sentenced to hard labor for the county for not more than twelve months, and for a third or any subsequent conviction with the same person, must be imprisoned in the penitentiary, or sentenced to hard labor for the county for two years."

Section 4189 of the same code declares that

"If any white person and any negro, or the descendant of any negro to the third generation, inclusive, though one ancestor of each generation was a white person, intermarry or live in adultery or fornication with each other, each of them must, on conviction, be imprisoned in the penitentiary or sentenced to hard labor for the county for not less than two nor more than seven years."

In November, 1881, the plaintiff in error, Tony Pace, a negro man, and Mary J. Cox, a white woman, were indicted under sec. 4189 in a circuit court of Alabama for living together in a state of adultery or fornication, and were tried, convicted, and sentenced, each to two years' imprisonment in the state penitentiary. On appeal to the supreme court of the state, the judgment was affirmed and he brought the case here on writ of error, insisting that the act under which he was indicted and convicted is in conflict with the concluding clause of the first section of the Fourteenth Amendment of the Constitution, which declares that no state shall "deny to any person the equal protection of the laws."

Mr. Justice Field delivered the opinion of the Court, and after stating the case as above, proceeded as follows:

The counsel of the plaintiff in error compares secs. 4184 and 4189 of the Code of Alabama, and assuming that the latter relates to the same offense as the former and prescribes a greater punishment for it because one of the parties is a negro or of negro descent, claims that a discrimination is made against the colored person in the punishment designated which conflicts with the clause of the Fourteenth Amendment prohibiting a state from denying to any person within its jurisdiction the equal protection of the laws.

The counsel is undoubtedly correct in his view of the purpose of the clause of the amendment in question—that it was to prevent hostile and discriminating state legislation against any person or class of persons. Equality of p[protection under the laws implies not only accessibility to each one, whatever his race, on the same terms with others to the courts of the country for the security of his person and property, but that in the administration of criminal justice, he shall not be subjected for the same offense to any greater or different punishment. Such was the view of Congress in the reenactment of the Civil Rights Act of May 31, 1870, c. 114, after the adoption of the amendment. That act, after providing that all persons within the jurisdiction of the United States shall have the same right, in every state and territory, to make and enforce contracts, to sue, be parties, give evidence, and to the full and equal benefit of all laws and proceedings for the security of person and property as is enjoyed by white citizens, declares, in sec. 16, that they shall be subject "to like punishment, pains, penalties, taxes, licenses, and exactions of every kind, and none other, any law, statute, ordinance, regulation, or custom to the contrary notwithstanding."

The defect in the argument of counsel consists in his assumption that any discrimination is made by the laws of Alabama in the punishment provided for the offense for which the plaintiff in error was indicted when committed by a person of the African race and when committed by a white person. The two sections of the Code cited are entirely consistent. The one prescribes generally a punishment for an offense committed between persons of different sexes; the other prescribes a punishment for an offense which can only be committed where the two sexes are of different races. There is in neither section any discrimination against either race. Section 4184 equally includes the offense when the persons of the two sexes are both white and when they are both black. Indeed, the offense against which this latter section is aimed cannot be committed without involving the persons of both races in the same punishment. Whatever discrimination is made in the punishment prescribed in the two sections is directed against the offense designated, and not against the person of any particular color or race. The punishment of each offending person, whether white or black, is the same.

*Judgment affirmed.*

*Source: Pace v. Alabama, 106 U.S. 583 (1883).*

# From *Loving v. Virginia*, 1967

U.S. Supreme Court

Virginia's statutory scheme to prevent marriages between persons solely on the basis of racial classifications held to violate the Equal Protection and Due Process Clauses of the Fourteenth Amendment. . . .

Mr. Chief Justice Warren delivered the opinion of the Court.

This case presents a constitutional question never addressed by this Court: whether a statutory scheme adopted by the State of Virginia to prevent marriages between persons solely on the basis of racial classifications violates the Equal Protection and Due Process Clauses of the Fourteenth Amendment. For reasons which seem to us to reflect the central meaning of those constitutional commands, we conclude that these statutes cannot stand consistently with the Fourteenth Amendment.

In June 1958, two residents of Virginia, Mildred Jeter, a Negro woman, and Richard Loving, a white man, were married in the District of Columbia pursuant to its laws. Shortly after their marriage, the Lovings returned to Virginia and established their marital abode in Caroline County. At the October Term, 1958 . . . a grand jury issued an indictment charging the Lovings with violating Virginia's ban on interracial marriages. On January 6, 1959, the Lovings pleaded guilty to the charge and were sentenced to one year in jail; however, the trial judge suspended the sentence for a period of 25 years on the condition that the Lovings leave the State and not return to Virginia together for 25 years. He stated in an opinion that "Almighty God created the races white, black, yellow, malay and red, and he placed them on separate continents. And but for the interference with his arrangement there would be no cause for such marriages. The fact that he separated the races shows that he did not intend for the races to mix."

After their convictions, the Lovings took up residence in the District of Columbia. On November 6, 1963, they filed a motion in the state trial court to vacate the judgment and set aside the sentence on the ground that the statutes which they had violated were repugnant to the Fourteenth Amendment. The motion not having been decided by October 28, 1964, the Lovings instituted a class action in the United States District Court for the Eastern District of Virginia requesting that a three-judge court be convened to declare the Virginia antimiscegenation statutes unconstitutional and to enjoin state officials from enforcing their convictions. On January 22, 1965, the state trial judge denied the motion to vacate the sentences, and the Lovings perfected an appeal to the Supreme Court of Appeals of Virginia. On February 11, 1965, the three-judge District Court continued the case to allow the Lovings to present their constitutional claims to the highest state court.

The Supreme Court of Appeals upheld the constitutionality of the antimiscegenation statutes and, after . . . modifying the sentence, affirmed the conviction. The Lovings appealed this decision, and we noted probable jurisdiction on December 12, 1966. . . .

The two statutes under which appellants were convicted and sentenced are part of the comprehensive statutory scheme aimed at prohibiting and punishing interracial marriages. The Lovings were convicted of violating 20–58 of the Virginia Code:

"Leaving State to evade law. If any white person and colored person shall go out of this State, for the purpose of being married, and with the intention of returning, and be married out of it, and afterwards return to and reside in it, cohabiting as man and wife, they shall be punished as provided in 20–59, and the marriage shall be governed by the same law as if it had been solemnized in this State. The fact of their cohabitation here as man and wife shall be evidence of their marriage."

Section 20–59, which defines the penalty for miscegenation, provides:

"Punishment for marriage. If any white person intermarry with a colored person, or any colored person intermarry with a white person, he shall be guilty of a felony and shall be punished by confinement in the penitentiary for not less than one nor more than five years."

Other central provisions in the Virginia statutory scheme are 20–57, which automatically voids all marriages between "a white person and a colored person" without any judicial proceeding. . . . The Lovings have never disputed in the course of this litigation that Mrs. Loving is a "colored person" or that Mr. Loving is a "white person" within the meanings given those terms by the Virginia statutes. . . .

Virginia is now one of 16 states which prohibit and punish marriages on the basis of racial classifications. Penalties for miscegenation arose as an incident to slavery and have been common in Virginia since the colonial period. The present statutory scheme dates from the adoption of the Racial Integrity Act of 1924, passed during the period of extreme nativism which followed the end of the First World War. The central features of this Act, and current Virginia law, are the absolute prohibition of a "white person" marrying other than another "white person," a prohibition against issuing marriage licenses until the issuing official is satisfied that . . . the applicants' statements as to their race are correct, certificates of "racial composition" to be kept by both local and state registrars, and the carrying forward of earlier prohibitions against racial intermarriage.

## I

In upholding the constitutionality of these provisions in the decision below, the Supreme Court of Appeals of Virginia referred to its 1955 decision in Naim v. Naim . . . as stating the reasons supporting the validity of these laws. In Naim, the state court concluded that the State's legitimate purposes were "to preserve the racial integrity of its citizens," and to prevent "the corruption of blood," "a mongrel breed of citizens," and "the obliteration of racial pride," obviously an endorsement of the doctrine of White Supremacy. . . . The court also reasoned that marriage has traditionally been subject to state regulation without federal intervention, and, consequently, the regulation of marriage should be left to exclusive state control by the Tenth Amendment.

. . . the State argues that the meaning of the Equal Protection Clause, as illuminated by the statements of the Framers, is only that state penal laws containing an interracial element . . . as part of the definition of the offense must apply equally to whites and Negroes in the sense that members of each race are punished to the same degree. Thus, the State contends that, because its miscegenation statutes punish equally both the white and the Negro participants in an interracial marriage, these statutes, despite their reliance on racial classifications, do not constitute an invidious discrimination based upon race. The second argument advanced by the State assumes the validity of its equal application theory. The argument is that, if the Equal protection Clause does not outlaw miscegenation statutes because of their reliance on racial classifications, the question of constitutionality would thus become whether there was any rational basis for a state to treat interracial marriages differently from other marriages. On this question, the State argues, the scientific evidence is substantially in doubt and, consequently, this Court should defer to the wisdom of the state legislature in adopting its policy of discouraging interracial marriages.

Because we reject the notion that the mere "equal application" of a statute containing racial classifications is enough to remove the classifications from the Fourteenth Amendment's proscription of all invidious racial discriminations, we do not accept the State's contention that these statutes should be upheld if there is any possible basis for concluding that they serve a rational purpose. . . . In the case at bar . . . we deal with statutes containing racial classifications, and the fact of equal application does not immunize the statute from the very heavy burden of justification which the Fourteenth Amendment has traditionally required of state statutes drawn according to race. . . .

The State finds support for its "equal application" theory in the decision of the Court in Pace v. Alabama. . . . In that case, the Court upheld a conviction under an Alabama statute forbidding adultery or fornication between a white person and a Negro which imposed a greater penalty than that of a statute proscribing similar conduct by members of the same race. The Court reasoned that the statute could not be said to discriminate against Negroes because the punishment for each participant in the offense was the same. However, as recently as the 1964 Term, in rejecting the reasoning of that case, we stated "Pace represents a limited view of the Equal Protection Clause which has not withstood analysis in the subsequent decisions of this Court." . . . As we there demonstrated, the Equal Protection Clause requires the consideration of whether the classifications drawn by any statute constitute an arbitrary and invidious discrimination. The clear and central purpose of the Fourteenth Amendment was to eliminate all official state sources of invidious racial discrimination in the States. . . .

There can be no question but that Virginia's miscegenation statutes rest solely upon distinctions drawn according to race. The statutes proscribe generally accepted conduct if engaged in by members of different races. Over the years, this Court has consistently repudiated "[d]istinctions between citizens solely because of their ancestry" as being "odious to a free people whose institutions are founded upon the doctrine of equality." . . . At the very least, the Equal Protection Clause demands that racial classifications, especially suspect in criminal statutes, be subjected to the "most rigid scrutiny," . . . and, if they are ever to be upheld, they must be shown to be necessary to the accomplishment of some permissible state objective, independent of the racial discrimination which it was the object of the Fourteenth Amendment to eliminate. Indeed, two members of this Court have already stated that they "cannot conceive of a valid legislative purpose . . . which makes the color of a person's skin the test of whether his conduct is a criminal offense." . . .

There is patently no legitimate overriding purpose independent of invidious racial discrimination which justifies this classification. The fact that Virginia prohibits only interracial marriages involving white persons demonstrates that the racial classifications must stand on their own justification, as measures designed to maintain White

Supremacy. We have consistently denied . . . the constitutionality of measures which restrict the rights of citizens on account of race. There can be no doubt that restricting the freedom to marry solely because of racial classifications violates the central meaning of the Equal Protection Clause.

## II

These statutes also deprive the Lovings of liberty without due process of law in violation of the Due Process Clause of the Fourteenth Amendment. The freedom to marry has long been recognized as one of the vital personal rights essential to the orderly pursuit of happiness by free men. Marriage is one of the "basic civil rights of man," fundamental to our very existence and survival. . . . To deny this fundamental freedom on so unsupportable a basis as the racial classifications embodied in these statutes, classifications so directly subversive of the principle of equality at the heart of the Fourteenth Amendment, is surely to deprive all the State's citizens of liberty without due process of law. The Fourteenth Amendment requires that the freedom of choice to marry may not be restricted by invidious racial discriminations. Under our Constitution, the freedom to marry, or not marry, a person of another race resides with the individual and cannot be infringed by the State.

These convictions must be reversed.

It is so ordered.

*Source: Loving v. Virginia,* 388 U.S. 1 (1967).

## A Personal Experience

The last document in this section is an oral history composed by Michele DeFreece, who grew up in Massachusetts, the daughter of a white mother and black father. She describes the opposition to her parents' relationship expressed by some members of both of their families. She also describes the close emotional attachment she has felt to several members of her extended family. Her discussion of her childhood, adolescence, and young adulthood illustrates some of the problems that can occur when a person feels forced to identify as either one race or another. Her personal experience provides a concrete example of the complications that arise through insistence on rigid categories—the kind of racial categories that are discussed in the first section of this chapter. Her story also reveals some of the pain that results from attempts to restrict loving relationships. Yet her story is ultimately one of strength and gratitude.

## Michele DeFreece, "Stop Explaining. My Name's Michele," 2014

I was born June 3, 1960 to a white Italian mother from western Massachusetts. She conceived me through a black man who was her high school sweetheart. They dated through high school but their dating had to be called "just friends." He went on to school; when he came back, I guess I was conceived. My grandmother was Catholic, and they put my mother in a Catholic hospital in the hopes that she would give me up because this just was not right as far as she was concerned. My father was on his way to college, and it was like this was a stumbling block for him. After I was born, I was put into foster care until my mother and grandmother found a place and the equipment to bring me home. There was never any doubt in my mother's mind that she was not going to give me up. She was determined to keep me. So around September of 1960, I finally ended up living with my mother and grandmother, and I took on the last name of my mother which was Miner.

When I was in high school and saw my birth certificate, I was very upset because my mother's name was the only one on it. It listed me as white, and I had no father. I was very, very disturbed with it because I knew who these people were.

When I was small I lived with my grandmother who was a waitress and my mother, but the weird thing was that my mother always had positive contact with my father's immediate family. I was told when I was very little my paternal grandfather didn't want anything to do with me, but everybody lived in the same town. My father's family weren't allowed to see me in the first couple months after I was born, but then my mother and my father's mother met at the railroad tracks down by where they lived so they could get the first glimpse of Michele. My aunt who was sixteen at the time also was there. Then after that my paternal grandfather accepted me. After

I was born, my mother's father disowned her for the rest of his life. I knew his face, and this sounds crazy, but he lived three doors away from my black grandparents. He spoke to them but he did not speak to his daughter nor did he ever talk to me. I didn't realize he was my grandfather until I was around ten or eleven.

When I was growing up, until I was eight or nine, I always called my paternal African American grandparents by their first names, Doris and Jackie. They babysat for me; they spoiled me; we went there for Christmas, all those kinds of things. I also went to my black father's grandmother's house. I called her Mrs. Barnes, but she was my great grandmother. I went there every Sunday. I looked forward to vanilla wafers. I was part of the Sunday dinner. My mother was there, and Edith Barnes loved my mother. But the only grandparent I really thought I had was my maternal grandmother who lived with me when I was little. She helped raise me with my mother. My maternal grandparents were divorced. My grandfather moved down by my black grandparents and lived there and remarried but never spoke to my mother again after she conceived me. My mother and I were living in an apartment, just the two of us, very low class, not even middle class. She's a hard worker. When I was around four, she started dating another black man who had been married before. They ended up getting married by the time I was five, and she married him because she was once again pregnant. I did not go to her wedding. I remember her coming home saying, "You need to call Donald Dad now." It was as simple as that. So I started calling this black man "Dad"—I wasn't used to being around a lot of blacks. I was being raised in my mother's culture. So I felt very uncomfortable. I just went along with it. I was an easy person to raise. After my mother married him, I was in first grade and she said, "Tell the teacher your name is not Michele Miner. Your name is Michele Scott." It took two years to get it through the school system that I was Michele Scott. Did the man ever adopt me? No. Before they married when they were dating, I do remember being caught on a neighbor's swing set, and my mother said, "Michele, get over here now. You can't be there." And the reason was that these neighbors did not like the idea of white woman dating a black man, so they didn't want me to be over there, but I didn't know.

In elementary school, I remember never really thinking that I was black. I was a star dancer so that's what I did a lot. My mother put me in talent shows, and I was Miss Tap Dancer of Greenfield, Massachusetts. She put me on stage. I had the Shirley Temple curls, and I believe part of her reason was to prove to the community that we were ok, because I'm sure it was very hard on her to have this biracial child alone. She pushed me a lot to be out in front. I don't know if I would have done it if it wasn't for her pushing. Look at what I've done; I've created this star.

I'm close to my great grandmother, and like I said, my mother used to take her to do her errands. She loved my mother. My dad was her favorite grandson. I knew some of my great cousins because they were my dad's cousins. My mother was a very active woman, so when she would go to the YMCA exercise class or do something else, my paternal grandfather would babysit me. So I grew up with these people, but I didn't get the connection truly of who they were until we moved to a house that had an attic, and I went up in the attic one day and looked through pictures. The pictures said "Mommy and Michele." "Aunty Berta and Michele." Oh, my goodness, Berta's my aunt? Then the next page, "Daddy and Michele." There's Herb! I'd been calling my father Herb for years, until I was probably twelve years old. It was crazy, but this is what happened. I remember every time he came home from college, he'd always see me. My mother and he seemed to be friends, and he would take me somewhere. When I was around four years old, he took me up the Mohawk Trail, and he said I could buy whatever I wanted. What I bought was a blue ring—turquoise—and then he brought me down to get a root beer float. He said he wanted to bring me to meet his girlfriend, and I told him, "No." I said, "you have to wait until I grow up because I want to marry you." I wanted to marry my father. I knew he had a special connection to me, and I knew the whole family had a special connection to me, but to think that he was my father, and to think that Berta was my aunt, because she'd always visit too, was just—Wow.

Did I run downstairs from the attic and tell anybody? No, I didn't. I kept it to myself. For probably a year I kept it to myself. When it finally came out, I think I told my dad's mother, Doris, that I knew because one Christmas people got tipsy, and she sat next to me and said, "You know you're my granddaughter." And I said, "I know, shhhh." Finally when I was with them, I made up names for them. I called Grandma Dodo and Daddy Jack. Daddy Jack called me

Zebe—can you imagine where that came from? Black and white, so he called me Zebe. That was my name with them. Finally I felt comfortable. But as comfortable as I wanted to be, what I noticed was that they were not comfortable. When I would introduce my grandmother to my friends, or when I would say my father's coming home and I can't wait to see him, they said, "Is it ok with your mother that you say that?" And I got really mad; I said, "I don't care if it's ok. This is the truth. I want to live the truth." It really bothered me. When I talked to my mother, I said, "How come you never told me?" She said, "I told you when you were little." What little kid remembers whatever she said? But I do remember my great grandmother, Herb's grandmother, buying me things. They'd go to all my dance recitals, all this loving support for this child, yet I was never able to call her Nana. I felt like I missed out on a lot because I didn't have that relationship with them until later on in my teens.

I developed the relationship. I believe there must have been something in me that I was determined to find out who I was. My self-esteem, my identity was so important. Looking at a certificate that says you're white with no father. Looking at these people who feel uncomfortable, including my dad. When I started calling him Dad, he said, "Oh, geez." I said don't worry about it. I was sad that I wasn't raised by my natural father.

In elementary school they used to tell me, "Oh you're a brownie." I used to be so hurt by that, but I would be so happy when my friends would say, "You're very light anyway, so you look like all the rest of us." I was so happy, and this went on until I got into ninth grade. In ninth grade, my father Herb and his wife invited me out to their home in Ohio, so I spent two weeks with them and my adopted sister out there, and I was ingrained in the black experience there because we were in communities that were all-black; we went to a Baptist church and everything. I came back—my mother was mad—saying black experience, black power. I am black. I went back to ninth grade, and I'd say, "I am black. That's right." I listened to all the black music. I was black. So there was no in-between anymore. I finally came to the conclusion that I don't have to identify as black because that doesn't celebrate the love I have for my mother or grandmother. It was like I am who I am.

In high school I wanted to date, but when I had some crushes on some boys, one of my friends came back and told me that one of the boys liked me, but his mother said, "Stay away from that colored girl." So that really hurt. And then another one, the same thing. So I never dated white men during high school. My second cousin grew up in the same town. He was telling me that his mother had to tell him that he couldn't date Michele because we were related. All the blacks, maybe four or five of us in the whole junior high and high school, were all related, so you couldn't date anybody, but his mother had to tell him because apparently he didn't know.

People would constantly ask me what I am, and I really got tired of it. It was so important for people to know what I am. They would ask me this. So what are you? They would start speaking Spanish to me. Are you Filipino? What bothered me most was myself because I always felt a need to explain. People always had to verify what I was because of how light I am. I always felt I had to explain it. I have this black father and white mother. Why? How about just caring for me as me? Now it's great to see that there's such a mix in society.

At the end of both my grandparents' lives, I was just so thankful that I took the initiative as a young child to make these relationships happen, the closeness with my grandparents from my dad's side. I just said to my mom, after Sunday school, I'm going down to spend Sundays with them. They came and picked me up and they were good friends—it's so wild how everybody hung out in the town, but nobody wanted to be truthful with each other. My mother insisted that the core normal family was her husband, herself, my half-brother, and me. But I never felt part of that family. I always felt that I belonged with the Peters side of the family—that was their last name. That was my family, and I did everything I could to be part of it. I got to know my dad's cousins and got to go to the family reunions. My mother had no problem with that.

I lost my grandfather Daddy Jack when he was sixty-six because he loved sweets and didn't listen to the doctor or take care of himself, so he died just before I had my first child. But my grandmothers ended up living in the same senior citizen complex for twenty years, from 1970 until they passed. One lived on the third floor, and one lived on the fourth floor. You talk about competition. I wanted to spend time with both, but my maternal grandmother would call down and say, "When are you coming up? I made some lasagna for you." Or "let's go out to eat." I'd say, "Grandma, I'll be there." I loved both of them in very different ways. My maternal grandmother was my heart and soul and best friend. My paternal grandmother and I did a lot of fun things. She liked to golf, so we would go golfing. She liked to bowl, so I'd go to the bowling alley. It's funny because when I went to the bowling alley, my stepfather's father was bowling, too. I'd always say hi to him, but I never connected to that family. I was a Peters and I was with Doris and Jackie all the time. I think I was blessed that they lived in the same area so that I could have their love. The more love you can have, the better. It's just love. People say, "Weren't you confused?" Yes, but as a parent, I'd probably try to help my child more in figuring out and exploring her identity. I believe that if it wasn't for me, I wouldn't have had the interactions and experiences I had being biracial but learning about myself. I think I was more passionate about learning about myself than anybody. I would do reports in college on the black experience, of being biracial, multiculturalism. I was always passionate about those subjects. I have used my experiences and my life to share with my students. I always have a heart toward our students of color and their needs. Some of them come from so many different backgrounds. They don't know how to explain themselves. I just said, "Stop explaining. My name's Michele DeFreece. That's my name."

When I got married to my first husband, I wanted to be married with a true name because my birth certificate said I was Michele Miner and I'd been going by Michele Scott. I felt like I was doing something wrong. I'd been using this false name for all those years. My mother said, "Oh, no, you've used it enough. It's all right." Not for me it wasn't. It really hurt. I did go to court. I had to fill out this form and say that for all these years I had been going by the name Scott. They asked if I felt comfortable with this name. I said yes. My mother was there, and I was there, and that was it. It was a couple months before I got married. So I got married as Michele Scott. I wanted to be married truthfully. When I took his name, that is the name I have felt most connected to because of the love for his family and the love of the children we have together. I will not change my name.

Dating was always hard. I had a lot of bad experiences with African American women in college because I was light. They were jealous. I didn't get it. I just wanted to get along. They didn't like that I was in a lot of leadership positions, but that was just because of my enthusiasm. But they didn't like it. I did not come from a city area. So being biracial, being light skinned and half-way attractive and being from a general hometown community did not sit well with inner city college women. There were times kids just wanted to beat me up. Some of their boyfriends liked me—I didn't like them, but they liked me—that created a problem. I like to get along with people. During events like graduation, marriage, birth, it was always important to me to make sure that my true family was acknowledged. I always wanted people to know the truth about who I was. It was so important to know that Doris and Jackie were my grandparents. And Annie Miner and my mother were on that side.

I did ask my dad one time later in life, "How come I didn't spend summers with you?" He said, "I just wanted to make everybody happy. I just wanted to keep the peace." What I said back was, "That's fine, but guess what. You didn't make me happy. As a matter of fact, it hurt." He said, "I am sorry, Michele." He needed to know that. Everybody was scared of my mother. They wanted to make her happy. I guess at the time these non-educated black people weren't going to challenge the white woman in this community. They weren't going to do it. It wasn't like she was well to do or anything, but in 1960–65, she was going to win. So everybody has always tip-toed around my mother, and then here comes her daughter as she got older, and her daughter really gave her a run for the money.

I like myself now, because I'm Michele, and I think more of the qualities and character I have than the color of my skin. I was telling somebody the other day that since it's winter, I love when I can get tanned. I think that's the perfect color for me. I like to be a little bit darker. When I was young, my grandmother used to say, "Sheeley, why don't you put on some rouge. You're getting kind of pale." God made me the way I am, and I'm pretty happy with it most of the time.

I'm glad to share. It makes me feel good.

*Source:* DeFreece, Michele. "Stop Explaining. My Name's Michele."
Oral history, 2014. Reprinted by permission of Michele DeFreece.

## Discussion Questions

1. Hold a debate in your class about what types of information persons engaged to marry can legitimately withhold from each other. Are

there facts that, if withheld from a spouse, could invalidate a marriage? Consider the fact that marriage is, among other things, a
legal contract and that fraud is a crime.

2. Although marriage is regulated by the government, it is also often
   regulated by religion. Research the understanding of marriage in
   one or more religions; do religious understandings of marriage
   include restrictions on race, either historically or currently?

3. Write an essay comparing and contrasting the presentation of marriage or romantic partnership in *Quicksand* and/or *Passing* with
   similar presentations in *Their Eyes Were Watching God.*

4. Discuss the titles of both of these novels as they relate to marriage.
   Is Larsen using the word "quicksand" to comment on marriage? Can
   marriage itself be considered a type of "passing"? Why or why not?

5. Read another novel published during the Harlem Renaissance or
   a more recently published novel and compare the representation
   of female characters with Helga Crane, Clare Kendry, or Irene
   Redfield.

6. Watch the movie *Guess Who's Coming to Dinner.* To what extent is
   this movie dated? In what ways does it remain current? If you were
   to produce a remake of it today, how would you change the script,
   and what would you retain?

7. Watch several hours of television on different networks at different
   times of the day. Record how many total relationships are portrayed
   during shows and commercials. How many of those relationships
   are between members of the same race? How many are interracial?
   Do the same survey examining print advertisements in magazines
   or online advertising.

8. Using data from the U.S. census or other sources, trace changes in
   the frequency of interracial marriage. You could also refine your
   research to focus on specific racial groups. Which racial groups are
   most or least likely to intermarry?

9. Research other laws focused on race before, during, or after the
   period of the Harlem Renaissance. You might consider the Johnson–
   Reed Immigration Act of 1924, the Indian Citizenship Act, and the
   Chinese Exclusion Act. What do these laws reveal about American
   values?

10. Research effects of government regulation of marriage—consider
    transmission of property, decisions regarding health care, child cus-
    tody arrangements, insurance availability, etc. Then hold a debate
    on whether or how government should regulate marriage.

11. Research the history of your state's laws on marriage. How have those laws changed over the last three centuries? What do current laws state about who can marry whom?
12. Research the frequency of interracial marriage in another country and compare those rates with rates in the United States. What factors might account for any differences?
13. Many laws classify people based on various categories—marital status, age, sexual orientation, citizenship—based on the assumption that an orderly society needs such categories. Choose a specific law as your primary example and write a paper arguing that such categories are or are not necessary.
14. Interview someone you know who is a member of an interracial family. Compare and contrast that person's experience with that of Michele DeFreece.

## Suggested Readings

Botham, Fay. *Almighty God Created the Races: Christianity, Interracial Marriage, and American Law.* Chapel Hill: University of North Carolina Press, 2013.

Childs, Erica Chito. *Navigating Interracial Borders: Black-White Couples and Their Social Worlds.* New Brunswick, NJ: Rutgers University Press, 2005.

Dabel, Jane. "'A Superior Colored Man . . . and a Scotch Woman': Interracial Marriages in New York City, 1850–1870." *International Social Sciences Review* 80, no. 3–4 (2005): 87–102.

Eubanks, W. Ralph. *The House at the End of the Road: The Story of Three Generations of an Interracial Family in the American South.* Washington, DC: Smithsonian Institute Press, 2009.

Fu, Vincent Kang and Nicholas H. Wolfinger. "Broken Boundaries or Broken Marriages? Racial Intermarriage and Divorce in the United States." *Social Sciences Quarterly* 92, no. 4 (2011): 1096–17.

Gullickson, Aaron. "Black/White Interracial Marriage Trends, 1850–2000." *Journal of Family History* 31, no. 3 (2006): 289–312.

Haizlip, Shirlee Taylor. *The Sweeter the Juice: A Family Memoir in Black and White.* New York: The Free Press, 1992.

Hamilton, Derrick, Arthur H. Goldsmith, and William Darity. "Shedding 'Light' on Marriage: The Influence of Skin Shade on Marriage for Black Females." *Journal of Economic Behavior and Organization* 72, no. 1 (2009): 30–50.

Hoewe, Jennifer and Geri Alumit Zeldes. "Overturning Anti-Miscegenation Laws: News Media Coverage of the Lovings' Legal Case against the State of Virginia." *Journal of Black Studies* 43, no. 5 (2012): 427–43.

Holder, Ann S. "What's Sex Got to Do with It? Race, Power, Citizenship, and 'Intermediate Identities' in the Post-Emancipation United States." *Journal of African-American History* 93, no. 2 (2008): 153–73.

Jacobson, Cardell K. and Bryan R. Johnson. "Interracial Friendship and African American Attitudes about Interracial Marriage." *Journal of Black Studies* 36, no. 4 (2006): 570–84.

Kennedy, Randall. *Interracial Intimacies: Sex, Marriage, Identity, and Adoption.* New York: Vintage, 2012.

Maillard, Kevin Noble and Rose Cuison Villazor, eds. *Loving v. Virginia in a Post-Racial World: Rethinking Race, Sex, and Marriage.* New York: Cambridge University Press, 2012.

Newbeck, Phyl. *Virginia Hasn't Always Been for Lovers: Interracial Marriage Bans and the Case of Richard and Mildred Loving.* Carbondale: Southern Illinois University Press, 2008.

O'Neill, Eugene. *All God's Children Got Wings.* In *Nine Plays.* New York: Modern Library, 1959.

Pascoe, Peggy. *What Comes Naturally: Miscegenation Law and the Making of Race in America.* New York: Oxford University Press, 2010.

Perry, Samuel L. "Racial Composition of Social Settings, Interracial Friendship, and Whites' Attitudes toward Interracial Marriage." *Social Science Journal* 50, no. 1 (2013): 13–22.

Perry, Samuel L. "Religion and Interracial Romance: The Effects of Religious Affiliation, Public and Devotional Practices, and Biblical Literalism." *Social Sciences Quarterly* 94, no. 5 (2013): 1308–27.

Robinson, Charles F. *Forsaking All Others: A True Story of Interracial Sex and Revenge in the 1800s South.* Knoxville: University of Tennessee Press, 2010.

Rothman, Joshua D. *Notorious in the Neighborhood: Sex and Families across the Color Line in Virginia, 1787–1861.* Chapel Hill: University of North Carolina Press, 2007.

Smith-Pryor, Elizabeth M. *Property Rights: The Rhinelander Trial, Passing, and the Protection of Whiteness.* Chapel Hill: University of North Carolina Press, 2009.

Sommerville, Diane Miller. *Rape and Race in the Nineteenth-Century South.* Chapel Hill: University of North Carolina Press, 2004.

Thaggart, Miriam. "Racial Etiquette: Nella Larsen's *Passing* and the Rhinelander Case." *Meridians: Feminism, Race, Transnationalism* 5, no. 2 (2005): 1–29.

Villazor, Rose Cuison. "The Other Loving: Uncovering the Federal Government's Racial Regulation of Marriage." *New York University Law Review* 86, no. 5 (2011): 1360–443.

Wallenstein, Peter. "Reconstruction, Segregation, and Miscegenation: Interracial Marriage and the Law in the Lower South, 1865–1900." *American Nineteenth Century History* 6, no. 1 (2005): 57–76.

Wallenstein, Peter. *Tell the Court I Love My Wife: Race, Marriage, and Law—An American History.* New York: Palgrave Macmillan, 2002.

Weierman, Karen Woods. *One Blood: Interracial Marriage in American Fiction, Scandal, and the Law, 1820–1870.* Amherst: University of Massachusetts Press, 2005.

# HISTORICAL EXPLORATION: EXPATRIATES

The last section of this chapter addresses the idea of the expatriate, someone who lives abroad, often as a means of intentionally withdrawing from the social or political milieu of his or her own country. Occasionally, this term implies that a person is renouncing allegiance to his or her country of origin, but this isn't generally true of the many American writers who lived abroad, particularly in Europe, during the early and mid-20th century. As we saw in Chapters III and IV of this book, several of the writers most prominent during the Harlem Renaissance spent time outside the United States. For African Americans particularly, part of the attraction of living in Europe was that they would experience substantially less racial discrimination than they had in the United States. International experiences were motivated in part by a desire to avoid discrimination and then also influenced the civil rights movement as it emerged in the late 1950s and 1960s. Because African Americans had experienced something closer to equality while living in Europe, they began to insist more vehemently on equality once they returned to the United States. Yet African American writers weren't the only ones who took advantage of the opportunity to live or travel in Europe during this era. Nearly all of the most well-known modernist American writers resided in England, Germany, France, or Spain at some point.

In *Quicksand,* Helga Crane immigrates temporarily to Denmark, and Larsen is able to use this portion of the novel to comment on life in the United States. In Denmark, Helga avoids the vicious racism that was so common in the United States; yet she isn't completely comfortable in Denmark either. Like virtually all expatriates, she is still identified by her foreign citizenship and still only a temporary resident. Nevertheless, her experience in Denmark permits her and readers of the novel to understand America from a different perspective—habits and assumptions that are so common as to be virtually invisible become suddenly noticeable, and once noticed even subject to change.

## Expatriate Experiences of American Writers

The three excerpts below illustrate the variety of experiences available to expatriate American writers. The final is from an autobiographical book by Ernest Hemingway, who lived in Paris during the early 1920s. Although he would become exceptionally well-known for his novels and stories later in his life, even eventually winning the Nobel Prize for literature, he was at this time a young newly married man without much income. He associated with several other English-speaking writers in France, but this brief description of his life there, with its attention to concrete detail, reveals how he and his wife struggled financially. The first excerpt is taken from the travel writing of John Dos Passos, a contemporary of Hemingway who shared many of Hemingway's European experiences. In this piece, Dos Passos describes ordinary Spanish public life, creating an analogy between Spanish cafes and American movie theaters. In describing movie theaters as such a democratic institution, Dos Passos obviously neglects the fact that racial segregation would undermine democratic access. The second excerpt is taken from the work of James Baldwin, who moved to Paris in 1948 and remained there for much of the rest of his life. He explicitly stated that one of his motives for living as an expatriate was to avoid the racism so common in the United States. In the passage included here, he describes the ambivalence of meeting other African Americans in Paris, individuals who would inevitably remind each other, intentionally or not, of the discrimination they would all experience were they to return to the United States.

---

# From John Dos Passos, "The Republic of Honest Men," 1934

The cafés . . . are always open, they are always cheerful. A man can sit brooding over a single cup of coffee from the time he gets up till it's time to walk home in the greyness of the early morning, or else he can talk with a group of friends or with a casual stranger. He's not on the make, there's nothing to be gained; jobs come from family pull, money comes from a salary or a stipend, or from the lottery or roulette; to have no money is no disgrace. Talk is a pure art. Its only limits are the patience of the listeners who, when they get tired, can always pay for their coffee or charge it with a friendly waiter and walk out. The only place of entertainment that can compare with a Spanish café in cheapness and democracy is an American movie palace. But at a movie we pay for forgetfulness, darkness, soft seats and the stupor induced by a narcosis of secondhand daydreams. In his café the madrileño pays for his mild stimulant and has free entrance to the agora of concepts and ideas where he can make his way on his own. As the Stock Exchange is the central nervous system of New York, the cafés are the brains and spinal column of Madrid.

> *Source:* Dos Passos, John. "The Republic of Honest Men." *John Dos Passos: Travel Books and Other Writings, 1916–1941.* New York: Library of America, 2003: 347–48. Reprinted by permission of Lucy Dos Passos Coggin.

# From James Baldwin, "Encounter on the Sein: Black Meets Brown," 1955

It is estimated that there are five hundred American Negroes living in this city, the vast majority of them veterans studying on the G.I. Bill. They are studying everything from the Sorbonne's standard *Cours de Civilisation Française* to abnormal psychology, brain surgery, music, fine arts, and literature. Their isolation from each other is not difficult to understand if one bears in mind the axiom, unquestioned by American landlords, that Negroes are happy only when they are kept together. Those driven to break this pattern by leaving the U.S. ghettos not merely have effected a social and physical leave-taking but also have been precipitated into cruel psychological warfare. It is altogether inevitable that past humiliations should become associated not only with one's traditional oppressors but also with one's traditional kinfolk.

Thus the sight of a face from home is not invariably a source of joy, but can also quite easily become a source of embarrassment or rage. The American Negro in Paris is forced at last to exercise an undemocratic discrimination rarely practiced by Americans, that of judging his people, duck by duck, and distinguishing them one from another. Through this deliberate isolation, through lack of numbers, and above all through his own overwhelming need to be, as it were, forgotten, the American Negro in Paris is very nearly the invisible man.

*Source:* Baldwin, James. "Encounter on the Sein: Black Meets Brown." *Notes of a Native Son. James Baldwin: Collected Essays.* New York: The Library of America, 1998: 85–86. Copyright © 1955, renewed 1983, by James Baldwin. Reprinted by permission of Beacon Press, Boston.

# From Ernest Hemingway, *A Moveable Feast*, 1964

You got very hungry when you did not eat enough in Paris because all the bakery shops had such good things in the windows and people ate outside at tables on the sidewalk so that you saw and smelled the food. When you had given up journalism and were writing nothing that anyone in America would buy, explaining at home that you were lunching out with someone, the best place to go was the Luxembourg gardens where you saw and smelled nothing to eat all the way from the Place de l'Observatoire to the rue de Vaugirard. There you could always go into the Luxembourg museum and all the paintings were sharpened and clearer and more beautiful if you were belly-empty, hollow-hungry. I learned to understand Cézanne much better and to see truly how he made landscapes when I was hungry. I used to wonder if he were hungry too when he painted; but I thought possibly it was only that he had forgotten to eat. It was one of those unsound but illuminating thoughts you have when you have been sleepless or hungry. Later I thought Cézanne was probably hungry in a different way.

After you came out of the Luxembourg you could walk down the narrow rue Férou to the Place St.-Sulpice and there were still no restaurants, only the quiet square with its benches and trees. . . .

From this square you could not go further toward the river without passing shops selling fruits, vegetables, wines, or bakery and pastry shops. But by choosing your way carefully you could . . . reach the rue de l'Odéon and turn up to your right toward Silvia Beach's bookshop and on your way you did not pass too many places where things to eat were sold.

*Source:* Hemingway, Ernest. *A Moveable Feast.* New York: Charles Scribner's Sons, 1964: 69–70. Copyright © 1964 by Mary Hemingway. Copyright renewed © 1992 by John H. Hemingway, Patrick Hemingway, and Gregory Hemingway. Reprinted with permission of Scribner, a division of Simon & Schuster, Inc.

## Discussion Questions

1. Choose a country you would like to live in for an extended period. Research the laws of that country that would affect your move. Would you be able to work there? Would you need a visa? How long would you be permitted to stay? If you earned money, would you still owe taxes in the United States?
2. Write an essay about a time when you felt out of place. What contributed to that feeling? Did you ever become comfortable in that situation?
3. Take a walk through an unfamiliar neighborhood and write an essay describing everything you see there.
4. Interview someone you know who moved to the United States as a teenager or an adult. What was most difficult about their experience? What was most surprising? At what point did they start to feel "American," if ever? Or, interview someone you know who has spent months or years in another country, focusing on similar questions.
5. Research the biography of a writer who lived as an expatriate. How did that experience seem to affect their writing? Examples include Henry James, Ernest Hemingway, Gertrude Stein, James Baldwin, Elizabeth Bishop, Hart Crane, e.e. cummings, T.S. Eliot, F. Scott Fitzgerald, Langston Hughes, Claude McKay, and Ezra Pound.

## Suggested Readings

Bruccoli, Matthew, ed. *American Expatriate Writers: Paris in the Twenties.* Detroit: Gale, 1997.

Campbell, James. *Exiled in Paris: Richard Wright, James Baldwin, Samuel Beckett, and Others on the Left Bank.* Berkeley: University of California Press, 2003.

Elkins, Marilyn. "Expatriate Afro-American Women as Exotics." In *International Women's Writing: New Landscapes of Identity,* edited by Anne E. Brown and Marjanne E. Goozé. Westport, CT: Greenwood, 1995.

Fitch, Noel Riley. *Sylvia Beach and the Lost Generation: A History of Literary Paris in the Twenties and Thirties.* New York: W. W. Norton, 1985.

Gabin, Jane S. *American Women in Gilded Age London: Expatriates Rediscovered.* Gainesville: University Press of Florida, 2006.

Gammel, Irene. "New Readings of American Expats in Paris." *Canadian Review of American Studies* 44, no. 1 (2014): 148–58.

Gilsdorf, Ethan. "Expat Literary Publishing in Paris Today." *Chronicle of Higher Education* 49, no. 24 (February 21, 2003): B14–15.

Gopnik, Adam. *Americans in Paris: A Literary Anthology.* New York: Library of America, 2004.

Gray, Jeffrey. "Essence and the Mulatto Traveler: Europe as Embodiment in Nella Larsen's *Quicksand." Journal of Transnational American Studies* 4, no. 1 (2012): 1–15.

Hansen, Arlen J. *Expatriate Paris: A Cultural and Literary Guide to Paris of the 1920s.* New York: Arcade Publishing, 2012.

Heath, Gordon. *Deep Are the Roots: Memoirs of a Black Expatriate.* Amherst: University of Massachusetts Press, 1996.

Hemingway, Ernest. *A Moveable Feast.* New York: Scribner, 2010.

Holcomb, Gary Edward and Charles Scruggs, eds. *Hemingway and the Black Renaissance.* Columbus: Ohio State University Press, 2012.

Katz, Daniel. *American Modernism's Expatriate Scene: The Labour of Translation.* Edinburgh: Edinburgh University Press, 2007.

Lim, Shirley Geok-lin. "First World 'Expats' and Expatriate Writing in a Third-World Frame." *New Literatures Review* 28–29 (1994–1995): 1–22.

Lloyd, Greg. *Eugene Bullard: Black Expatriate in Jazz-Age Paris.* Athens: University of Georgia Press, 2006.

Luczak, Ewa Barbara Lewiston. *How Their Living Outside America Affected Five African American Authors: Toward a Theory of Expatriate Literature.* Lewiston, NY: Edwin Mellen Press, 2010.

Lunde, Arne. "Helga Crane's Copenhagen: Denmark, Colonialism, and Transnational Identity in Nella Larsen's *Quicksand." Comparative Literature* 60, no. 3 (2008): 228–43.

Monk, Craig. *Writing the Lost Generation: Expatriate Autobiography and American Modernism.* Iowa City: University of Iowa Press, 2008.

Pizer, Donald. *American Expatriate: Writing and the Paris Moment: Modernism and Place.* Baton Rouge: Louisiana State University Press, 1997.

Rogers, Kelly. *Extraordinary, Ordinary Women: Questions of Expatriate Identity in Contemporary American Paris.* Lanham, MD: University Press of America, 2014.

Schatt, Stanley. "You Must Go Home Again: Today's Afro-American Expatriate Writers." *Negro American Literature Forum* 7, no. 3 (1973): 80–82.

Stovall, Tyler. "The Fire This Time: Black American Expatriates and the Algerian War." *Yale French Studies* 98 (2000): 182–200.

Van Koppen, Amanda Klewkowski. *Migrants or Expatriates? Americans in Europe.* New York: Palgrave Macmillan, 2014.

Winnett, Susan. *Writing Back: American Expatriates' Narratives of Return.* Baltimore: Johns Hopkins University Press, 2012.

Wiser, William. *The Great Good Place: American Expatriate Women in Paris.* New York: W. W. Norton, 1991.

Zwerdling, Alex. *Improvised Europeans: American Literary Expatriates in London.* New York: Basic Books, 1998.

# WHY WE READ *QUICKSAND* AND *PASSING* TODAY

Despite their initial critical success, these novels had fallen out of print and remained out of print as Nella Larsen herself disappeared from public notice. In this way, her experience resembles that of Zora Neale Hurston. Like many nearly forgotten pieces of women's literature that scholars recovered, the novels were brought back into print in 1986, and they likely have more readers in the 21st century than they did when they were originally published. So the fact is that people do continue to read *Quicksand* and *Passing;* the more important question is why.

Although some of the issues explored in these novels can seem dated today, when we think about those issues more deeply, we gain insight not only into the past but also into the present. The social differences between America at the beginning of the 20th century and the beginning of the 21st are profound yet also sometimes superficial. Because of changes in immigration laws, the United States has become a much more diverse society, yet Americans remain constantly aware of race and ethnicity. Americans are frequently asked to identify themselves by race, even if only for research or statistical purposes; such continuous attention to race suggests that Americans believe racial identity remains important—even when they cannot provide a satisfactory definition of "race." Although interracial marriage has been legal throughout the United States for several decades, interracial couples continue to experience discrimination, in some regions or neighborhoods more than others. And many social organizations, even if they don't describe themselves as interested in race or ethnicity, nevertheless appeal to one or two racial groups more than to others. What this means is that race is displayed and responded to differently in the 21st century than it had been a hundred years earlier, but it remains a significant category of notice. Clare Kendry might not feel as tempted to "pass" in today's society, but she would still at least occasionally be treated differently than a woman with a darker complexion, and she would still be expected to label herself according to categories created by others.

Another reason these novels continue to be read is that women's writing is received much more seriously than it once had been. *Quicksand* and *Passing* both feature female protagonists; they can, therefore, provide insight into American experience generally and African American experience specifically that novels focusing on male characters cannot. As more and more women are pursuing higher education, courses in women's studies and women's literature have proliferated, and Nella Larsen's work fits well in these courses. However, an assumption that a novel with a female protagonist requires an audience composed of women is no more valid than an assumption that only male readers will be interested in Langston Hughes or Claude McKay.

Neither of these novels is pleasurable in the way that *Their Eyes Were Watching God* is—for although Tea Cake dies and Janie is tried for his murder at the end of that novel, Janie nevertheless experienced a fulfilling relationship with Tea Cake and has grown into a self-assured woman who is grateful for her experience. The characters in Larsen's novels, however, experience very little satisfaction and are no less frustrated by the end of the novels than they were at the beginning. Larsen's novels provide substantial social and political commentary; they are less engaged in exploring the details of personal relationships. This doesn't mean that personal relationships aren't important to the novels, but readers will likely remember the issues that are addressed better than they will remember the characters. Yet readers will empathize with the personal frustrations experienced by Helga Crane, Clare Kendry, and Irene Redfield, even if the sources of those frustrations are different, and it is this evocation of empathy that keeps the novels alive.

# VI

# *Their Eyes Were Watching God*

## HISTORICAL BACKGROUND

*Their Eyes Were Watching God* was originally published in 1937, in the midst of the Great Depression and toward the end of the period we call the Harlem Renaissance. It was Hurston's second novel and third book. Although the book is generally perceived today as Hurston's finest work and is beloved by many readers, its initial reception was mixed. Many other African American writers, particularly men, criticized the novel for not being radical enough. They argued that the novel doesn't sufficiently challenge the intensity of racial discrimination in the United States. *Their Eyes Were Watching God* is not a directly political novel like *Native Son*, which Richard Wright would publish just three years later, nor are relationships among black and white characters a central concern of Hurston's novel. It is not a social protest novel. In her autobiography, *Dust Tracks on a Road,* Hurston argues that her refusal to address racial tension directly does not imply that she is ignoring the significance of race, for African American people (and implicitly African American characters) are never able to forget their racial identity.

**Zora Neale Hurston was an American novelist, folklorist, anthropologist, and prominent member of the circle of writers associated with the Harlem Renaissance of the 1920s. (Library of Congress)**

Instead, Hurston has created a space where black characters exercise autonomy, establishing their own town, electing their own leader, managing their own businesses. This choice to represent black characters as independent agents can also be interpreted as a progressive move, for it refuses to acknowledge white privilege and power as dominating forces in black lives. White characters are not central to the novel or to the characters' lives; black characters are. Yet white critics sometimes refused to believe that such towns as Eatonville could exist in the United States. Hurston, in other words, was criticized by some readers for writing a story that was not radical enough and by others for writing a story that was too radical.

The novel fell out of print repeatedly between its original publication and the late 1970s. During the 1960s and 1970s, many universities created African American Studies programs, and both African American literature and women's literature courses were increasingly offered at colleges and universities and eventually in many high schools. Part of the task of scholars who offer such courses is the recovery of valuable but forgotten texts. During this period, many literary critics rediscovered *Their Eyes Were Watching God.* Their enthusiasm for the novel encouraged publishers to bring the novel back into print, and it has now remained continuously in print since 1978. Due to its consistent popularity (as well as to technological developments in the publishing industry), it is not likely to fall out of print again anytime soon.

*Their Eyes Were Watching God* is unusual among novels published during and after the Harlem Renaissance for its focus on rural life. Jean Toomer's *Cane* is also set in the rural South, but many other books are set in metropolitan areas, as the period title "Harlem Renaissance" would suggest. The setting is one factor that permits Hurston to exclude most white characters from her book, for although several all-black towns existed in the United States, there were no large all-black cities. The setting also permits the plot to develop as it does, with Joe Starks rising to political prominence and with Janie and Tea Cake working together on the muck and suffering through the hurricane together.

This novel has been particularly well received by female readers and critics, not simply because it features a female protagonist, but also because the protagonist, Janie, is initially thwarted in her desires because she is female. Attempting to protect her and to secure her future, Janie's grandmother arranges a marriage to Logan Killicks, an older man Janie does not love or even find attractive. This decision by Janie's grandmother reminds us of how near in time the Harlem Renaissance was to the Civil War and emancipation. Janie's grandmother had been born in slavery and had already given birth to Janie's mother before she experienced freedom. Her desire to protect Janie is not simply economic; it is a desire to protect her from the sexual exploitation she and her own daughter experienced. Janie, though, has come of age in a different era and has her own dreams that cannot be fulfilled in a marriage to Logan Killicks. Hoping for freedom and self-determination, Janie marries Joe Starks, but Joe eventually also forces Janie into a restrictive role that he believes will reflect well on himself. Joe has achieved middle-class status economically, and his influence in the town exceeds his class status; he believes the wife of a man such as himself should not appear too common, which means that he forbids Janie from joining in many social activities. As far as Joe is concerned, Janie exists in order to be an object of envy for other men; her desirability needs to reflect on himself. Although their relationship had begun in delight, Janie and Joe fail to grow as partners, and they are nearly estranged from each other by the time Joe dies.

OPRAH WINFREY PRESENTS
THEIR EYES WERE WATCHING GOD

**From the book by Zora Neale Hurston: Movie poster advertises "Their Eyes Were Watching God" (ABC, 2005), starring Halle Berry, 2005. (John D. Kisch/Separate Cinema Archive/Getty Images)**

Finally, when Janie meets Tea Cake, she is more fully able to express her own desires and to function as a full member of their community. In many ways, Janie's experience serves as a microcosm for women's experiences through the 20th century, as they attained political equality with the vote in 1920 but continued to work toward economic and social equality, a task that is not yet complete.

The end of *Their Eyes Were Watching God* may seem tragic, with Tea Cake's death and Janie's subsequent trial. Indeed, as an expression of their impotent grief, the spectators at the trial wish to see Janie punished. The courtroom scene is the one passage in the book where white people retain the power and authority they typically have in much of the rest of the country—the judge and the jury consist entirely of white men. The novel acknowledges, therefore, that the comparative freedom the characters experienced living in an all-black town did not extend far beyond its boundaries. Despite these events during the last several pages, however, the novel circles back to its beginning, as Janie returns, mildly triumphant, certainly content with her experience and survival.

## ABOUT ZORA NEALE HURSTON

Zora Neale Hurston was born in Alabama on January 7, 1891, although she herself claimed several other birthdates between 1898 and 1903. When she was three years old, her family moved to Eatonville, Florida, an all-black community near Orlando, the model for the town where Janie and Joe make their home in *Their Eyes Were Watching God*. Hurston's father was a carpenter and minister, and her mother had been a teacher. Hurston's mother died in 1904. After her father remarried, Hurston attended boarding school, but she left without earning a high school diploma. She worked at several jobs until she entered Morgan Academy, a high school in Baltimore. Because she was 26 years old by this time, she lied about her age, claiming to be only 16 so that she could be admitted. She later attended Howard University in Washington, D.C., where she earned an Associate's Degree in 1920.

In 1925, she enrolled in Barnard College in New York, where she studied anthropology with Franz Boas, one of the founders of modern anthropology. She earned her Bachelor's Degree from Barnard in 1928, and she later studied for a PhD in anthropology at Columbia University. She did some research for Boas in Harlem, but she is more well known for her studies of folk traditions and religion in Florida, Jamaica, and Haiti. While she was living in New York, she became acquainted with other writers affiliated

Zora Neale Hurston, anthropologist, author, and prominent figure of the Harlem Renaissance. The setting of this photograph foregrounds her identity as a writer, the activity for which she remains most well-known today. (Library of Congress)

with the Harlem Renaissance, particularly Langston Hughes, with whom she would coauthor a play, *Mule Bone: A Comedy of Negro Life.*

Hurston had a spirited personality, and she brought her lively presence to many social encounters. She dressed flamboyantly, and she defied social convention by participating in such scandalous activities as smoking cigarettes in public. One story has it that when a particular man attempted to flirt with her, she punched him and kept right on walking. Although her enthusiasm sometimes had to be reined in when she was a child, this same enthusiasm served her well as an adult. Her pleasure in singing and reciting folk tales is apparent not only through the stories of people who knew her but also from recordings she made to document her research.

Hurston had begun to write fiction, essays, and poetry before she moved to New York; her first published piece was a story, "John Redding Goes to Sea," that appeared in Howard University's literary magazine. She began to publish frequently in *Opportunity* magazine, a journal devoted to the study of African American life. She continued to publish short pieces in other periodicals. In 1930 she worked with Langston Hughes on *Mule Bone,* but the collaboration ended with a bitter falling-out between the two writers. The once close friends never reconciled.

In 1934, Hurston published her first book, a novel, *Jonah's Gourd Vine,* which was a Book-of-the-Month Club selection. Between then and the end of that decade, she published two additional novels, including *Their Eyes Were Watching God,* and two collections of folklore. Hurston wrote *Their Eyes Were Watching God* while she was conducting research in Haiti, and she said that she was able to compose the entire novel in seven weeks because the material had been welling up inside her. In 1942, she published an autobiography and then in 1948 a final novel. Her interests in folklore and literature overlap in many of her books, and the research she'd done interviewing African Americans who lived in the South in order to collect folk tales clearly informs her fiction. She won many accolades for her work, including a Guggenheim fellowship in 1936, an honorary doctorate from Morgan State College, and Howard University's Distinguished Alumni Award. Despite the attention that is paid to her work today, she did not earn substantial royalties from these books, and she funded some of her research trips through the support of a white patron, Charlotte Mason. Hurston's relationship with Mason was complex, as is often the case with patrons and their beneficiaries.

Hurston published no more books after 1948, but she continued to publish essays in popular magazines such as *The Saturday Evening Post* and *Negro Digest.* During this period, she publicly supported conservative political causes. She objected to the decision of the Supreme Court in the *Brown v. Board of Education* case that mandated school integration with its famous phrase, "separate educational facilities are inherently unequal." Not surprisingly, her opposition to this decision was controversial, but Hurston's rationale reflected her childhood experience in Eatonville, where all authority and leadership rested in black citizens. Once integration occurred, she believed, access to even local power would evaporate for African Americans.

During the last years of her life, Hurston functioned much less as a public figure. She wrote a few articles for a local newspaper but no longer had a national presence. In 1959 she suffered a series of strokes and was forced to move into a county welfare home. She died on January 28, 1960, virtually forgotten, just a few years too soon to see her work receive renewed fame. She was buried in an unmarked grave, but fortunately her story does not end there. In 1973, writer Alice Walker sought out her grave and purchased a headstone, which she had engraved with the phrase "A Genius of the South." Walker's work was a significant factor in creating renewed critical and popular interest in Zora Neale Hurston. Although *Their Eyes Were Watching God* sold only 5,000 copies when it was initially published, it now sells approximately 100,000 copies each year, and thousands of tourists visit Eatonville, Florida, which hosts the Zora Neale Hurston Festival.

# HISTORICAL EXPLORATION: ALL-BLACK TOWNS

One of the unusual plot points of *Their Eyes Were Watching God* is Joe Starks's ability, with apparent ease, to establish and preside over a town that had been little more than an intersection when he and Janie arrived. He purchases the land from Cap'n Eaton (who never actually appears in the novel), sells individual lots at a profit, runs a post office and general store, and gets himself elected mayor. All of the residents of this town are African American. Without historical knowledge of some American small towns during the late 19th and early 20th centuries, this portion of the novel might seem like Hurston's wishful thinking. Even in Hurston's own day, some readers refused to believe that such a place could exist.

Yet several such towns did in fact exist, in some of the former Confederate states subsequent to the Civil war, and in Oklahoma, which had been known as "Indian Territory" at that time. Advantages for African American residents were numerous, some obvious and some more subtle. Individuals would have a greater chance of achieving success based on merit, and no one would be excluded from positions of power or authority because they had once been slaves or because of their African ancestry. Children could witness models of success that resembled them. People could relax their guard, relieved of constant awareness that at any given moment they could become victims of racially inspired violence and slurs. Whether or not true equality was achieved in any given town, inequalities resulting from racial discrimination would not provide unfair advantages to some citizens and not others. Residents of these towns could avoid many of the daily effects of Jim Crow, the legally entrenched system of racial segregation that functioned throughout the South during these decades.

View of Washington Street in Nicodemus, Kansas, circa 1885. Nicodemus was an African American town settled by former slaves. The existence of these towns was sometimes questioned by readers of *Their Eyes Were Watching God,* who were skeptical of Hurston's representation of Eatonville. (Library of Congress)

## Zora Neale Hurston's Eatonville

The first excerpt below is taken from Hurston's autobiography, which she originally published five years after *Their Eyes Were Watching God.* The actual town of Eatonville was founded a few years before Hurston's birth, so she was not a witness to that event in the way that Janie is in the novel, but she had clearly absorbed the narrative. You will notice the resemblance between this historical event, at least as Hurston presents it in her autobiography, and the fictionalized version in the novel. Eatonville, Florida does claim to be the first all-black incorporated town in the United States, though other towns also make similar claims.

## From Zora Neale Hurston, *Dust Tracks on a Road,* 1942

Joe Clarke asked himself, why not a Negro town? Few of the Negroes were interested. It was too vaulting for their comprehension. A pure Negro town! If nothing but their own kind was in it, who was going to run it? With no white folks to command them, how would they know what to do? Joe Clarke had plenty of confidence in himself to do the job, but few others could conceive of it.

But one day by chance or purpose, Joe Clarke was telling of his ambitions to Captain Eaton, who thought it a workable plan. He talked it over with Captain Lawrence and others. By the end of the year, all arrangements had been made. Lawrence and Eaton bought a tract of land a mile west of Maitland for a town site. The backing of the whites helped Joe Clarke to convince the other Negroes, and things were settled.

Captain Lawrence at his own expense erected a well-built church on the new site, and Captain Eaton built a hall for general assembly and presented it to the new settlement. A little later, the wife of Bishop Whipple had the first church rolled across the street and built a larger church on the same spot, and the first building was to become a library, stocked with books donated by the white community.

So on August 18, 1886, the Negro town, called Eatonville, after Captain Eaton, received its charger of incorporation from the state capital, Tallahassee, and made history by becoming the first of its kind in America, and perhaps in the world.

*Source:* Hurston, Zora Neale. *Dust Tracks on a Road.* New York: Harper Perennial, 1991: 5–6. Copyright © 1942 by Zora Neale Hurston. Copyright renewed © 1970 by John C. Hurston. Reprinted by permission of HarperCollins Publishers, Inc.

## The All-Black Town of Langston, Oklahoma

The next two articles provide background to the founding of another all-black town, Langston, Oklahoma. After the Civil War, for a period of approximately 50 years, essentially until the beginning of World War I, over 60 all-black towns were founded in the United States, generally in the South and Southwest. Twenty of these towns were founded in Oklahoma, in part because of Oklahoma's earlier status as "Indian Territory." The federal government was opening up land in Oklahoma for settlement as the attraction of all-black towns was increasing. Of course, the government's treatment of Native Americans in Oklahoma, many of whom resided there as a result of the Trail of Tears, is also problematic, but sympathetic questions about Native Americans weren't being asked by very many other Americans who sought Oklahoma land at the time.

Both of these articles urge African American people to migrate west. The articles are written by black journalists to a black audience. They describe the advantages available for people who wish to reside in all-black towns generally, and they also present Langston as an idealized option. Yet the articles also warn that such a choice should be made only by people of sturdy character. On the one hand, this is simply honest. Pioneering, even at that late date, was hard work. But the articles also permit their readers to compliment themselves; by seriously considering such a move, they are defining themselves as hard working, reliable, and potentially success-ful individuals. Notice how the articles fill several rhetorical roles; they're persuasive but also instructional. The articles warn readers that potential settlers have to be prepared for hardship, but they also provide information about how to become prepared.

---

## "Home, Sweet Home. A Home for You and Your Children. Millions! of Acres in the Cherokee Strip Soon to Be Given to the People for Homes. This Will Tell You How You Can Get the Benefit," 1892

### Begin to Prepare Now

The fact that it now seems almost certain that a trade will be made with the Cherokee Indians whereby they will relinquish all their right, title and interest in the tract of land known as the Cherokee strip. It is time that our people should possess a thorough understanding of the situation in order that they may be able to take advantage of what will be about the last chance to secure free homes on government domain. Since the opening of the Oklahoma country the fertile lands in the reservations around it have been the principal objective points of thousands of homemakers.

The Iowa, Sac and Fox and Pottawatomie reservations were opened for settlement on the 22nd day of September, 1891. Thousands of persons have found homes there and the country is being rapidly developed and has a great future before it. It is estimated that nearly a thousand colored families secured homes in these reservations. This result was brought about through the influence of the Herald.

A conservative estimate of the amount of wealth acquired by the colored people in Oklahoma by securing homesteads is placed at from two hundred and fifty thousand to four hundred thousand dollars. By this we mean that the property which they have secured here within the last six months will sell today for four hundred thousand dollars more than it cost them.

The Herald is proud of what it has done for the advancement of the Negro. We point to the past as an evidence of what you may expect in the future. Follow its advice and you will be the winner. Below we give full instructions as to how to proceed to secure these homes. Study it carefully and you will have no trouble in knowing just how to proceed.

### Who Can Take Homesteads

The law says that any citizen of the United States who is the head of a family or who is twenty one years of age and who is not already the possessor of more than 160 acres of land in any state or territory shall be entitled to enter 160 acres of unoccupied public land.

### How to Take a Homestead

When the lands are open to settlement you select wherever you can find it 40, 80, or 160 acres of land and claim that as your homestead. As evidence that you do claim it, you must make some visible improvements. Drive a stake with your name on it; cut timber to lay the foundation of a home, do a little plowing or some other act that will show to others that you have occupied that particular piece of land. These first improvements should at the earliest possible moment be followed by others of a permanent nature.

### Making Your Filing

After having made settlement on the land proceed, in person, as soon as possible to the government land office for the district in which your land is located and there make your filing as follows:

First. You must file an application with the officers of the land office, which application must be on the blank form used by the land office. The application will state that you have made settlement on a certain tract of land, the proper description of which can be readily ascertained, and that you claim the same under the homestead law.

Second. You must file an affidavit in which you swear that you are properly qualified to take a homestead, that is that you are a citizen of the United States and that you are either the head of a family or that you are 21 years of age, and that you have taken the land for your own use and benefit and for the purpose of cultivating the same and making it your home.

Third. You must pay to the receiving of the land office the filing fee which is six dollars for 40 acres, seven dollars for 80 acres, or fourteen dollars for 160 acres.

This done, you have complied with all the requirements of the law necessary to take a homestead.

## Making Final Proof

At any time after one year from the date of settlement you can make your final proof before the local land office and pay for land you have taken at the government price and get a deed to your land from the United States. The price to be paid in the Cherokee strip cannot yet be told. It will be whatever price the government has to pay the Indians. Probably a dollar and twenty five cents an acre. Or it may be a dollar and fifty cents per acre.

## May Have Seven Years

However if you wish to do so you are allowed to live on the land seven years before making proof and paying for the land, and until you make your final proof the land cannot be taxed for any purpose, which is a great advantage.

## Actual Value

It should not be understood that the price you pay the government for the land represents its actual value. Far from it. Very little of the land is actually worth less than eight or ten dollars an acre.

Just so soon as you have completed your entry on 160 acres of land in this country, you are worth at least one thousand dollars more than before you make your filing.

Is this worth trying for? If it is why don't you try for it?

Remember This.

No one can do this for you. *You must make settlement yourself. You must go to the United States land office and make your filings yourself. You and your family, if you have one, or your family at any rate must live on it. You must make the final proof yourself.*

## Beware of Frauds

If any man tells you that you can get a homestead in any other way look out for him. He is either ignorant and does not know what he is talking about, or he is willfully deceiving you, and probably *trying to defraud you,* so be on your guard and do not be deceived.

## Old Soldiers

The government favors its old soldiers by making one exception in their favor, which is as follows: an old soldier can if he wants to appoint an agent who through power of attorney can file papers at the land office for such soldier. But *within six months* from the filing of the declaratory statement *the soldier and his family* must take up their actual residence on the land, and in every other respect conform to the law as stated above.

## When to Come

Come any time when you are prepared to do so. By prepared we mean just what we have always said, *don't come to this country unless you are prepared to support yourself and family until such time as you can raise a crop.*

We make this point strong. It is right and good for you to understand the circumstances. It will not do to come here expecting to depend on getting employment to support yourself. While hundreds have done it and come out all right, we still say that it will not do to depend on it. We cannot afford to deceive you. We want you to come with your eyes wide open, and to know as near as possible what you are coming to, in order that you may meet and successfully overcome the hardships of a new country, and in order that the race here may make the highest possible development in the shortest possible space of time.

## When Will the Lands Open?

We answer you frankly, we don't know, but we shall give our readers all the fresh news in regard to it from week to week. Read the Herald and keep posted. The probabilities are that it will be opened in the spring or early summer, and we hope to see it opened early in the spring so that the people can make a full crop after the opening if possible.

## Where Shall You Come?

We answer without any hesitation whatsoever. *Come to Langston City.* It is the place for you to wait the opening of the Strip. Here you can for a few dollars secure a good lot and put up a cheap house that will shelter you and your loved ones. Here you will find plenty of noble men and women, who like yourselves have turned their backs upon their old associations, have arisen in the strength of their manhood and womanhood and come to make for themselves homes in this fair land where every man is a man and every woman is a woman, provided they conduct themselves as such, without regard to the color of their skin.

In case the opening of the lands should be delayed longer than is expected, you can rent land close by Langston and you can make a crop on it and at the same time live on your lot, where your children can have school privileges and yourselves and families have society.

Then when the opening comes you will be right here on the ground and will know just what steps to take and will be much more likely to secure a claim than if you wait until the last minute to come.

If you are doing reasonably well where you are and have employment it will be better for you to stay where you are until late in the winter, but in the mean time you should be making your arrangements, so that when this time comes you will have nothing to interfere with your plans, and remember that this may be your last chance for a free home. If you contemplate coming do not delay but secure a lot in Langston City at once while they are cheap all things considered, in that you will have a place of your own to come to and at the same time you will have an investment that will be rapidly increasing in value.

*Source:* "Home, Sweet Home. A Home for You and Your Children. Millions! of Acres in the Cherokee Strip Soon to Be Given to the People for Homes. This Will Tell You How You Can Get the Benefit." *The Langston City Herald,* November 17, 1892: 2.

# E. P. McCabe, "Freedom. Peace, Happiness and Prosperity, Do You Want All These? Then Cast Your Lot with Us and Make Your Home in Langston City," 1892

Do you ask why? We will tell you. Langston City is a Negro city, and we are proud of the fact. Her city officers are all colored. Her teachers are colored. Her public schools furnish thorough educational advantages to nearly two hundred colored children. The country is as fertile as ever was moistened by nature's falling tears, or kissed by heaven's sunshine. Here, too, is found a genial climate—about like that of southern Tennessee or northern Mississippi—a climate admirably adapted to the wants of the Negro from the southern states. A land of diversified crops, where every staple crop of both north and south can be raised. . . .

One of the finest fruit growing countries in the union, a land where a few dollars judiciously invested in real estate will yield returns in the future that cannot be estimated.

Do you want to build for the future? If so you can do no better than to invest a few dollars in Oklahoma soil. It does not matter whether you contemplate coming here at once or not. Real estate is the basis of all wealth. There is nothing in which money can be so safely invested. Do you wish to build for the future? If you do, you cannot do anything that will be more to your advantage than a small investment in Langston City property. This property combines everything that it needs to commend it to homeseekers or investors, viz: Reasonable prices, easy payments, steady and rapid increase in value, sure returns, absolute safety, good society, church privileges, school privileges, and last but not least, absolute political liberty and the enjoyment of every right and privilege every other man enjoys under the constitution of the country. What more do you want? Young men, if you will save the money that many of you now squander and invest it in Langston City property, ten years from now you will be independent.

Remember it is not a picnic we are inviting you to, but to join hands with us in an active and earnest effort to better our conditions and to open to the race new avenues through which they may obtain more of the good things of life.

In another column will be found an accurate plot of the townsite. All that portion north of Drexel Boulevard and west of Michigan Avenue has recently been plotted and put out on the market, and is known as the first addition. With the exception of perhaps a dozen, all the lots front on Washington Boulevard, and all those lying south of it are sold. For business purposes, all things considered, the cheapest and best property now offered is that on Drexel Boulevard. The post office is located on lot 7 in block 4; the office of the Langston City Herald is on lot 10, block 3; the First Baptist church is in block 78; and the public school is in block 76, as shown in the plot.

Before the first of February $3,000 worth of machinery will be on the ground for the grist mill and cotton gin which is to be located on the site shown on the plot. Plans have been drawn and work will commence on the hotel building, which, when completed, will cost from $2,000 to $2,500; it will be located in block 69, as shown in the plot.

All the lots which remain unsold to this time are good ones—there is not a rough or bad one in the entire number. Washington Boulevard is the leading street in the city at present, being located exactly in the center of the townsite. Lots can be obtained at reasonable prices and on easy terms. For particulars address

E.P. McCabe,

Guthrie, Oklahoma

*Source:* McCabe, E. P. "Freedom. Peace, Happiness and Prosperity, Do You Want All These? Then Cast Your Lot with Us and Make Your Home in Langston City." *The Langston City Herald,* November 17, 1892: 3.

### The All-Black Town of Mound Bayou, Mississippi

In the next two articles, Booker T. Washington and Day Allen Willey describe another town, Mound Bayou, Mississippi. Their purpose is not to persuade potential settlers to move to this town, but to celebrate the success of the original founders and current residents. Notice how much attention each writer gives to Isaiah Montgomery and his background. Why is his birth as a slave such a significant detail of his history? Notice that the writers seem to be unaware of Eatonville, Florida. Why would a town's status as a unique example of a "Negro town" be important?

Booker T. Washington's article would have been particularly influential because he was among the leading African American intellectuals of his day. He remains most well-known as the founder of Tuskegee Institute, a college emphasizing practical education, and as the author of *Up from Slavery,* his second autobiography and a best seller when it was published in 1901. Both authors emphasize the good character of the residents of Mound Bayou, attempting to demonstrate that African Americans, even those who had once been slaves, embody many of the values other Americans also appreciate. Both articles, without naming any racial stereotypes, subtly attempt to counteract negative stereotypes that denigrate the abilities and efforts of African Americans.

## From Booker T. Washington, "A Town Owned by Negroes: Mound Bayou, Miss., An Example of Thrift and Self-Government," 1907

Bolivar County is noted among the counties of Mississippi for two reasons: it contains the richest soil in the famous Yazoo Delta, and it possesses the only regularly constituted Negro town in the Southern States. This town, called Mound Bayou, gets its name from a large mound, a relic of the prehistoric inhabitants of the country, which marks the junction of two of the numerous bayous that make so important a part of the natural drainage system of this low and level land.

Situated in the heart of the wide alluvial plain between the Mississippi and the Yazoo Rivers, Mound Bayou is the centre of a negro population more dense than can be found anywhere else outside of

Africa. The Negroes outnumber the whites seven to one throughout the Delta. There are whole sections of these rich bottom-lands where no white man lives. Mound Bayou and the territory for several miles around it on every side is one such section—a Negro colony, occupying 30,000 acres, all of which is owned by Negroes, most of them small farmers who till 40 and 80-acre tracts. The town itself has, at present, a population of about 500. Of these, eighty-three are registered voters.

Mound Bayou is a self-governing community. That is one of the interesting things about it. It has had, since it was incorporated in 1898, a mayor, three aldermen, a constable, and a town marshal, all of them Negroes. This was necessarily so, because no white man has ever lived in this community since it was established, except the man who introduced the telephone system, and he remained only long enough to teach some of the townspeople how to manage the exchange. . . .

Local entrepreneur Mrs. Annice R. Christmas, sits on a bale of cotton, circa 1920. She owned 50 percent of a cotton gin in the town of Mound Bayou, Mississippi and acted as the manager. Mound Bayou was a predominantly African American town, similar to Eatonville as Zora Neale Hurston portrays it in *Their Eyes Were Watching God*. (Bettmann/ Corbis)

One morning in the fall of 1887, a northbound train stopped in the midst of this wilderness, a party of Negroes stepped off, and the train went its way. The leader of the group, a small, slender man, with strongly marked features and a deliberate and thoughtful manner, held in his hand a plot, which he looked at from time to time. This was Isaiah T. Montgomery and the men with him were the first contingent of prospective settlers.

It was not easy, as I have often heard Mr. Montgomery say, to find settlers in that early day. The task of taming this wild country seemed hopeless to men with so few resources and so little experience. On this particular morning, Mr. Montgomery thought it best to make a little speech before proceeding with the work that had brought them thither.

"You see," he said, waving his hand in the direction of the forest, "this is a pretty wild place." He paused, and the men looked hesitatingly in the direction he had indicated, but said nothing.

"But this whole country," he continued, "was like this once. You have seen it change. You and your fathers have, for the most part, performed the work that has made it what it is. You and your fathers did this for some one else. Can't you do as much now for yourselves?"

The men picked up their axes and attacked the wilderness. The idea of the thing got hold of their minds of some of them, so they went back home and prepared to return and take up the work of pioneers. It was not until February, 1888, however, that the first permanent settlers moved in. A month later, the ground was cleared sufficiently to set up a small store. Two dwellings were also erected. A few more of these early buildings may still be seen in remote corners of the community. . . .

It was not the ordinary Negro farmer who was attracted to Mound Bayou colony. It was rather an earnest and ambitious class prepared to face the hardships of this sort of pioneer work. The scheme was widely advertised among the Negro farmers throughout the state and drew immigrants from all parts of Mississippi, and a certain number from other states. . . .

There are some special difficulties in the financial direction and development of a town and colony like Mound Bayou. For instance, it has been the constant aim of the men who founded the colony to preserve it as a distinctively Negro enterprise. Separated from, yet intimately bound up with the commercial and political interests of the other communities about it, the problem of preserving this isolation has often been a perplexing one. A difficulty arose a few years ago when the Louisville, New Orleans, and Texas Railway was sold to the Yazoo and Mississippi. Practically all the lands purchased from the railroad company had been subject to a lien for deferred payments. With the change of ownership in the railroad, a wholesale foreclosure of these mortgages seemed imminent. Charles Banks and his associates in the bank managed, however, to have the loans renewed and upon terms by which the mortgages were to bear 6 per cent. interest instead of 8 per cent.

In time, all of the original purchase money for these lands was paid, but many of the colonists had borrowed money for improvements. There was, therefore, a constant danger that farmers who were not able to discharge the mortgages when they came due would lose their holdings. To provide against this, the Mound Bayou Loan and Investment Company was formed, with a capital stock of $50,000. W. T. Montgomery was made president of this company and Charles Banks secretary and treasurer. The plan of this company was to sell stock to the farmers in the community. The price of shares was fixed at $50, payable in monthly instalments of one dollar. By this means, a capital was secured to take over the mortgages of those members of the community who were not able to pay the loans as they fell due, and at the same time provide a way by which the owners of the land might accumulate a sum sufficient to pay off the indebtedness for which the mortgage was issued. It is expected that the capital accumulated in this way will eventually be used to assist settlers coming into the colony to acquire and pay for lands, and in this way extend the holdings and the influence of the colony. . . .

During the whole twenty years of the town's existence, only three persons have been sent to the circuit court for trial. Two of these were men convicted of theft. Since the town obtained its charter in 1898, there have been, up to February, 1907, but 163 criminal cases tried in the town. Of these, fifty were committed by strangers or by men who had come into town from the surrounding community. Twenty-eight cases were either never tried or were of so trivial a nature that no fine was imposed. Sixty-four were cases of disturbing the peace. . . .

During the year 1905, there were several disturbances in the town which were traced directly to the illicit liquor sellers. Men would come into town on Saturdays to do their marketing, fall to drinking, and end in a fight. Things became so bad at last that a public meeting was held in regard to the matter. As a result of this meeting, the town marshal, the mayor, and the treasurer were appointed to get evidence and secure the conviction of those who were guilty. Six persons were convicted and fined at that time. One of these, a woman, left town. Another is still under suspicion and the rest, now on their farms, have become respectable citizens. To my mind, the interesting fact in regard to these prosecutions is that they served not merely to correct a public abuse but to reform the men who were prosecuted. In most cases, these men went back to the farms and became useful members of the community.

It seems to be pretty well agreed that the moral conditions of the Mound Bayou colony are better than those in other Negro settlements in the Delta. Some years ago, when the question was an "issue" in the community, a committee was appointed from each of the churches to make a house to house canvass of the colony, in order to determine to what extent loose family relations existed. The report of this committee showed that there were forty families in the colony where men and women were living together without the formality of a marriage ceremony. As a result of this report, the people of the town gave notice that these forty couples would have to marry within a certain length of time or they would be prosecuted. Nearly all of them acted upon this suggestion; the others moved away. . . .

One thing that has helped to maintain order in the colony is the fact that Bolivar County prohibits the sale of liquor. More than once the liquor men have attempted to pass a law that would license the selling of liquor in the county. Some years ago a determined effort was made to repeal the prohibition law. In order to secure the vote of Mound Bayou, which seems to have the balance of power in the county on this question, a "still hunt" was made among the voters in the community. A plan was arranged by which a saloon was to be established in the town and one of the citizens made proprietor.

"This scheme came very near going through," said Mr. Montgomery. "The plan was all arranged before we heard of it. Then we called a meeting and I simply said to the people that experience in our own town had taught us that a saloon was a bad thing to have in the community. I said that if the law was passed, a colored man might run the saloon here, but in the rest of the county they would be in the hands of white men. We would pay for maintaining them, however, and we would be the ones to suffer. We voted the law down and there has been no serious attempt to open the county to the liquor traffic since." . . .

The story of Mound Bayou would not be complete without some account of the man who founded the colony and to whose patience and wisdom it owes the greater part of its success. Isaiah T. Montgomery was born on the plantation of Joseph E. Davis, a brother of Jefferson Davis, the President of the Confederate States. The plantation where he was born, in 1847, was known as "The Hurricane," and was situated in Warren County, Miss. His father, Benjamin Thornton Montgomery, came originally from Virginia. He was purchased in Vicksburg by Mr. Davis, while he was still a boy. He had picked up a little education form his young master in Virginia before he was sold South. After he came into the possession of Mr. Davis, he managed to acquire, in some way that Isaiah could never account for, a very good practical education, so that he was able to make surveys and draw plans for buildings, and for years he was in practical control of the plantation upon which he was employed. There were four children, all of whom received the rudiments of an education from their father.

When he was nine years of age, Isaiah was set to work sorting and filing letters and papers in Mr. Davis's office, and from that time he lived in his master's home. He had a great deal of copying to do for Mr. Davis and it was in this way that he gained a practical knowledge of written English that has stood him in good stead ever since. As he grew older he became the special attendant of Mr. Davis, having charge of all his public and private papers, and he worked steadily in his office until the breaking out of the Civil War. In 1863, Mr. Davis retired, upon the approach of the Federal armies, to the interior of the state, taking with him his slaves. Young Montgomery was left behind with his father, however, to assist in taking care of the plantation.

After the destruction of the Federal gunboat *Indianola,* at Hurricane, and the passage of the Federal gunboats under the batteries of Vicksburg, Isaiah entered the service of the United States as a cabin-boy for Rear-Admiral Porter. He was present, in his capacity as cabin-boy, at the battle of Grand Gulf, accompanied the first expedition up Red River, and was a witness of the operations of the siege and capitulation of Vicksburg. In the winter of 1863, he lost his health and was discharged from the navy at Mound City. From there he went to Cincinnati, where, through the kindness of Admiral Porter, his parents had been able to precede him. . . .

Isaiah Montgomery is hopeful and confident of the future. He is now sixty years old, but takes an active part in every movement that relates to the upbuilding of the colony which he founded. He believes that his work at Mound Bayou is only just begun and his townsmen share that belief.

*Source:* Washington, Booker T. "A Town Owned by Negroes: Mound Bayou, Miss., An Example of Thrift and Self-Government." *The World's Work* (July 1907): 9125–34.

# From Day Allen Willey, "Mound Bayou—A Negro Municipality," 1907

Up in the northwest corner of the state of Mississippi, in the heart of the rich country which forms the delta region, where the Yazoo river mingles its waters with the Mississippi, is a community which is of more than ordinary interest, from the fact that it forms a proof of the ability of the Negro race to become successful in trade, agriculture and other vocations, though absolutely independent of the white man. . . .

The origin of the settlement forms a tale that is well worth the telling, for it was founded by a man who spent the early years of his life as a human chattel, being a slave in the days before the war. A few years ago the National Negro Business League, an organization comprising tradesmen, bankers and others of this race, met in the city of Chicago. One of the delegates to the meeting was the founder of Mound Bayou, and at that time its mayor. To talk with Isaiah Montgomery on ordinary topics, one would never think he was at one time a slave, for there is no indication of it in the appearance or conversation of this prosperous business man, but he does not hesitate to speak freely of his early life as a servant of Jefferson Davis, the president of the Confederacy.

Mr. Montgomery tells many entertaining stories about the life on the Davis plantation, one of the largest and most remarkable of the great cotton plantations in the entire South. His father was a foreman on the place, and he himself was taken into the "big house" at an early age to be made a "house" servant. Because he showed unusual aptitude, he was taught to read and write, and in time became a sort of office boy for Joseph Davis, the older brother of Jefferson Davis, coming in this way to have an intimate knowledge of the household and of many of the business and political matters in which his masters were interested. . . .

Montgomery's life on the big plantation gave him not only valuable ideas concerning farming, but of business methods. With the close of the war he did not join the exodus of his race to the North, but remained on the "old place," assisting his father, who had been employed as farm boss. He saw that the Negroes were drifting hither and thither, for their freedom tended to make them unsettled. Noticing their increase in idleness and shiftlessness, the idea occurred to him of securing a large tract of land and renting or selling it to those of his own color—in short, forming a community among themselves. He knew of the rich bottom land in the delta of the Yazoo and managed to obtain control of several thousand acres of it. The news of Montgomery's scheme spread throughout that part of the South, and he had no difficulty in getting enough people to cultivate it. As they received a revenue from the crops of corn, cotton and other staples that they "made," many bought their little farms outright. This money, with the rent from the leased land, put the settlement on a sound financial basis.

Assured that it would not be a failure, the ex-slave added more and more territory to the holdings of the "colony," if it can be termed such. This was also taken up by additional settlers. Meanwhile the town of Mound Bayou began to grow, and on account of its location and the fact that it was dominated by Negroes, it naturally became the market of this region. Here the farmers brought their produce to sell. Here they purchased their clothing, groceries, farm implements and other supplies. They borrowed any money they needed from its people, and when its bank and loan association were organized, utilized these institutions to care for their savings and to transact any banking business they had to do. . . .

The little metropolis of this interesting settlement is not inhabited entirely by Negroes. About 250 white people have drifted into it since it was established, tempted by the opportunity to earn a living as clerks, mechanics, even at unskilled labor. But in numbers they represent only about a tenth of the town population, and none of them hold any public offices. Mound Bayou is absolutely controlled by Negroes today, just as it was when it came into existence as a town. Its mayor and board of aldermen are colored. Its doctors, lawyers and ministers are Negroes, as is the postmaster, the town clerk, the railroad agent and the editor of the local paper. Of its score of stores all but one or two smaller shops are owned by colored merchants. The opportunities for banking business caused the formation of the Bank of Mound Bayou, which opened in 1904. . . . To quote a few other statistics it may be added that in addition to the stores the town has a saw mill, two blacksmith shops, a machine shop, a printing plant, while so much cotton is marketed here that two cotton gins are in continual operation in the season. Four churches, three schools minister to the religious and educational needs.

It may be needless to say that when Mound Bayou chose its first mayor its founder was honored with the office, filling it for several terms. At last he retired to give place to another, but still continues to take an important interest in the community, for Mr. Montgomery is part owner of one of the largest stores, a director in the bank and investment company, besides having large holding of the farm lands. He can be called the leading citizen, but he does not stand alone. . . . While there have been occasional failures to succeed these have been caused more by idleness and neglect than any other factors. Obviously the settlement has attracted some of the idle and vicious of the race, who have naturally drifted into it thinking to get enough to provide for themselves without working for it, but anything of this sort is discouraged by the townsfolk and, as a rule, the worthless ones remain but a short period. In fact, so well ordered is the community that thus far it has not needed a jail or lock-up and is probably the only town of its size in Mississippi which has no cell for the criminal.

*Source:* Willey, Day Allen. "Mound Bayou—A Negro Municipality." *Alexander's Magazine,* July 15, 1907: 159–66.

## Discussion Questions

1. Compare and contrast Hurston's description of the origins of Eaton-ville in her autobiography with her description of it in *Their Eyes Were Watching God.*

2. Compare and contrast the actions of the characters in *Their Eyes Were Watching God*'s Eatonville with characters in segregated neighbor-hoods of larger cities in other pieces of literature. Examples might include *A Raisin in the Sun* by Lorraine Hansberry, *Native Son* by Richard Wright, or *Plum Bun* by Jessie Redmon Fauset.

3. Research the racial composition of your neighborhood, city, or county. To what extent does the amount of racial diversity among elected or appointed leaders reflect the diversity of the general population?

4. Research the history of your neighborhood, city, or county, and then write a short piece of fiction that draws on this history for its plot or characters.

5. Research the history of Native Americans in Oklahoma. What hap-pened to members of the tribes after Oklahoma was opened for settlement by others?

6. Compare and contrast the persuasive strategies the author of "Home Sweet Home" and E. P. McCabe use in their attempts to convince people to move to Langston, Oklahoma. Which strategies do you find most effective? Why?

7. Look up articles that encourage people to move west when the fed-eral government opened up other regions for settlement. Are the points made by E. P. McCabe generally similar to or different from those in articles that don't specifically focus on African American settlers?

8. Read Booker T. Washington's "Atlanta Exposition Address." How do the ideas in that speech correspond to his interpretation of the success of Mound Bayou?

9. Discuss why Booker T. Washington and Day Allen Willey empha-size Isaiah Montgomery's relationship with Jefferson Davis in the excerpts printed above.

10. Discuss the effects of using vocabulary like "pioneers," "settlers," and "colony" in the articles by Washington and Willey.

11. Make a list of common American values. How are these values illustrated in the descriptions of all-black towns?

12. Research utopian communities that were established during the middle of the 19th century. Examples include Brook Farm and Fruitlands, Massachusetts; New Harmony, Indiana; and Oneida,

New York. How do plans for these utopian communities compare to descriptions of Langston, Oklahoma or Mound Bayou, Mississippi in the articles mentioned earlier?

13. Write a newspaper article in which you attempt to persuade people to move to your town or neighborhood.

14. Based on all of the readings mentioned earlier, write an essay or hold a debate in your class responding to this question: What is more crucial for the success of a town or other organization, an inspired and talented founder or the work of many ordinary people?

15. Read Toni Morrison's novel *Paradise* and compare and contrast the setting in that novel with the setting of *Their Eyes Were Watching God.*

16. Compare the assumptions made in the articles above about how people of the same race will get along with passages that illustrate conflict from *Their Eyes Were Watching God.*

17. Look up material about the annual Zora Neale Hurston festival held in Eatonville, Florida. How do the festival materials describe the town?

18. Imagine that you are attempting to found a new town in an area with very little infrastructure. How would you design your town's street plan? What kinds of businesses would you need to attract? Where would you situate schools, hospitals, and other public service buildings? How would you attract these businesses, workers, and other residents? What would you name your town?

## Suggested Readings

Bordelon, Pam. "New Tracks on Dust Tracks: Toward a Reassessment of the Life of Zora Neale Hurston." *African American Review* 31, no. 1 (Spring 1997): 5–21.

Cobb-Moore, Geneva. "Zora Neale Hurston as Local Colorist." *The Southern Literary Journal* 26, no. 2 (1994): 25–34.

Cooper, Jan. "Zora Neale Hurston Was Always a Southerner Too." In *The Female Tradition in Southern Literature*, edited by Carol S. Manning, 57–69. Urbana: University of Illinois Press, 1993.

Crockett, Norman L. *The Black Towns*. Lawrence: The Regents Press of Kansas, 1979.

Dearborn, Mary V. "Black Women Authors and the Harlem Renaissance." In *Pocahontas' Daughters: Gender and Ethnicity in American Culture*, 61–70. New York: Oxford University Press, 1986.

Glassman, Steve and Kathryn Lee Seidel, eds. *Zora in Florida*. Orlando: University of Central Florida Press, 1991.

Hemenway, Robert E. *Zora Neale Hurston: A Literary Biography.* Urbana: University of Illinois Press, 1977.

Humphrey, Charles A. and Donald E. Allen. "Educational and Social Needs in Small All-Black Towns." *The Journal of Negro Education* 47, no. 3 (1978): 244–55.

Hurston, Lucy Anne and the Estate of Zora Neale Hurston. *Speak, So You Can Speak Again: The Life of Zora Neale Hurston.* New York: Doubleday, 2004.

Hurston, Zora Neale. *Dust Tracks on a Road.* New York: HarperPerennial, 1991.

Jessee, Sharon. "The Contrapuntal Histography of Toni Morrison's Paradise: Unpacking the Legacies of the Kansas and Oklahoma All-Black Towns." *American Studies* 47, no. 1 (Spring 2006): 81–112.

Phillips, Kimberley L. *Daily Life during African American Migrations.* Westport, CT: Greenwood, 2012.

"The Queen of the Harlem Renaissance: Her Words Were Lost, but Not Forever." *The Journal of Blacks in Higher Education* 37 (Autumn 2002): 52–53.

Reese, Linda Williams. "'Working in the Vineyard': African-American Women in All-Black Communities." *Kansas Quarterly* 25, no. 2 (1993): 7–17.

Reich, Steven A., ed. *The Great Black Migration: A Historical Encyclopedia of the American Mosaic.* Westport, CT: Greenwood, 2014.

Trefzer, Annette. "'Let Us All Be Kissing-Friends?': Zora Neale Hurston and Race Politics in Dixie." *Journal of American Studies* 31 (1997): 69–78.

Trubek, Anne. "Zora's Place." *Humanities* (November/December 2011): 38–42.

Walker, Alice. "In Search of Zora Neale Hurston." *Ms.* (March 1975): 74–79, 85–89.

# HISTORICAL EXPLORATION: MIGRANT AND SEASONAL LABOR

In *Their Eyes Were Watching God,* Tea Cake and Janie go down to the Florida everglades to work on the "muck," picking beans during the harvest season. They do not own the farm, and they do not necessarily plan to stay in the area after the season is over. These facts mean that they are both "migrant workers" and "seasonal workers." These terms are often treated as if they are interchangeable, but they have precise definitions that do not entirely overlap. A migrant worker is someone who relocates for a comparatively short period in order to perform temporary labor; often a migrant worker then relocates to another place for the same purpose. Migrant workers usually perform agricultural labor, as Janie and Tea Cake and the other minor characters in this portion of the novel do. Migrant workers may follow crops north according to the growing seasons of specific crops. Seasonal workers, on the other hand, are hired for a specific season only, and they may or may not have relocated. Harvest season would be one period when seasonal workers are hired by farmers, but retail outlets often hire extra employees over the holiday season also. Employment laws generally treat seasonal workers differently than workers intended to be hired permanently; the obligations of the employers are different for each class of worker.

The life of a migrant worker is often stereotyped as miserable. While we always want to be wary of stereotypes, migrant workers have often been abused by their employers. They might be provided poor housing or charged exorbitant rates for the meals they eat while working. They might not be provided appropriate medical care, even if they are injured on the job. The work can be hot and dangerous; agricultural work generally is among the most dangerous types of employment due to the machinery that is required. But in *Their Eyes Were Watching God,* Janie finds her time as a migrant seasonal worker among the most pleasurable of her life. This novel's purpose is not to protest against economic inequalities promoted by the agricultural system; rather, one of its themes is that women desire personal fulfillment just as men do. Janie feels socially included when she's working with Tea Cake as she had not when she worked in Joe Clarke's store or when she was married to Logan Killicks. For Janie and Tea Cake, working at this temporary job provides them with conviviality and pleasure because of their relationships with the people they're working with. The work itself is often secondary.

Today, many people assume that migrant workers employed in the United States are not originally from the United States, and often people also assume that these workers have entered the United States illegally, generally from Mexico. These assumptions are often inaccurate. *Their Eyes Were Watching God* does not address questions of immigration. When the novel was published, the question of illegal immigration was not nearly as prominent in American politics as it is currently; however, the challenge of unemployment was significant for many people at that time, the decade of the Great Depression. The novel is set earlier, however, so readers will notice a contrast between the most crucial social problems at the time the novel is set and those at the time it was published.

## Migrant Loggers

The first excerpt below describes the life of itinerant loggers in the northwest. The type of work is much different from picking beans or harvesting other vegetables, and the natural environment of the northwestern forests is obviously also different from the environment of the southeastern everglades, but the circumstances are nevertheless similar. Logging is particularly dangerous, and the companies often retain much more power than individual workers can. Yet the excerpt also points out that if working conditions or wages are too unreasonable, the workers will quit and seek employment elsewhere. For this strategy to be effective, the workers would have to be united, even if they weren't formally organized within a union.

# From Charlotte Todes, *Labor and Lumber,* 1931

The majority of workers in western logging camps are single, homeless and possessionless. Relative absence of family ties and years of struggle against boss domination have given many of the workers in the woods a fearless and unconquerable attitude toward the job and employer. They unhesitatingly complain against unsatisfactory conditions and if these are not remedied, they protest by quitting. Oppressive life in the camps, the isolation, the hard and hazardous work and frequent shutdowns force the workers in the camps to be constant job hunters. Loggers must seek jobs five or six times a year in the best of times. Although they often travel many miles to new jobs, the loggers do not leave the region where they have had experience in logging a particular species of trees. . . . When the camps are down for long periods, and jobs are difficult to find, the workers are compelled to move on to other regions where they take jobs in the harvest fields, on construction gangs, in the mines or in the canneries. They join the vast group of migratory workers who follow the job market from California to Washington and then to Montana and the Dakotas riding freight cars and living in 'jungles' and cheap lodging houses. . . .

In their efforts to 'decasualize' the industry, the lumber companies give preference to married workers and young workers. A few days' training does not make an experienced logger but the companies take on young workers who work at lower wages. Inexperience endangers the lives of these young workers but does not damage the product. . . . [Y]oung workers are used to 'stabilize' the labor situation and prevent unionization. . .

Source: Todes, Charlotte. Labor and Lumber. New York:<br>International Publishers, 1931: 75–76.

## Migrant Farmers

This next document is an excerpt from a book by Robert Coles, who has written many sociological studies, often focusing on children. In this book, he interviews many people associated with migrant labor, presenting the complicated relationships among growers, migrant workers, and other farm employees. In the excerpt below, Coles is interviewing a grower, Hugh Bates, who employs many migrant laborers. In the extended interview, Bates discusses his frustrations, especially with repairing property after the migrants have left for the season. In the section below, he discusses the differences in values between his employees and himself, differences that are often pointed to in discussing values aligned with social classes. Bates assumes that if the migrant workers wanted the lifestyle he has, they would work more autonomously and be frugal with their earnings. *Their Eyes Were Watching God* does not feature much interaction between Janie or Tea Cake and their employers when they are picking beans; the novel's primary critique of social class occurs earlier, when Janie's life is so constrained by the desire of Joe Starks to be perceived as superior to his fellows. In the novel, the workers are carefree—at least until the hurricane arrives—and Tea Cake does embody many of the characteristics that Hugh Bates criticizes below. Tea Cake, however, is not unhappy with his lot in life. The novel may romanticize migrant labor; on the other hand, it may also illustrate the possibility that the value differences that frustrate Hugh Bates are not only real, but perhaps incomprehensible to outsiders.

## From Robert Coles, *Migrants, Sharecroppers, Mountaineers,* 1971

I've seen those children working in the fields beside their parents and I've wondered why. It's not because they need the money. I've asked the parents, and they'll say no, it's not because of money; it's because the children want to, they want to go out there with their mothers and fathers and pick beans, and they even race with them to see who can do the most work . . . but, I'll tell you, it's not long before those same kids are behaving just like their parents. I mean, they take their money and they squander it. They buy one chocolate bar after another and all those Cokes. They learn gambling, at ten years old they do. They don't care about school. . . . We'd like to do what we can for them, especially the children. But it's hopeless. . . . We realize now that people are different, and you can't go and impose your ideas and your values on others. . . .

I'm for paying them the best wage we can afford to people, in return for an honest day's work. I try to keep their quarters halfway presentable. I can't give them palaces; like I say, they'd be lost in a home like mine. . . . I'll grant that we need them, and they *are* experts of a kind. But we could be rid of most of them right now if we really had to; there are machines that will do almost anything a man does on a farm. . . . I'd hate to see them go, in a way I would. You get attached to them, after all these years you do. As I said, they're like children; and you get attached to them.

*Source:* Coles, Robert. *Migrants, Sharecroppers, Mountaineers.* Boston: Little, Brown, & Co., 1971: 454–57. Copyright © 1971 by Robert Coles. Reprinted by permission of Hachette Book Group, Inc.

## Labor Laws Regarding Migrant and Seasonal Labor

This next excerpt contains the content of a poster that the federal government requires agricultural employers to post where their employees have easy access to it. Some of the rights listed might seem self-evident, but they became required by law because some unscrupulous employers refused to recognize them. Historically, employers would require their employees to purchase goods at the company store, which might have inflated prices. Or they might have been provided housing that lacked running water or was otherwise unsanitary. This document specifies that employees can rightfully expect their health and safety not to be unnecessarily compromised by their employers.

# From U.S. Department of Labor Poster Required to Be Displayed by Employers, Migrant and Seasonal Agricultural Worker Protection Act, 1983

This federal law requires agricultural employers, agricultural associations, farm labor contractors and their employees to observe certain labor standards when employing migrant and seasonal farmworkers unless specific exemptions apply. Further, farm labor contractors are required to register with the U.S. Department of Labor.

Migrant and Seasonal Farmworkers Have These Rights

- To receive accurate information about wages and working conditions for the prospective employment
- To receive this information in writing and in English, Spanish or other languages, as appropriate
- To have the terms of the working arrangement upheld
- To have farm labor contractors show proof of registration at the time of recruitment
- To be paid wages when due
- To receive itemized, written statements of earnings for each pay period
- To purchase goods from the source of their choice
- To be transported in vehicles which are properly insured and operated by licensed drivers, and which meet federal and state safety standards
- For migrant farmworkers who are provided housing
- To be housed in property which meets federal and state safety and health standards
- To have the housing information presented to them in writing at the time of recruitment
- To have posted in a conspicuous place at the housing site or presented to them a statement of the terms and conditions of occupancy, if any

Workers who believe their rights under the act have been violated may file complaints with the department's Wage and Hour

Division or may file suit directly in federal district court. The law prohibits employers from discrimination against workers who file complaints, testify or in any way exercise their rights on their own behalf or on behalf of others. Complaints of such discrimination must be filed with the division within 180 days of the alleged event.

*Source:* U.S. Department of Labor Poster Required to Be Displayed by Employers. Migrant and Seasonal Agricultural Worker Protection Act. P.L. 97–470 (January 14, 1983).

## Discussion Questions

1. Read *The Grapes of Wrath* by John Steinbeck and compare the experience of the Joad family as they seek employment in California with the experience of Tea Cake and Janie.
2. Read novels or pieces of nonfiction that focus on work. Discuss what you notice about the types of work described and the attitudes of characters toward their work. Compare and contrast these materials to the descriptions of work in *Their Eyes Were Watching God.* Some examples include *The Jungle* by Upton Sinclair, *Working* by Studs Terkel, and *Nickled and Dimed to Death* by Barbara Ehrenreich.
3. Write an essay describing your efforts to find a job. If you succeeded, describe the factors in your success. If you did not succeed, analyze the factors that impeded your success.
4. Write an essay based on your own experience or interview someone you know about how relationships with coworkers affect one's enjoyment of a job.
5. Interview someone you know who has moved at least 100 miles in order to secure employment. What was most difficult about this experience? What were the benefits?
6. Research how farm labor has changed since the 1930s. You might consider developments in machinery and technology, the presence or absence of family farms, genetic modifications of plants, or laws affecting farmers and other agricultural workers.
7. Research the reliance on migrant labor in your own region.

8. Choose a specific fruit or vegetable available in your local grocery store. Research where that product was grown, the working conditions of the people who might have grown it, and how it was shipped to your store.

9. Write an essay analyzing the rights of workers and the rights of employers.

10. Watch several different television shows. What types of work are presented? What types of work are not represented? How do the characters feel about their work? Write an essay exploring your observations.

11. Write an essay exploring how work is presented in popular music. Some examples of songs are "Take This Job and Shove It," "She Works Hard for the Money," "9 to 5," "Wichita Lineman," and "Work in' for a Livin'."

12. Write a poem, song, or short story that describes a specific kind of job.

## Suggested Readings

Borjas, G.J. "Immigration, Minorities, and Labor Market Competition." *Industrial and Labor Relations Review* 40 (1987): 382–92.

Branz-Spall, Angela Maria, Roger Rosenthal and Al Wright. "Children of the Road: Migrant Students, Our Nation's Most Mobile Population." *The Journal of Negro Education* 72, no. 1 (Winter 2003): 55–62.

Bruns, Roger. *Encyclopedia of Cesar Chavez.* Westport, CT: Greenwood, 2013.

Coles, Robert. *Migrants, Sharecroppers, Mountaineers.* Boston: Little, Brown, 1971.

Congressional Research Service. "Report RL33372. Migrant and Seasonal Agricultural Workers: Protective Statutes." August 29, 2007.

Ferriss, Susan, Ricardo Sandoval, and Diana Hembree. *The Fight in the Fields: Cesar Chavez and the Farmworkers Movement.* New York: Harcourt Brace, 1997.

Friedland, William H. and Dorothy Nelkin. *Migrant Agricultural Workers in America's Northeast.* New York: Holt, Rinehart and Winston, 1971.

Krull, Kathleen and Yuyi Morales. *Harvesting Hope: The Story of Cesar Chavez.* San Diego: Harcourt, 2003.

Laskas, Jeanne Marie. *Hidden America: From Coal Miners to Cowboys, an Extraordinary Exploration of the Unseen People Who Make This Country Work.* New York: G. P. Putnam's Sons, 2012.

López, Ann Aurelia. *The Farmworkers' Journey.* Berkeley: University of California Press, 2007.

Murphy, A. D., Blanchard, C., and Hill, J. A., eds. *Latino Workers in the Contemporary South.* Athens: University of Georgia Press, 2001.

Nicholls, David G. "Migrant Labor, Folklore, and Resistance in Hurston's Polk County: Reframing Mules and Men." *African American Review* 33, no. 3 (Autumn 1999): 467–79.

Palley, Howard A. "The Migrant Labor Problem: Its State and Interstate Aspects." *The Journal of Negro Education* 32, no. 1 (Winter 1963): 35–42.

Quiñones-Hinojosa, Alfredo and Mim Eichler Rivas. *Becoming Dr. Q: My Journey from Migrant Farm Worker to Brain Surgeon.* Berkeley: University of California Press, 2011.

Rothenberg, Daniel. *With These Hands: The Hidden World of Migrant Farmworkers Today.* New York: Harcourt Brace & Co., 1998.

Schwartzman, Kathleen C. "Lettuce, Segmented Labor Markets, and the Immigration Discourse." *Journal of Black Studies* 39, no. 1 (September 2008): 129–56.

United States Department of Agriculture, Economic Research Service. "Farm Labor: Background." 2013.

Valle, Isabel. *Fields of Toil: A Migrant Family's Journey.* Pullman: Washington State University Press, 1994.

# HISTORICAL EXPLORATION: HURRICANES

In the climactic section of *Their Eyes Were Watching God*—and the section from which the novel gets its title—Janie and Tea Cake and their friends experience a major hurricane. Readers know that this is a significant moment in the plot because Hurston devotes one entire chapter and part of the next to the storm; these chapters occur just before the final short chapter when the novel returns to its frame story, with Janie talking to Pheobe. Initially, several characters had refused to believe that the storm could be coming because of their desire to continue working, earning what for them was very good money. So they refuse to leave the area while they can, and by the time they admit that they should evacuate, it is too late.

They huddle together, terrified of what they see. The storm becomes much more severe than any of the characters had anticipated, and it is during this hurricane that Tea Cake suffers the dog bite that eventually leads to his death.

After the hurricane has subsided, Tea Cake along with several other men is enlisted to help bury the dead. Ironically, even in these dire circumstances, Tea Cake is instructed to separate the bodies of white people from those of black people, but because of the decomposition of the corpses, sometimes race is difficult to distinguish. The white people will be buried in cheap hastily built coffins, but the black people won't receive even that dignity.

Hurston based this section of her novel on the Okeechobee Hurricane of 1928, also known as San Filipe II, a category 4 hurricane that resulted in the deaths of nearly 3,000 people. It began in the Atlantic on September 10th; from September 12th through 15th, the hurricane struck several islands, including St. Croix, Puerto Rico, and Haiti. It made landfall in Florida on September 16th, where the winds were estimated to have peaked at 160 miles per hour. By September 18th, the hurricane had made its way to North Carolina and then continued up the East Coast of the United States. During the week of the hurricane, Florida received over 18 inches of rain, and the storm surge on Lake Okeechobee was 15 feet.

Although Hurston was writing a novel rather than a piece of journalism, her description of the hurricane and the events following were quite consistent with the Okeechobee Hurricane. As in the novel, the Seminole Indians warned that a storm was coming, but their warnings were generally ignored by others. And as in the novel, white and black bodies were buried separately, with most white bodies being identified and buried in marked graves while most black bodies were buried in a mass grave that remained unmarked until 2004.

## A Flood in Folklore

In the first excerpt below, from a collection of Hurston's folklore, we hear a story related to another flood, in Johnstown, Pennsylvania. The humor of the story rests with the identity of a man who seems unimpressed by such natural disasters—because he has survived perhaps the greatest natural disaster of all. Although this piece depends on hyperbole for its effect, it reveals the true concerns of people who have survived such events, and the reality of death that often results.

# From Zora Neale Hurston, *Mules and Men,* 1935

In one place they call Johnstown they had a great flood. And so many folks got drownded that it looked jus' like Judgment day. . . .

De colored man was named John, so John ast Peter, says, "Is it dry in dere?"

Ole Peter tole 'im, "Why, yes it's dry in here. How come you ast that?"

"Well, you know Ah jus come out of one flood, and Ah don't want to run into no mo.' Ooh, man! You ain't *seen* no water. You just oughter seen dat flood we had at Johnstown." . . .

Way after while he went over to Ole Peter and said: "Thought you said everybody would be nice and polite?"

Peter said, "Yeah, Ah said it. Ain't everybody treatin' you right?"

John said, "Naw. Ah jus' walked up to a man as nice and friendly as Ah could be and started to tell 'im 'bout all dat water Ah left back there in Johnstown and instead of him turnin' me a friendly answer he said, 'Shucks! You ain't seen no water!' and walked off and left me standin' by myself."

"Was he a *ole* man wid a crooked walkin' stick?" Peter ast John.

"Yeah."

"Did he have whiskers down to here?" Peter measured down to his waist.

"He sho did," John tol' 'im.

"Aw shucks," Peter tol' 'im. "Dat was Ole Nora [Noah]. You can't tell *him* nothin' 'bout no flood."

## Personal Experiences of the Okeechobee Hurricane

The next two excerpts describe the experiences of people who were directly involved in the Okeechobee Hurricane. In the first passage, a naval officer describes his experience at sea as the hurricane passes over. His description is objective, focusing on the actual features of the storm rather

Coffins stacked along the bank of a canal, after the hurricane of 1928. Belle Glade, Florida. (Courtesy of the State Archives of Florida)

than his own emotional response. In the second passage, Eliot Kleinberg features an adolescent girl who sees her family home destroyed as her mother drowns. She survives as much through luck as determination. While Helen Sherous in Kleinberg's narrative reveals the severity of the storm by describing her fear, the officer conveys the severity of the storm by focusing on more factual evidence. Both passages, though, depend on personal experience and achieve their power through the intensity of this experience.

## From Charles L. Mitchell, "The West Indian Hurricane of September 10–20, 1928," 1928

The German steamer *August Leonhardt* en route from New York to Puerto Colombia, was hove to . . . when the center of the hurricane passed over it about 3 P.M. of the 15th. . . . After the barometer had remained stationary and the wind had calmed down for a short time, the hurricane started again at 3:10 P.M., "this time blowing from the south-southeast, according to the report of Second Officer

R. Sievers, 'with an undescribable force. The force of the wind, if more or less, could only be judged by the noise made by the storm, which reminded me of the New York subway going full speed passing switches. Rain and spray were carried away horizontally and our whistle started to blow loudly due to the force of the wind pressing the wire. The foam and spray went up to the masthead (40 meters above the water), this being proved by our antenna and insulators which we had to take down in order to clean off the salt. Hatch tarpaulins, boat ventilators, covers, etc., were torn to pieces and carried away. It is impossible to describe the sea and swell. Spray, rain, and foam was so dense that we could not see our forecastle head.'"

*Source:* Mitchell, Charles L. "The West Indian Hurricane of September 10–20, 1928." *Monthly Weather Review,* September 1928: 347–50.

## From Eliot Kleinberg, *Black Cloud: The Great Florida Hurricane of 1928*, 2003

Helen Sherouse was thirteen. Her family had heard the storm would pass. But on Sunday morning, her uncle went to Belle Glade to deliver milk and came back with grim news: the hurricane would strike any minute. Sherouse's mother said she'd rather stay than fight the road in the family's car, roofless in the style of the times and open to the elements. Nineteen relatives gathered around the table that night. . . . Water started coming through the door. Helen watched as someone cut a hole in the roof. The piano was now floating, and men pushed it across the room like a boat. People climbed onto the piano and onto the roof and huddled on one corner. Helen was holding on and calling to her mother. She'd shout, "Mama, are you there?" and her mother would answer. After a while, she didn't answer anymore.

Suddenly Helen found herself in the water. . . . She would learn later that the house had fallen away from her, turning over onto its roof like a capsizing boat. She could feel furniture falling around her. Her stepfather had instructed her that there was less chance of being struck by something if she were underwater, so she stayed under. She worked her way back to the house and inside. But the house was upside down, with part of it underwater.

She was freezing and exhausted. She heard someone stomping above and screamed. Believing all her relatives were still on what had been the bottom of the house, which was now the top, she continued to scream until her stepfather swung down and grabbed her. They huddled in a doorway until the morning.

*Source:* Kleinberg, Eliot. *Black Cloud: The Great Florida Hurricane of 1928.* New York: Carrol & Graf Publishers, 2003: 102–3. Copyright © 2003 by Eliot Kleinberg. Reprinted by permission of Perseus Book Publishers, a member of Perseus Books, LLC.

## The Federal Emergency Management Agency

The next excerpt is taken from a federal government document that shows how significantly responses to natural disasters have changed since the Okeechobee Hurricane. In *Their Eyes Were Watching God,* Tea Cake mentions that the Red Cross had arrived to assist survivors of the hurricane. The Red Cross had, in fact, worked vigorously in Florida after the Okeechobee Hurricane, but coordinated relief efforts weren't yet common practice. Within a few decades, however, the federal government would attempt to address this weakness through the creation of a federal agency specifically devoted to emergency response. The Federal Emergency Management Agency, or FEMA, responds to many types of disasters, not simply hurricanes, although it receives much media attention during hurricane season. This document traces the history of FEMA as it has evolved to address an increasing range of disasters. The document persuasively argues for the need for an agency like FEMA, and the success of its persuasion rests in great part on the specific narrative examples it includes. It is using some of the techniques of fiction, in other words, to create an engaging piece of writing, even in the form of a government report.

## From "The Federal Emergency Management Agency Publication 1," 2010

"The History of FEMA"
Federal Disaster Response and Emergency Management 1802–1979

In the early morning hours of December 26, 1802, fire ripped through the city of Portsmouth, New Hampshire, destroying large areas of this important seaport. The fire was a devastating event and threatened commerce throughout the northeast section of the newly founded Nation. Nineteen days later, Congress suspended bond payments for several months for the merchants affected by the fire, thus implementing the first act of Federal disaster relief in American history.

Large fires were a significant hazard for cities in the 19th century. Fire disasters, including one in New York City in 1835 and the Great Chicago Fire in 1871, led to more ad hoc legislation from Congress, most often authorizing the suspension of financial obligations for disaster survivors. It was not until the early 20th century that two catastrophic disasters affected public opinion and changed the role the Federal Government would play in future disasters.

The Galveston Hurricane in 1900 and the San Francisco Earthquake in 1906 remain the two deadliest disasters in U.S. history. In both cases, local governments led response and recovery efforts with support and assistance from volunteers and wealthy members of the respective communities. The Federal Government provided only token aid to both cities. These incidents spurred a national debate over the Federal Government's role in providing assistance following domestic disasters.

In response to the Great Mississippi Flood of 1927, President Coolidge designated Commerce Secretary Herbert Hoover as the flood "czar" to coordinate the Federal disaster response for this catastrophic event, which affected ten States. The executive-level response, led by Hoover, marks the first time the Federal Government directly assisted disaster response and recovery efforts.

Hoover used his authority to marshal Federal resources and integrate them with the efforts of the American Red Cross and private sector interests. The Federal Government actually provided very little financial aid. Instead, it successfully urged American citizens to donate to the relief effort.

In 1950, Congress enacted the Federal Disaster Assistance Program. For the first time, the Federal Government was authorized to respond to major disasters. This law defined a disaster as "[a]ny flood, drought, fire, hurricane, earthquake, storm, or other catastrophe in any part of the United States which in the determination of the President is, or threatens to be, of sufficient severity and magnitude to warrant disaster assistance by the Federal government." The Federal Disaster Assistance Program gave the President broad powers to respond to crisis, and those powers have been confirmed in all subsequent Federal disaster legislation. . . .

Although strides had been made to define and expand the Federal Government's role in emergency management, critics cited a lack of coordination and the fact that, at the Federal level, no single entity was responsible for coordinating Federal response and recovery efforts during large-scale disasters and emergencies. . . .

FEMA: 1979–2001

President Carter's 1979 executive order consolidated many separate Federal disaster-related responsibilities within FEMA. . . .

FEMA faced many challenges during its first years and experienced the real complexities of the business of Federal emergency management. Disasters and emergencies early in FEMA's history included the contamination of the Love Canal, the eruption of Mount St. Helens Volcano, the Cuban refugee crisis, and the radiological accident that the Three Mile Island nuclear power plant. Later, widespread problems in the Federal response to the Loma Prieta Earthquake and Hurricane Hugo in 1989 focused major national attention on FEMA. And despite important advances, . . . FEMA's response to Hurricane Andrew later that year [1992] brought additional criticism and calls for reform from Congress. Some members of Congress even threatened to abolish the agency. . . .

FEMA: 2001–Present

On September 11, 2001, terrorists attacked the United States, and FEMA was immediately engaged in supporting New York, Virginia, and Pennsylvania officials in the response. The deployment of 25 Urban Search and Rescue teams, mobile communication equipment, and thousands of staff was just the beginning of one of the agency's largest emergency response operations. The attacks on New York's World Trade Center and the Pentagon were the catalyst for major changes in legislation and policy that affected how the Federal Government would be organized to prevent subsequent attacks and respond to disasters. The changes led to the creation of the Department of Homeland Security (DHS).

When DHS was created in 2003, it integrated FEMA and 21 other organizations. . . .

In the aftermath of the September 11th attacks and the formation of DHS, the focus throughout the Federal Government was on terrorism preparedness, prevention, protection, and response. And although FEMA reflected this focus, the agency continued to respond to a string of significant natural disasters, including the historic hurricane seasons of 2004 and 2005.

In 2004, four hurricanes struck Florida in a matter of two months. Hurricanes Charley, Frances, Ivan, and Jeanne devastated the State and marked the first time in more than 100 years that four hurricanes had impacted a single State in the same year. These hurricanes provided FEMA's first opportunity to conduct a large-scale response operation as an entity within DHS. The need for an even greater response effort would come just a year later.

In August 2005, Hurricane Katrina passed over south Florida and grew into a Category 5 hurricane in the Gulf of Mexico. At the time, it was the fourth most powerful hurricane ever recorded in the Gulf. When it struck the Gulf shores as a strong Category 3 storm, Katrina became the costliest and one of the deadliest disasters in U.S. history. Louisiana, Mississippi, and Alabama suffered the greatest impact, but all 50 States were ultimately affected as they cooperated in the evacuation and relocation of more than one million displaced residents. Hurricane Katrina required the largest response effort to a disaster in U.S. history and presented unprecedented challenges at the local, Tribal, State, and Federal levels. The response to Hurricane Katrina by FEMA and others was roundly criticized in the media and in studies conducted by the White House, Congress, and policy/research organizations. As a result, major reforms and changes were instituted within FEMA. . . .

In summary, FEMA's existence represents a small part of the long history of Federal participation in emergency management. Although FEMA may be the best-known brand of Federal emergency management assistance, it is just one member of a much larger team. Other Federal departments play important roles in preparing for, responding to, recovering from, and mitigating disasters. State, Tribal, and local governments have significantly enhanced and expanded their capabilities since 2003, and communities, as always, continue to provide the first line of defense for and response to disasters and emergencies.

*Source:* "The Federal Emergency Management Agency Publication 1,"
November 2010: 3–14.

## The Saffir-Simpson Hurricane Wind Scale

This final document summarizes the "Saffir-Simpson Hurricane Wind Scale." Most readers will be impressed with the high wind speeds of severe hurricanes, but the description is more effective because it also provides additional data that readers will likely have more experience with. It includes the types of damage that will occur at particular wind speeds, and it also projects how long areas will remain uninhabitable after a hurricane. These facts can seem unbelievable, which is one reason why many people are unprepared for a storm of this magnitude.

# National Weather Center, "Saffir-Simpson Hurricane Wind Scale," 2013

The Saffir-Simpson Hurricane Wind Scale is a 1 to 5 rating based on a hurricane's sustained wind speed. This scale estimates potential property damage. Hurricanes reaching Category 3 and higher are considered major hurricanes because of their potential for significant loss of life and damage. Category 1 and 2 storms are still dangerous, however, and require preventative measures. In the western North Pacific, the term "super typhoon" is used for tropical cyclones with sustained winds exceeding 150 mph.

| Category | Sustained Winds | Types of Damage Due to Hurricane Winds |
|---|---|---|
| 1 | 74–95 mph<br>64–82 kt<br>119–153 km/h | Very dangerous winds will produce some damage: Well-constructed frame homes could have damage to roof, shingles, vinyl siding and gutters. Large branches of trees will snap and shallowly rooted trees may be toppled. Extensive damage to power lines and poles likely will result in power outages that could last a few to several days. |
| 2 | 96–110 mph<br>83–95 kt<br>154–177 km/h | Extremely dangerous winds will cause extensive damage: Well-constructed frame homes could sustain major roof and siding damage. Many shallowly rooted trees will be snapped or uprooted and block numerous roads. Near-total power loss is expected with outages that could last from several days to weeks. |

*(Continued)*

| Category | Sustained Winds | Types of Damage Due to Hurricane Winds |
|---|---|---|
| 3 (major) | 111–129 mph 96–112 kt 178–208 km/h | Devastating damage will occur: Well-built framed homes may incur major damage or removal of roof decking and gable ends. Many trees will be snapped or uprooted, blocking numerous roads. Electricity and water will be unavailable for several days to weeks after the storm passes. |
| 4 (major) | 130–156 mph 113–136 kt 209–251 km/h | Catastrophic damage will occur: Well-built framed homes can sustain severe damage with loss of most of the roof structure and/or some exterior walls. Most trees will be snapped or uprooted and power poles downed. Fallen trees and power poles will isolate residential areas. Power outages will last weeks to possibly months. Most of the area will be uninhabitable for weeks or months. |
| 5 (major) | 157 mph or higher 137 kt or higher 252 km/h or higher | Catastrophic damage will occur: A high percentage of framed homes will be destroyed, with total roof failure and wall collapse. Fallen trees and power poles will isolate residential areas. Power outages will last for weeks to possibly months. Most of the area will be uninhabitable for weeks or months. |

*Source:* "Saffir-Simpson Hurricane Wind Scale." National Weather Service, National Hurricane Center, 2013.

## Discussion Questions

1. Look up recommendations for hurricane preparedness or recommendations for the type of weather emergencies that are likely to occur in your region. Discuss these preparations with the other members of your household.
2. In your classroom, discuss the effect of the hurricane on the development of the plot, major and minor characters, and theme of *Their Eyes Were Watching God.*
3. Read another novel or story that features severe weather and compare the experiences of the characters with those in *Their Eyes Were*

*Watching God*. Some examples include *Power* by Linda Hogan, *Tracks* by Louise Erdrich, "The Open Boat" by Stephen Crane, and *The Wizard of Oz* by Frank Baum.

4. Read a piece of nonfiction that explores a natural disaster. Some examples are *The Perfect Storm* by Sebastian Junger, *Into Thin Air* by Jon Krakauer, or *Into the Wild* by Jon Krakauer. How does nonfiction present this material differently from fictionalized accounts you have read? What narrative strategies are similar?

5. Read another novel set in Florida and compare the significance of the setting with that in *Their Eyes Were Watching God*. Some examples include *Continental Drift* by Russell Banks, *Power* by Linda Hogan, and *The Yearling* by Marjorie Kinnan Rawlings.

6. The title of *Their Eyes Were Watching God* comes from a scene that suggests the hurricane is as powerful as a god. Research the mythology of other cultures—perhaps Greek or Roman, Norse, or Native American—to identify other stories in which gods or other supernatural creatures control or embody the weather.

7. The narrator of *Their Eyes Were Watching God* suggests that the animals knew a storm was coming. Research other stories about animals that suggest they can predict the weather.

8. Analyze the relief efforts following a recent natural disaster. What did the federal and state governments and private agencies do well? What could be improved?

9. Create a myth or folk tale that explains a particular weather phenomenon or features characters responding to severe weather. Write one version that incorporates humor and another version that is intended as a cautionary tale.

10. Interview someone who has experienced a hurricane, tornado, or flood. How were their daily lives affected by this disaster? How have they recovered?

11. Research how local agencies respond to natural disasters in your region.

12. Choose one of the disasters mentioned in the History of FEMA document to research. Write a paper or deliver a report to your class explaining your discoveries about that event.

13. Read several newspaper reports of the hurricane from 1928 and compare the evidence reported during the hurricane to later discussions of it.

14. Visit your state museum or local history society to research the significance of natural disasters in your area.

15. Choose a state where you've never lived and research the history of disasters that have occurred in that state—hurricanes, tornadoes, floods, fires, droughts, blizzards.
16. Explore the website of The National Weather Service. What information does the site provide that is useful for people who are not professional meteorologists?

## Suggested Readings

Barnes, Jay and Steve Lyons. *Florida's Hurricane History.* Charlottesville: University of North Carolina Press, 1998.

Brinkley, Douglas. *The Great Deluge: Hurricane Katrina, New Orleans, and the Mississippi Gulf Coast.* New York: HarperPerennial, 2007.

Colten, Craig E. and Alexandra Giancarlo. "Losing Resilience on the Gulf Coast: Hurricanes and Social Memory." *Environment* 53, no. 4 (June 2011): 6–19.

Cooley, Nicole. *Breach.* Baton Rouge: Louisiana State University Press, 2010.

Dunn, Gordon E. and Banner I. Miller. *Atlantic Hurricanes.* Baton Rouge: Louisiana State University Press, 1964.

Dyson, Michael Eric. *Come Hell or High Water: Hurricane Katrina and the Color of Disaster.* Philadelphia: Basic Civitas Books, 2005.

Emanuel, Kerry. *Divine Wind: The History and Science of Hurricanes.* New York: Oxford University Press, 2005.

"Find 200 More Dead in Florida Village." *The New York Times.* September 24, 1928.

Fischetti, Mark. "Storm of the Century Every Two Years." *Scientific American* 308, no. 6 (June 2013): 58–67.

"544 Bodies Recovered." *The New York Times.* September 22, 1928.

"Florida Deaths Mounting, Now 800, Many Are Missing; Disease Imperils Living." *The New York Times.* September 21, 1928.

Frattaroli, Jessica Lucia. "A State's Duty to Prepare, Warn, and Mitigate Natural Disaster Damages." *Boston College International and Comparative Law Review* 37, no. 1 (Winter 2014): 173–208.

Gannon, Michael, ed. *The History of Florida.* Gainesville: The University Press of Florida, 2013.

Grunwald, Michael. *The Swamp: The Everglades, Florida, and the Politics of Paradise.* New York: Simon & Schuster, 2007.

Kantha, Lakshmi. "Classification of Hurricanes: Lessons from Katrina, Ike, Irene, Isaac, and Sandy." *Ocean Engineering* 70 (September 2013): 124–28.

Keller, Edward A. and Duane E. DeVecchio. *Natural Hazards: Earth's Processes as Hazards, Disasters, and Catastrophes.* Upper Saddle River, NJ: Prentice Hall, 2011.

Larson, Erik. *Isaac's Storm: A Man, a Time, and the Deadliest Hurricane in History.* New York: Vintage, 2000.

Longshore, David. *Encyclopedia of Hurricanes, Typhoons, and Cyclones.* New York: Checkmark Books, 2008.

Mykle, Robert. *Killer 'Cane: The Deadly Hurricane of 1928.* Lanham, MD: Cooper Square Press, 2002.

Norcross, Bryan. *Hurricane Almanac: The Essential Guide to Storms Past, Present, and Future.* New York: St. Martin's Press, 2007.

Oppel, Frank and Tony Meisel, eds. *Tales of Old Florida.* Secaucus, NJ: Castle, 2008.

Pfost, Russell L. "Reassessing the Impact of Two Historical Florida Hurricanes." *Bulletin of the American Meteorological Society* (October 2003): 1367–72.

"Relief Need Grows, Red Cross Reports." *The New York Times.* September 21, 1928. 23.

Schumacher, Michael. *November's Fury: The Deadly Great Lakes Hurricane of 1913.* Minneapolis: University of Minnesota Press, 2013.

Smith, Mike. *Warnings: The True Story of How Science Tamed the Weather.* Austin, TX: Greenleaf Book Group, 2010.

"Threat of Disease Grows in Florida." *The New York Times.* September 28, 1928. 10.

Williams, Jack and Bob Sheets. *Hurricane Watch: Forecasting the Deadliest Storms on Earth.* New York: Vintage, 2001.

Williams, John M. and Iver W. Duedall. *Florida Hurricanes and Tropical Storms, 1871–2001.* Gainesville: University Press of Florida, 2002.

# WHY WE READ *THEIR EYES WERE WATCHING GOD* TODAY

For many readers, Janie Crawford is a favorite character. Despite the hardships she experiences, she remains optimistic, and she generally aims to respond to others fairly, even when she has been treated unfairly herself. We witness her mature from an adolescent girl to a middle-aged woman, and we empathize with her confusion and disappointment. She begins in hope, and she even ends in hope, despite all of the events that have intervened. As with most literature that endures for decades and even centuries, we continue reading *Their Eyes Were Watching God* because it is enjoyable. Twenty-first century readers can rejoice that Hurston's work did not fall into complete obscurity before it was rediscovered and made available to a contemporary audience.

This novel is not only frequently taught in classes, especially women's studies and African American literature courses but it is also taught in American literature surveys and fiction classes. Adolescent readers empathize with Janie as she dreams of romance, but the complexity of Janie's life and life choices, as well as the personalities of the male characters and the challenges of Janie's marriages, appeal to adult readers particularly. Readers approaching the novel from a feminist perspective find it representative of the restricted lives of women during the early to mid-20th century. Most of Janie's significant decisions are made for her, even the man who will become her first husband. Admittedly, in arranging this marriage, Janie's grandmother Nanny intends to protect her and provide for her security—advantages that Nanny never enjoyed herself—but Nanny's choice is particularly disappointing for Janie. Her husband is not someone she ever comes to love, and through his own fear, he mistreats her rather than charm her into a more intimate relationship.

When Janie begins her relationship with Joe Starks, she hopes to both bring joy to it and receive joy from it. Initially, it seems that her desires will be fulfilled. But Joe also treats her as someone who should not be consulted about her own life. To Joe, Janie is evidence of his success, and she must act as he believes the wife of a successful man should act. He instructs her to remain apart from the community rather than become integrated into it.

Finally, Janie does create a more fulfilling relationship with Tea Cake, who not only permits Janie to be who she is but enjoys who she is. In her relationship with Tea Cake, Janie achieves the inner freedom she has sought. She has become the subject of her own life rather than whatever object someone else wants to make of her. Modern readers will likely be disturbed by the scene of domestic violence that occurs when Tea Cake believes he needs to assert his dominance in his home. By physically abusing her, he makes of Janie a lesson to gossiping neighbors, especially Mrs. Turner. This scene, and Janie's apparent acquiescence to Tea Cake's behavior, precludes the novel from being absolutely feminist in any simplistic sense. Yet it also reveals how complicated cultural interpretations of literature must be.

*Their Eyes Were Watching God* also holds a prominent place in African American literature. It is a prominent text within the Harlem Renaissance, which is itself a prominent period in African American literature and American literature more generally. Because of its nearly exclusive focus on African American characters, it reveals some fractures within African American communities, particularly as characters like Mrs. Turner privilege lighter complexions. *Their Eyes Were Watching God* positions itself temporally at the point when slavery recedes as a primary identifier of African American characters and other civil rights concerns begin to emerge. In this novel, Nanny identifies herself as a former slave, but she is elderly and dies fairly early in the novel. The other characters negotiate discrimination—for the novel certainly does not suggest that with the passing of the last generation of people born in slavery, African Americans will be entirely equal to other Americans—but they are more concerned to influence their own futures than they are to memorialize the past.

After 1940, African American literature will again shift its focus, reflecting (and helping to create) the energy that will be devoted to the civil rights movement during the middle of the 20th century. With the discussion of segregated burials for African American and white characters in the penultimate chapter, *Their Eyes Were Watching God* may anticipate the civil rights movement, but it is not fully part of it.

Stylistically, the novel is lyrical and poetic; sentence by sentence, it's pleasurable to read. But its consistent attention on Janie propels the plot. These factors prevent it from feeling dated, despite some of the references and Hurston's use of dialect. The dialect can be distracting to some readers, but it generally occurs to mark dialogue, and that dialogue is often energetic and amusing, so the dialect rewards any effort required to comprehend it. As a novel, this book is obviously not simply an oral tale. When the last chapter returns to Janie and Phoebe, however, readers recall that the entire book has been a story told in Janie's voice. Phoebe feels raised up through Janie's story, and Janie herself celebrates her experience as a gift rather than a tragedy. The story keeps readers riveted, but Janie is the reason readers return to read *Their Eyes Were Watching God* and to read it again.

# Index

# About the Author

**Lynn Domina** is a professor of English at the State University of New York at Delhi. Her books include *Understanding a Raisin in the Sun: A Student Casebook to Issues, Sources, and Historical Documents; Understanding Ceremony: A Student Casebook to Issues, Sources, and Historical Documents; Poets on the Psalms;* and two collections of poetry, *Framed in Silence* and *Corporal Works*. She earned a PhD in literature from the State University of New York at Stony Brook.